The Essential Garden Design Workbook

Rosemary Alexander

Second Edition
Revised and Updated with New Eco-Design Tips

Timber Press

Portland | London

All photographs by Rosemary Alexander.

All illustrations by Joseph Kent except those appearing on pages 31, 34, 42–43, 61–62, 65, 86–90, 92–94, 142, 196, 199, 232, 236, 253, 259, 269 and 273 by Carel Lucas; and pages 33, 75–77, 107, 110 (bottom), 112, 118 (left), 119 (bottom five), 121, 124 (lower left), 125 (left), 126 (upper left, lower left), 128 (lower right), 130 (top left, middle left, bottom left), 132, 133 (lower), 135 (top), 136 (upper), 137–138, 139 (bottom four), 165, 170 (all except top left), 171 (left), 179 (lower right), 185 (lower), 189 (right), 193 (bottom three), 194 and 225 by Roger Sweetinburgh.

Mood boards and designs by Rochelle Greayer (page 257), Sarah Haigh (page 237) and Rachel Myers (pages 200 and 251).

Published in 2009 by Timber Press, Inc.

The Haseltine Building
133 S.W. Second Avenue, Suite 450
Portland, Oregon 97204-3527
www.timberpress.com

2 The Quadrant
135 Salusbury Road
London NW6 6RJ
www.timberpress.co.uk

ISBN-13: 978-0-88192-975-1

Second printing 2010

Designed by Dick Malt
Printed in China

Catalogue records for this book are available from the Library of Congress and the British Library.

Contents

Acknowledgements   7

Introduction   9

Chapter 1   **Research, Preparation and Design Appraisal**   13
The Garden Owner's Requirements   15
Making a Site Survey   18
Surveying the Site   22
Basic Drawing Skills   35
Recording Information for the Site Inventory:
  The Checklist   45
The Garden and Its Setting   46
Recording Existing Conditions   52
Legal Considerations   58
Moving Towards the Design Stage   64
Consolidating the Information   64

Chapter 2   **Developing the Design: Focusing on the Ground Plane**   67
Approaching the Design Process   69
Drawing Skills for Presentation Plans   69
Designing with Patterns and Shapes   78
Creating Grids for Different Sites   83
Theme Plans   91
Planning an Outdoor Space   97
Space   97
Light   99
Scale and Proportion   101
Water   103
Refining Ideas for the Preliminary Garden Layout Plan   115
The Ground Plane or Garden Floor: Horizontal Elements
  in the Design   115
Materials   120
Vertical and Overhead Elements   133
The Preliminary Garden Layout Plan   141
Colour plates   145

Chapter 3   Finalizing the Garden Layout Plan   153
The Role of the Vertical Plane   155
Vertical Features   156
Materials   162
Structural Planting: Barriers and Enclosures   167
The Role of the Overhead Plane   171
Overhead Features   172
Garden Accessories   178
Practical Considerations   191
Finalizing a Scheme for the Final Garden Layout Plan   195
Colour plates   201

Chapter 4   Creating a Planting Plan   207
The Role of Planting   209
Principles of Planting Design   211
Seasonal Changes in Plant Compositions   216
Practical Considerations   217
Planting Styles   219
Creating a Planting Plan   223
Colour plates   238

Chapter 5   Visualizing and Constructing the Design   247
Enhancing the Plan   249
Using Colour   249
Applying Tone and Rendering Texture   251
Using Photographs   254
Mood Boards   256
Drawing Sections and Elevations   258
Axonometric Projections   263
Construction, Planting and Maintenance   272
Your Role as Garden Designer   275

Appendices   277
Keeping a Plant Notebook   278
Core Plant List   283
Glossary   288
Recommended Reading   294
Index   298

Acknowledgements

Writing and updating a design manual is often a partnership. As with the previous edition, I have been able to draw on a very talented team.

Firstly my thanks go to Anthony du Gard Pasley, whose vast experience and discerning eye taught me so much in the formative years of The English Gardening School, and who made a great contribution to the original text. My thanks, secondly, to my editor, Anna Mumford, whose encouragement and tenacity greatly improved the first edition and now to Erica Gordon-Mallin, who encouraged me to bring the book up to date with the latest garden design developments. I am indebted to Susanne Haines, project editor of the first edition, for her valuable work and to Dick Malt for the excellent design. My thanks also to Joe Kent, Carel Lucas and especially to Roger Sweetinburgh, who were invaluable in providing the line drawings and chapter plans; to Rochelle Greayer for advice on the American perspective; to Rochelle Greayer, Sarah Haigh and Rachel Myers for allowing me to show their plans; to Amanda Crabb for her invaluable and reliable support and for giving some semblance of order to my erratic computer skills; and to Barbara Linton for her patience and experience in dealing with the original plans and drawings.

And above all I am grateful to past, present and future students of garden design worldwide, whose enthusiasm and encouragement motivates me to share and expand my knowledge.

There is more pleasure in making a garden than in contemplating a paradise.

Anne Scott-James

Introduction

Introduction

Since the first edition of this book was published in 2004, our approach to garden design has changed in several essential ways. While creating beautiful and thoroughly enjoyable spaces remains top priority, our growing concern for saving the planet for future generations has made many of us think carefully about what we do with our homes and gardens.

Drawing upon the very latest eco-friendly methods of sensitive design, planting and sustainability can make our gardens, and the experience of working in them, far more rewarding. For instance, we can use recycled household water instead of irrigation systems, seek out permeable and sustainable materials, and encourage wildlife to enhance our garden's ecosystems. To this end I have added new information, easy-to-follow illustrations and inspirational photographs to show how innovations such as green roofs or rainwater harvesting systems can be constructed, how gardens and planting have been adapted to the challenging bio-diverse conditions that now concern us, and much more.

Garden design is all about organizing and shaping spaces, and in this respect it is closely related to architecture. It covers many different elements, beginning with surveying the site and understanding the soil and the climate, through to selecting the plants, ornaments and lighting. Because it encompasses so many different disciplines, it is also one of the most complex art forms. But just as someone can be taught how to paint, anyone who is new to garden design can be taught how to make a beautiful garden.

Most of what I have written is based on what I practise in the garden and teach in the classroom. Whether you are starting from scratch or revamping a neglected, overgrown or outdated site, my aim is to take you logically through the various stages of planning a garden. It is a process that begins with assessing the site, the soil and the surroundings and involves everything from this initial survey through to constructing pergolas and terraces, using water wisely, choosing plants and placing them to best effect.

Factors to Consider

To be a good designer, two qualities are essential: firstly the ability to see things clearly and to understand their intrinsic nature, and secondly the ability to analyze the value of what is seen, identifying good and bad points and deciding how best they may be used or concealed. For the professional designer, identifying what is wanted in possible and practical terms results from collaboration with the owners.

Gardens are for people as well as plants, and the space must be comfortable and appropriate for both. Family needs evolve as children grow up, or as the owners find they have less time or energy. A garden should enhance the lives of those who use it, without imposing a stressful burden; it is crucial to understand how much maintenance can realistically be devoted to the garden before beginning the design process. Once you have thoroughly consulted with the owners, take time to consider your new ideas, experimenting with different styles or themes until you find a suitable and workable scheme.

Cost may also be a critical factor. Fortunately, using recycling existing or local materials is cost-effective as well as eco-friendly. Legal constraints now imposed by many civic authorities require the use of permeable and sustainable materials, and in many countries scarcity of water has affected what can be grown.

Choosing the plants is usually the most exciting part of designing a new garden, but it is also the most exacting. Plants have their individual preferences, and it is crucial that you select those that will thrive in your locality. When using plant material, the scene is constantly evolving as the plants' shapes, colours and textures mature or respond to seasonal changes. This book will show you how to choose, combine and arrange plants to create a display suited to your garden's climate and soil conditions.

Stages in the Design Process

In order to effectively explain and develop your design, it is vital that you present your ideas on paper. This book takes you step-by-step through the process, with a sequence of plans for a large suburban garden providing drawn examples of how a site develops through the various stages. You need not be artistic to draw up a presentable plan; in this book I go back to basics, explaining which drawing materials are needed and how to use them, showing you how to draw a plan to scale and, finally, describing how to create other back-up or presentation material, such as details, visuals and mood boards. Very encouraging results can be achieved with no previous drawing experience.

Designing a garden is a gradual process, and the sample plans shown throughout the book chart the different stages. The site survey, site inventory and site appraisal are the first drawings made during the research and preparation phase. In researching them and drawing them up you will become familiar with the advantages and constraints of the site. Concept diagrams illustrate options for reorganizing the site to fulfil your needs.

The design process is then progressed on the drawing board, using the information previously gathered on site. Experimenting with different design themes and relating these to a grid springing from the house will ensure that your new garden sits comfortably within the property.

Gardens are, of course, three-dimensional, and while it is helpful to develop the design initially on a tracing-paper plan, the three-dimensional effects of your ideas must also be considered. The experimental design theme will then probably need considerable amendment before it moves on to the next stage, the preliminary garden layout plan, which includes both areas of hard landscaping, or inert materials, and spaces for plants.

From this evolves the final garden layout plan—the most crucial part of your design. The garden will be built to this plan, so it must be accurately drawn to scale, complete with details of all hard and soft materials, their dimensions, their construction, and how they are to be used. A good garden designer should aim to use the materials most practically suited to the situation, with imaginative detailing.

Although the garden layout plan normally gives a broad indication of planting intentions, often there is insufficient room to detail each plant—hence the next stage of the design process is to produce an itemized and clearly labelled planting plan. This can be used as an inspirational proposal, or as a working document to show where each plant should be placed in the new borders. Sometimes the planting plan is accompanied by an elevation showing the plants' different outline heights and shapes.

Many people cannot visualize how the garden will look by studying a flat plan, so this book shows you how to produce accompanying drawings to make your intentions clear. For professional garden designers, the resulting illustrations are often key to securing the commission.

What Will You Achieve by Reading This Book?

Garden design is among the most creative of endeavours, encompassing an understanding of nature and a love of plants. By following the processes described here, you will be well equipped to analyze a site, define its problems and potential, and then develop your ideas into an original and workable design, achieving a professional standard in design and presentation. As you proceed, you will develop a heightened critical appreciation for gardens in general. Above all, I hope that you use this book to create an outdoor space that is beautiful and thoroughly rewarding.

Chapter 1
Research, Preparation and Design Appraisal

Research, Preparation and Design Appraisal

Garden design is a form of art, and just as with painting or music, there are guidelines that, once absorbed, help to make the creative process easier. The most important tools for understanding any form of visual art are our eyes, but often we look but do not see. This chapter provides the basis for design, explaining the various processes that will lead to the eventual layout or plan, taking you logically through the preliminary stages of garden design. It will help you to develop an observant yet practical approach to creating a garden.

Before any planning can begin, it is vital to assess how a garden is going to be used.

A climbing frame for children can be replaced by a pergola (right) when the children have grown up.

The Garden Owner's Requirements

It is vital that any design for a private garden should satisfy the needs of those who own and use it. If you are designing your own garden you will probably have thought about how you want the garden to function, and the resources, time and skills that you can devote to it, but it is still useful to get this information down on paper. When designing for others you will need to assess what they want and need through sensitive discussion with them. Sometimes they do not know what they want and will hope for your guidance. The garden should reflect not only their needs but also something of their personalities.

By deliberating on site you can also consider the setting. No garden should be conceived in isolation. Every outdoor space, however small or restricted, is part of a larger whole with which it interacts, apparently fitting naturally into its surroundings. It may only extend to the back of neighbouring houses, or it may stretch to distant woods and hills. So, in contemplating your garden project it is necessary to look beyond the immediate boundary of the site and decide how to create your own personal paradise within the wider context while still supplying the practical necessities.

Today, with outdoor space an expensive domestic asset, gardens often need to serve as outdoor rooms for eating, cooking, entertaining and so on. Children may use the garden for riding bicycles or for a climbing frame, but as they grow older these needs will change. Try to cater for this by making your proposed design sufficiently flexible to be easily adapted for later changes in use.

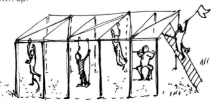

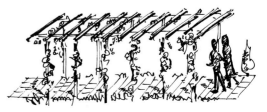

Three possible designs for a small, featureless site. The chosen design should reflect the architecture and interior style of the house.

Linking Garden and House

If the garden is directly adjacent to the house, it is important that the two are linked so that they appear to function as one entity. You will need to study the architecture and the interior style of the house to achieve this. Note the type of building materials used to construct the house, and incorporate some of the same materials into the hard landscaping of the garden. Try to carry the colour schemes used inside, and the style of furniture and furnishings, through to the design of the garden. It is often possible to create a subtle, unified effect simply by carefully selecting and painting one or two pieces of garden furniture in the same colour as used inside, or by echoing, in nearby plantings, the colours of furnishing fabrics.

Questions to Ask

There are numerous important points to consider at this early stage concerning how the garden will be used. Start with the broad questions of use and budget:

– What time of day is the garden most used, and by whom?
– Will it be used year-round or only on summer weekends?
– What family and friends may visit?
– How much time and energy will be available for maintenance?

Try to establish a budget for building and planting the garden and for future maintenance. There is no point in creating a high-maintenance garden if there are no resources to look after it. Then consider more specific practical points:

– Is a greenhouse or garden shed required?
– How might water-saving devices be incorporated?
– Where will tools, toys and garden furniture be stored?
– Where are dustbins kept, and are they easily accessible for rubbish removal?
– Are compost bins for recycling household waste required?
– Is there parking space for cars, if required, and sufficient room to turn vehicles?
– Is lighting required for security, safety or for simply enjoying the garden in the evening?

Once it has been established how the garden is going to be used, you can consider the aesthetics:

– Is a particular style of garden required?
– Are there any materials that you particularly like or dislike?
– Do you have any preferences for plantings?
– Do you favour a particular colour scheme?
– Is attracting wildlife desirable?

GARDEN OWNER'S CHECKLIST

1. Resident Family Members (including pets)

Name	Age	Hobbies (if relevant)
Dr. A. Williams	45	→ Love travel; Mediterranean climates gardens – Both enthuse about La Mortola gardens.
Mrs. E Williams	43	
Karen	11	Both children use garden year-round for wild play. Quote "It hasn't got any hidden corners to hide in"
Peter	9	

2. Existing Problems (visual and functional)

Fences and walls dominate the scene
No views to park – fence blocks view
SIDE BEDS empty except for rose bushes
Front Garden, though small, needs 'more excitement'
House elevation AB is bare of plants.

3. Positive elements to be retained or enhanced

Trees T1, T3, T5, T6   Brick WALL (good colours + texture)
Garage is v. attractive but cluttered with wall decoration + accessories (hose, light, bird table etc.)
Garage has human scale and a charming roof.

4. Desired Character of site (formal/ informal, etc.)

Informal – a variety of places required – a sense of mystery in places
– to contrast with a sense of openess elsewhere.

5. Favourite Plants (if any)

Exotic, Mediterranean

6. Planting effects

- Emphasis on foliage ✓
- Flowers for cutting – flowers from shrubs preferred
- General all year interest ✓
- Spring interest
- Summer interest
- Autumn interest
- Winter interest ✓ Winter flowering shrubs w/ long lasting flowers - clients emphatic!

7. Favoured materials for hard landscaping

- Brick ⎫
- Gravel ⎬ Any of these – but watch costs!
- Stone ⎪
- Concrete ⎭
- Setts No
- Cobbles No – Client says "I loathe cobbles"
- Timber No
- Iron NO

8. Other elements to be included

- Lighting Integrated w/ some flexibility.
- Irrigation ✓
- Furniture ✓ Not "country house", more "Italian café"
- Water ✓ must be ok for wildlife – several small ponds preferred.
- Ornaments ✓ A free hand but not too expensive
- Other structures ✓ + not too formal. A vine covered arbour for meals and drinks but "I don't want leaves dangling in our coffee" (height required)

9. Client requirements

- Parking area - soften area near garage
- Sitting area ✓
- Play area ✓ Should invite play + exploration
- Vegetable garden No X
- Herb garden ✓
- Fruit garden - Retain existing trees. Quince + Apricot needed.
- Flowers for the house (cutting garden) X
- Greenhouse X – No tender plants
- Dust bin storage ✓
- Firewood storage X No
- Tool and storage shed – improve
- Compost ✓

10. Budget

Initial costs £ 24,000 excluding new shed
Annual maintenance cost £ 500 – Clients would like maintenance guide

— Do you want to include any special features, such as ponds or garden artwork?
— Which water-saving devices will fit in with your garden's style?
— Would you like to incorporate new innovations such as green roofs and living walls?

Preceding page: Whether you are designing a garden for yourself, a friend or a client, it is useful to make a checklist of everything that will be required of the garden.

Garden Owner's Checklist

As a garden designer, reconciling visual requirements with practical necessities is one of your biggest challenges. These issues need careful assessment from the start, culminating in the checklist which you will need to refer back to when you begin to design. It is useful to complete a garden owner's checklist to clarify what is actually wanted.

Making a Site Survey

In order to produce an accurate plan of your intentions for the design of the garden, you will need to produce a scale drawing of the site, called a site survey. If you are lucky, there may be an existing ground plan that you can use (even house plans can help by providing the exact location of doors and windows). But usually you will need to measure the site yourself. In this way you will become much more familiar with the site and at the same time you will have the opportunity to notice all aspects of the garden that need to be considered.

For the survey you will need to locate the house, boundaries and any existing features (good or bad) that are likely to remain unchanged. These will include man-made structures, such as manhole covers, oil tanks and telegraph poles, and existing vegetation, such as mature trees, hedges, shrubs and perennials.

Before any work begins on the garden you must establish the ownership of any boundary walls. You may find, for instance, that the owner is responsible for one wall, an adjacent neighbour for another and a neighbour opposite responsible for the rear wall. If in doubt, ask your local council at an early stage for advice on ownership and responsibilities.

At this stage it is also important not to make any hasty decisions about removing established plants. On closer examination you may well discover that the position of a particular tree or large shrub has a specific purpose—for instance, to obscure some eyesore.

"Well, for a start, that boring tree will have to go."

"Ah… I think I may have made a mistake."

Trees and hedges also provide a garden with a sense of maturity, so unless you have a good reason for removing these, try to incorporate them into the new scheme. Some plants, such as herbaceous perennials and shrubs with a fibrous root system (for example, rhododendrons), can be moved and reused quite easily. Others, such as trees and shrubs with stringy roots that do not retain soil (for example, broom), are less likely to survive.

The positions of all of these fixed elements can be measured and plotted on the site survey plan, first as a sketch and then drawn up to scale. At the next stage of the design process, the many other factors that cannot be measured with a tape or ruler are recorded on the plan for the site inventory (see page 61). Following this, an assessment of existing elements and action to be taken is evaluated on the plan for the site appraisal (see page 62). However, it is useful to bear these things in mind when preparing the site survey. They include visual elements such as views and the style of the house, practical matters such as the state of existing plants, and local conditions such as climate, orientation, ambient noise levels and soil type.

You will need the following equipment to make a survey of the site:

– Measuring tape (30 m or 100 ft.)
– Metal skewer
– Flexible metal tape (2–3 m or 6–10 ft.)
– Small plastic spirit level
– Clipboard
– Graph paper (A4 or 8.5 × 11 in.)
– Notebook
– Camera and film
– Trowel
– Small plastic bags, ties and labels
– Torch (flashlight)

And you will need the following equipment to draw up the plan of the survey:

– Drawing board
– Parallel motion rule or T-square
– Set square
– Circle template
– Compasses with beam attachment

– Graph paper (A2 or 17 × 22 in.)
– Tracing paper (A2 or 17 × 22 in.)
– Scale rule (make sure that the scale rule coordinates with the measuring system that you plan to use)
– Masking tape
– Pencils and eraser
– Technical drawing pens
– Felt-tip pens
– Coloured pens

Taking Measurements

You will be using two types of measuring tapes. The flexible, retractable metal tape is straightforward to use and requires no explanation. However, if you have never used the very long 30-m (100-ft.) tape outdoors, you may find it unwieldy and prone to tying itself—and you—up in knots! To avoid this, keep the case under your left arm (if you are right-handed), and pay out, or gather in, with your right hand.

Loop the tape over your arm when walking about, to avoid becoming entangled.

Once you have begun the operation, avoid winding the tape back into the case. Instead, treat the length of tape rather like rope, looping it over your arm. Once you have finished measuring all the dimensions, you can then wipe the moisture and dirt from the tape with a cloth or tissue as you wind in. This method will help keep this expensive piece of equipment in good condition.

A metal skewer tied to the hook at the end of the tape and anchored into the ground is useful for securing the tape, particularly if you are surveying on your own. When measuring from a hard surface, you will need to fix the end of the tape with a brick or something similarly heavy, and then begin to read off any measurements.

If the distances to be measured are longer than your 30 m (100 ft.) tape, you can use a ball of string to set out the line first. The string line can then be measured in stages.

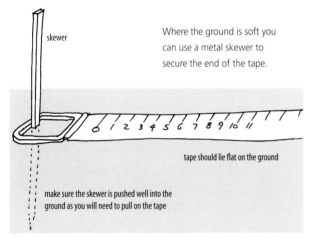

skewer

Where the ground is soft you can use a metal skewer to secure the end of the tape.

0 1 2 3 4 5 6 7 8 9 10 11

tape should lie flat on the ground

make sure the skewer is pushed well into the ground as you will need to pull on the tape

Taking and recording accurate measurements in your garden is quite simple once you know the correct way to proceed. There are three main methods, and often all three need to be used to accurately locate and fix the different elements on the plan. They are baseline measuring (also called running dimensions), offset measuring and triangulation measuring.

Baseline measuring

When measuring up a site accurately, there will be many points that you need to record along one straight line: for example, recording where the doors and windows are located along the front of the house. Rather than measuring from the house edge to the window edge, then shifting the tape and measuring another separate length (which is time-consuming and may cause inaccuracies), align

the tape as closely as possible along a fixed line (the baseline—in this case the exterior wall of the house) and read off each point that needs to be measured. These measurements are sometimes referred to as running dimensions because they are progressive.

Measure the side of a house using baseline measuring.

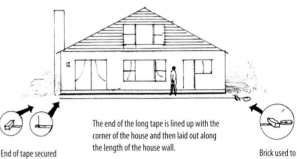

End of tape secured with a brick or skewer

The end of the long tape is lined up with the corner of the house and then laid out along the length of the house wall.

Brick used to keep tape taut while measuring

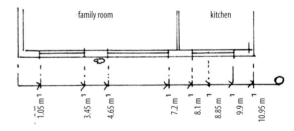

family room   kitchen

1.05 m   3.45 m   4.65 m   7.2 m   8.1 m   8.85 m   9.9 m   10.95 m

Above: Running measurements are used to record the position on the ground plan of such items as doors and windows and the length of the wall.

Below: The information is recorded on a sketch, drawn freehand on graph paper (not to scale).

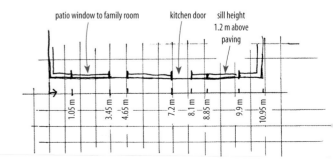

patio window to family room   kitchen door   sill height 1.2 m above paving

1.05 m   3.45 m   4.65 m   7.2 m   8.1 m   8.85 m   9.9 m   10.95 m

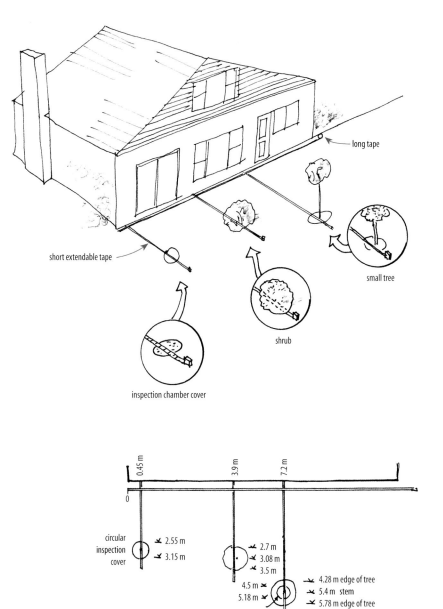

short extendable tape

long tape

small tree

inspection chamber cover

shrub

Take offsets to measure elements close to the house wall.

The long tape, laid against the house wall, is used to measure "how far along" the element occurs, and the shorter tape is used to measure the offset, or "how far out" the element occurs. Manhole covers are particularly important to locate accurately—they will often affect paving patterns around the house.

0.45 m

3.9 m

7.2 m

0

circular inspection cover

2.55 m
3.15 m

2.7 m
3.08 m
3.5 m

4.28 m edge of tree
5.4 m stem
5.78 m edge of tree

4.5 m
5.18 m

paving cutout

Offset measuring

While measuring from a baseline, you may also wish to take offset measurements to record elements that do not fall on the line itself but are located close to it, such as a manhole cover or a tree near the house wall. In this case you simply note from the long tape how far along the element is situated and then, placing the rigid tape at right angles to it, record how far out the element occurs.

Triangulation measuring

The triangulation method is used to locate a third point in relation to two known points or an established baseline. Since the starting point for

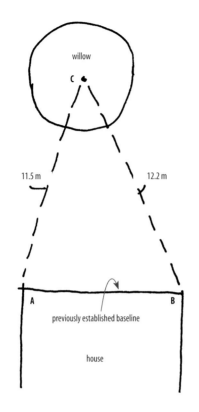

When locating a point by triangulation, first you need to establish a baseline (two fixed points or previously located points) from which you can measure. On site, measure the length of the baseline (from point A to point B), then measure from each point to the feature that you are locating (here, the willow tree at point C). Record the measurements of A–C and B–C on a sketch, as shown.

surveying a garden is usually the house, two of the house corners usually act as the two known points from which trees, boundary corners and so forth can be measured. On site you simply measure and note down the distance from each corner of the house to the object (such as a tree). You can then plot the measurements later, using compasses as shown.

Surveying the Site

Begin by sketching a rough outline plan of the house on A4 (8.5 × 11 in.) graph paper. If the garden is only on one side of the house, you need only sketch that side. Make your sketch as large as possible, leaving some room to write measurements. The graph paper will help you to keep the drawing neat and reasonably proportioned, but do not attempt to draw the house to scale at this point. The sketch of the exterior of the building should include the position of all doors and windows and their

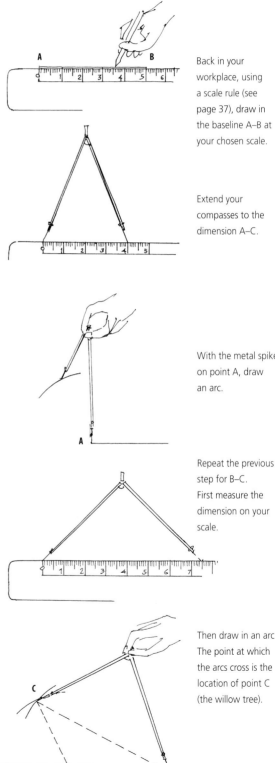

Back in your workplace, using a scale rule (see page 37), draw in the baseline A–B at your chosen scale.

Extend your compasses to the dimension A–C.

With the metal spike on point A, draw an arc.

Repeat the previous step for B–C. First measure the dimension on your scale.

Then draw in an arc. The point at which the arcs cross is the location of point C (the willow tree).

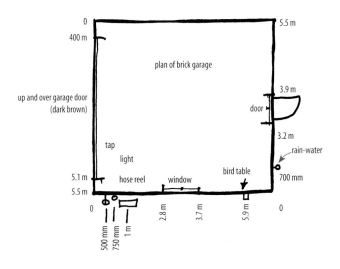

First sketch a rough plan of the buildings on graph paper. Indicate the position of doors and windows and make a note of any items attached to the building that you will need to measure. Then, starting on one side, measure each wall using running measurements and record these neatly on your drawing, as shown.

direction of opening, as well as elements close to the house, such as drains and manhole covers. If there are any other buildings on the site, such as a garage or shed, you should make sketches of these on separate sheets of paper. These rough sketches will be the drawings on which you note down the dimensions of the buildings. Later they will be drawn to scale on a larger sheet of tracing paper.

Measuring Buildings Using Running Dimensions

Once you have drawn the rough sketch plan you are ready to begin measuring, using running dimensions as described on page 20. It is usually sensible to begin with the house because the walls are generally straight and provide a firm surface for establishing a baseline, but it does not matter if the walls are not straight, or if there are indents or protrusions along its length.

Using a skewer or brick to fix the tape securely to the starting point (usually one corner of the house), pay out the tape along the length of the house as close to the house wall as possible, then lay the reel down on the ground. Go back to the beginning of the tape and read off the position of all corners, doors, windows, taps, drains and so on, along the

house wall, and record these neatly. Now plot the running dimensions of the other buildings in the same way.

Measuring Heights and Nearby Features Using Offsets

Use the shorter tape to take offset measurements (see page 21) for the heights of window sills, lights, taps and any irregularities along the line of the building. Start with the house, and then take measurements for any other buildings on the site. Also use offset measurements to locate any nearby features, such as manhole covers.

Measuring More Distant Elements Using Triangulation

When you have completed the house survey, take another piece of graph paper and roughly sketch on it the site boundary by eye. Within this, using triangulation (as described on previous pages), draw the house, or house wall, and any other elements that you wish to locate, such as trees, paths and garden buildings.

When you choose a baseline, or two fixed points from which to measure, try to select the longest unobstructed line from which all or most of the area can be seen. For most sites, however, particularly when the house is surrounded by the garden, you will need more than one baseline.

Triangulation is very useful for establishing the position of elements that are not parallel or at right angles to a building, such as paths and boundaries. Before you start to measure, it is helpful to label on the sketch all the points that will need to be located and the known points from which they will be triangulated.

Measuring Heights and Widths of Features

As well as locating the exact position of fences, railings, steps and so on, you will need to record their heights and widths. These measurements can be recorded in detail beside each feature on the sketch plan or separately in a notebook.

It is incorrect to represent a wall, fence or railing by a single line. When measuring, make sure that you take detailed notes of the width and height of the main supporting posts, plus the width and height of the panels or metal bars between each upright.

If there is a lot of information, record heights on a separate sketch as shown here. Draw a separate elevation for each side of the building that you need to measure.

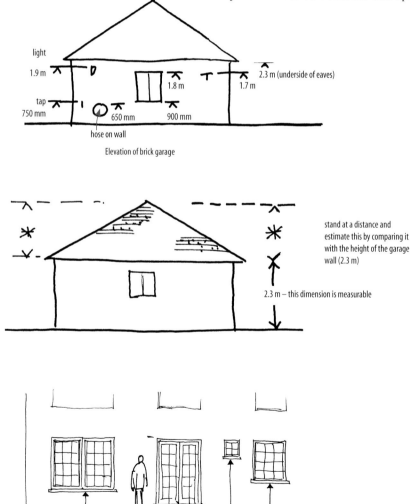

Elevation of brick garage

You can estimate the height of a roof by photographing the building and scaling off from a print later (see page 27), or by comparing it with a measurable dimension, as shown.

stand at a distance and estimate this by comparing it with the height of the garage wall (2.3 m)

2.3 m – this dimension is measurable

It is most important to measure sill heights accurately, particularly if you are intending to plant up against or close to the house. Your measurements will dictate the size of suitable plants.

Even a wire fence (which has minimal thickness) will be supported by fence posts, which should be surveyed and recorded on the sketch of the site.

If the posts of a wooden fence are positioned on the garden side, these too should be surveyed and drawn on the correct side of the fence panels.

Walls of any thickness are drawn as a double line, the thickness also being noted on the survey.

If a brick wall is supported by piers or buttresses, these too should be measured and the spacing between them recorded.

Where a wall abuts a building it is important to locate the exact position of the join.

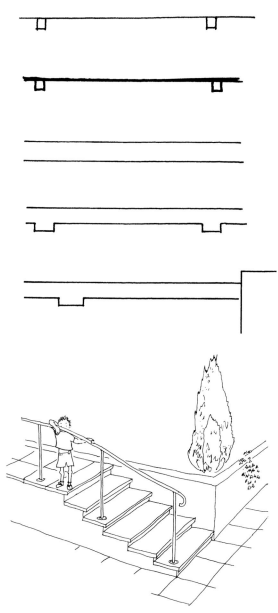

When measuring steps it is important, from a safety aspect, to survey the handrail—both its height and the position of the uprights. Often, as shown here, handrails do not provide a sufficient barrier to prevent small children from slipping through. If you design such a feature you may well be liable if an accident occurs.

Below: the overhang increases the tread size and produces shadow on the step below, which is both attractive and a safety feature, as the cast shadow emphasizes the change in level.

In the case of steps you will need to note the sizes of both risers and treads, as well as the number of steps. While taking the dimensions, look also at the state of these features. Are the steps cracked and in need of repair?

overhang or nosing

tread

riser

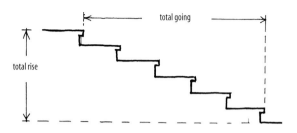

For most formal garden steps, such as these, the dimensions of treads and risers will be the same for every step. Instead of measuring each one individually, you can get an average tread measurement by dividing the total going by the number of treads, and an average riser measurement by dividing the total rise by the number of risers.

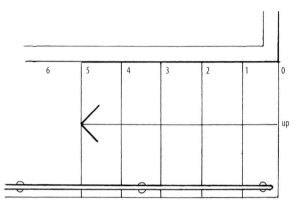

It is useful to number the steps when recording them on the sketch plan.

Estimating Measurements

If a wall is too high to measure with a tape, its height can be estimated. If the wall is made of brick, since an average brick is 75 mm (3 in.) high, the height can be calculated first by counting the number of brick courses, then working out the number of brick courses to 300 mm (1 ft.). Walls made of other materials can be measured against the height of a person, as shown. When checking heights and widths, notice the state of the wall (for instance, whether it has been rebuilt recently), and remember to record these details later on the site inventory.

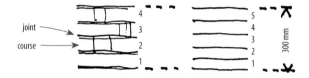

Above: Count the number of brick courses in a typical foot (or 300 mm). Often this is 4 courses, but sometimes slim bricks are used.

Below: There are 12 brick courses in this wall. By dividing by 4 (where there are 4 courses per 300 mm or 1 ft.) the height of the wall can be estimated as 900 mm (3 ft.).

If the wall you want to measure is high, you may find it easier to count the number of brick courses, rather than measure with your tape.

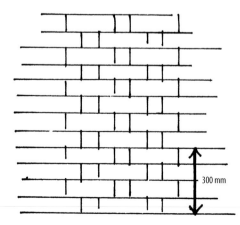

If the wall is not constructed in a material that is convenient to measure (such as brick or cut stone), use a different approach. Photograph a person, a 2 m (6.6 ft.) rod or an extended tape, against it. When the photograph is printed, you will be able to estimate the height surprisingly accurately by scaling off the photograph, using your "unit of measurement" as a reference. Here, the height of the building is approximately five times the height of the person, or 1.8 m (6 ft) × 5 = 9 m (29.5 ft.).

Measuring Trees

If there are any trees on the site that you wish to retain, use triangulation to locate the position of each trunk on the plan. In addition to this measurement you should note the type of tree, the diameter of the trunk, the spread of the tree canopy, the height of the lowest branches and the overall height of the tree. The latter can be estimated by using the height of a person standing near the tree as a unit of measurement (in the same way as for a wall). If there is not enough space for all this information on your plan, record it in a notebook.

It is often worth measuring the height of the lowest branches of a tree as these may have an effect on views and underplanting.

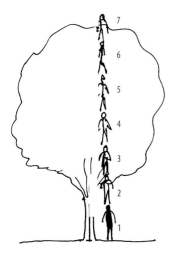

Left: To estimate the height of a tree, place an extended tape against its trunk or ask an assistant to stand next to the tree.

Right: Use running dimensions to record the diameter of the tree canopy, the location of the trunk and its thickness. Always name the tree, if possible, and record its height.

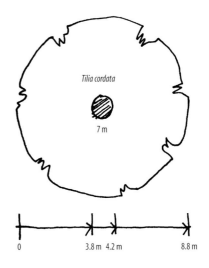

Tilia cordata

7 m

0   3.8 m 4.2 m   8.8 m

When surveying trees, it is important to record the outline form of the tree, particularly of any lower branches that you may wish to remove. Photograph the tree so that you remember the outline shape.

existing tree outline

after removing the lower branches

Measuring Curves

Curving lines that delineate features such as paths, beds or boundaries are measured using offsets taken at regular intervals from a baseline or a triangulation line. When taking offsets you must ensure that the measurements are taken at right angles to the baseline. You may find it useful to use a rectangular object, such as a cardboard box, to make the right angle.

Right: Use a rectangular object, such as a box, to establish a right angle.

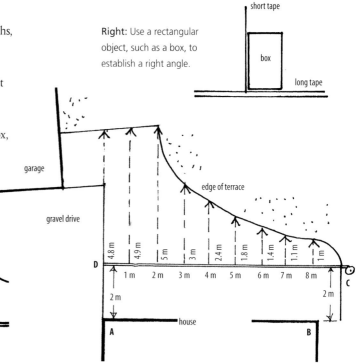

Above: The long tape forms the baseline. Offsets are taken at regular intervals—in this case one-metre intervals using the shorter tape.

Above: Use offset measurements to measure the curve of an existing terrace from a baseline. For accuracy, always try to use a baseline as close to the curve as possible. In this example, offsets are taken from the baseline D–C, established by moving the house baseline, A–B, two metres in the direction of the curve.

Assessing Slopes or Changes in Level

In most gardens there will inevitably be slopes or gradients and areas which to the naked eye look level but which are in fact at odds with each other. It is very important to be aware of any changes of level before working up the design. Squat down as near as possible to the ground in the flat part of the site to get the best view. You may notice that there is a slight slope to one side or another, or that one retaining wall is lower than the one opposite. A change in level or slope can drastically affect the garden layout. Soil may need to be brought in to make up the ground, or the surface may need to be regraded by machine.

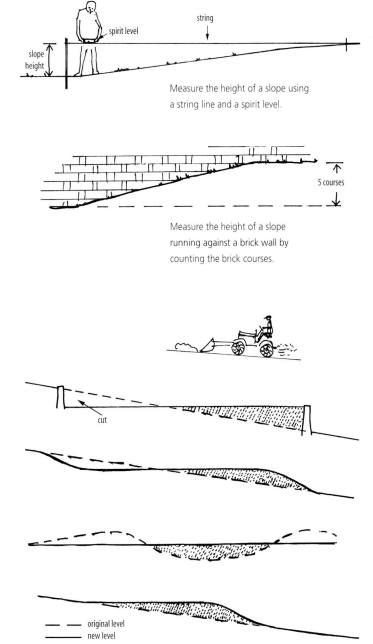

Measure the height of a slope using a string line and a spirit level.

Measure the height of a slope running against a brick wall by counting the brick courses.

Judge the slope of a garden feature by viewing it through a small plastic spirit level. The spirit level must be held directly in front of your eyes, not at an angle. When it is level, you will be able to estimate at what degree the particular feature slopes away from the horizontal. In this case, the ground is level.

By observing the line of the earth against a brick wall, the slope of a garden can be assessed. Brickwork is usually horizontal.

– – – original level
——— new level

If you intend to create a level area in a sloping garden, the slope must be measured accurately to assess the work required. There are two main ways of levelling an area: by the "cut and fill" method, which involves cutting into the slope and using the "spoil" or removed soil to fill an adjacent area, or by importing soil on to a site.

Drawing a Sketch Plan of the Site Survey

The first stage of drawing up the garden plan brings together on one sketch all the initial surveying information that is recorded about the existing features on the site. It should be kept carefully together with the supporting sketches and notes that you make for future reference.

1. Start by attaching a sheet of graph paper to a clipboard, and—without worrying about scale at this stage—sketch the outline of the house or the part of the house that is adjacent to the garden. Mark the position of any doors and windows, showing the direction in which they open, plus any elements close to the house, such as drains and manhole covers.

2. On the sketch outline, mark the major points, such as the corners of the house, buildings and the main changes of direction in the site boundary, labelling them alphabetically in running order. You can then survey to or from these reference points, and they will be very useful when you come to draw up the survey to scale. If you are using a notebook to record the dimensions, these should tally with the points on the rough sketch plan.

3. Using either imperial or metric dimensions (but not mixing the two), measure one side of the house by laying the long tape along and close to the house wall. Use a skewer or brick to keep the tape in place.

4. Read off the running dimensions and record these accurately on the sketch plan.

5. Keep the long tape in place and use the short rigid tape to record the heights of windowsills, lights, taps and any other relevant features or irregularities along the building line. Add these to the sketch plan.

6. With the long tape still in place, take offsets to measure and record any influencing elements close by, such as manhole covers.

7. If necessary, repeat this exercise around each house wall.

8. On a fresh sheet of graph paper, sketch out the site boundary. Within this, locate and draw in the house (or part of it, as necessary).

9. Using triangulation or offsets, locate and draw in any other influencing elements, such as outbuildings, trees (numbering them T1, T2 and so on, if necessary), paths and planting beds.

10. In a notebook, write down information about each of the trees (using the numbers for identification): the diameter of the trunk, the spread or width of the tree canopy, the height of the lowest branches and the overall height of the tree. This information will be useful later.

11. Measure and record the height and width of walls, fences, gates and the treads and risers of steps in your notebook.

12. Having located the major trees and shrubs, try to name them. This may help you to decide whether or not to keep them in your new design.

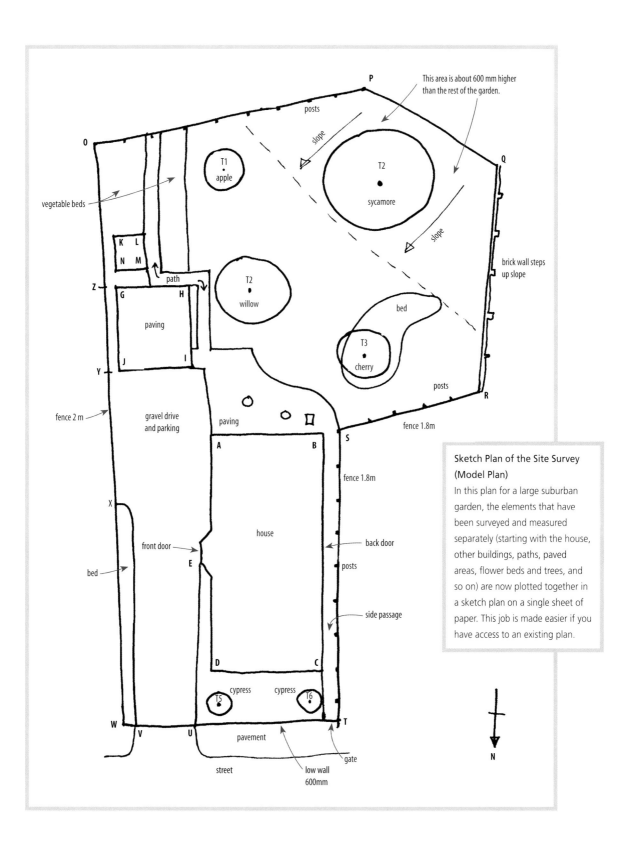

This area is about 600 mm higher than the rest of the garden.

P

posts

slope

O

T1
apple

T2
sycamore

slope

Q

vegetable beds

brick wall steps up slope

K L
N M

path

Z

G H

paving

T2
willow

bed

J I

Y

T3
cherry

posts

R

fence 2 m

gravel drive and parking

paving

S

fence 1.8m

A B

X

bed

house

back door

front door

posts

E

side passage

D C

cypress cypress

T5 T6

W

V U

T

pavement

gate

street

low wall
600mm

N

Sketch Plan of the Site Survey (Model Plan)

In this plan for a large suburban garden, the elements that have been surveyed and measured separately (starting with the house, other buildings, paths, paved areas, flower beds and trees, and so on) are now plotted together in a sketch plan on a single sheet of paper. This job is made easier if you have access to an existing plan.

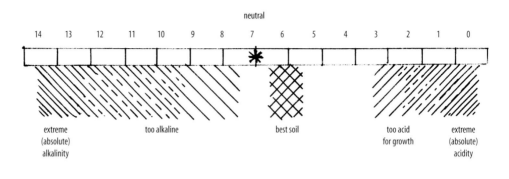

neutral

| 14 | 13 | 12 | 11 | 10 | 9 | 8 | 7 | 6 | 5 | 4 | 3 | 2 | 1 | 0 |

extreme (absolute) alkalinity   too alkaline   best soil   too acid for growth   extreme (absolute) acidity

Soil can be tested with a kit to determine the pH factor. The pH scale ranges from 0 to 14, but plants can only tolerate a range from pH 4 to pH 7.5. The consistency of the soil and the type of plants that naturally occur on it are also useful indicators of soil type.

Testing the Soil

It is important to establish what type (or types) of soil you are dealing with and to record your findings on the plan. The acidity or alkalinity of the soil will govern what type of plants can be grown in the garden. This is known as the pH value and usually ranges from 4 (very acid) to 7.5 (very alkaline). A neutral or middle-range soil with a pH value of around 6 will support both types of plants.

Soil varies enormously from area to area. Under trees, for instance, there may be an accumulation of decaying leaf matter, which will render the soil in this area with a more acidic reading or lower pH value than elsewhere. A dry area at the base of a sunny wall may give a different reading with a higher pH. A damp boggy area may give a low pH reading.

You will therefore need to take soil samples (using a trowel, small plastic sandwich bags and labels) from several parts of the garden; sample points may include a spot adjacent to the house, under various trees and in existing beds. These samples will be tested later when they have dried (see opposite page).

A second test to check the soil structure should be made on the spot at each sample point. Simply take a tablespoonful of soil and rub it between your fingers or squeeze it in the palm of your hand. If it sticks

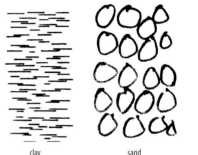

clay   sand   loam

To determine the soil structure, squeeze a soil sample in the palm of your hand—note its consistency and texture.

together or can be squeezed into a largish lump, the soil will be made up of many tiny particles and will be clay. If, instead, the sample disintegrates into sandy, fibrous material, the soil is sandy or peaty. If there is an even balance between the two, you will have the best type of texture—a loam high in organic content. Very poor soil structure will result in poor plant growth, and you may need to consider improving the soil before you plan the planting.

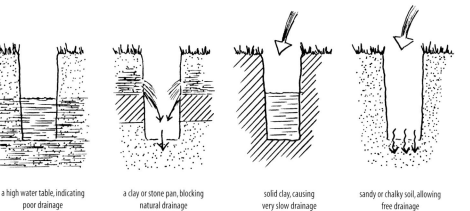

a high water table, indicating poor drainage

a clay or stone pan, blocking natural drainage

solid clay, causing very slow drainage

sandy or chalky soil, allowing free drainage

Digging test pits and observing the rate of water drainage over twenty-four hours can give insight into the garden's soil structure.

Thin, sandy soil drains very quickly. This leaching of nutrients and minerals causes nutrient deficiencies in plants, which in turn requires applications of fertilizers to redress the balance. Heavy clay soils may retain water for much of the year, but dry out and crack in warmer climates. In some gardens the soil varies from wetter (softer) to drier (harder).

Water tables, or the level at which water lies naturally in the soil, may vary from area to area. While you are surveying the site, take a spade and dig two or three soil profile test pits. Leave these for at least twenty-four hours in dry weather. If the bottom of the pit fills with water that does not drain away, this indicates a high water table, requiring either improved drainage or specially adapted planting techniques. If water drains away very quickly, an irrigation system may be needed.

Another test relies on your observation of the vegetation that naturally occurs on the site, and this is described on page 58.

Collecting Soil Samples

1. Decide where soil tests would be most appropriate and mark these positions on the sketch plan, labelling them SS1 (soil sample 1), SS2, SS3 and so on (see page 34).
2. Take a sample from each by inserting a trowel to approximately 100–150 mm (4–6 in.) below the surface, collecting about a tablespoonful of soil. Deposit this into a plastic sandwich bag and then seal and label the bag in the same way.
3. At the same time, in each chosen position, test the structure of the soil in your hands (as shown opposite).
4. On returning to your workplace, tip each soil sample onto a separate saucer, then sit each one on top of the labelled bag and allow it to dry out naturally under cover overnight.
5. When completely dry, test the soil using a kit that contains a mixture of dyes which, when added to the soil sample and shaken with water, will change colour according to the pH value. Note your findings carefully (SS1: pH 6.5, SS2: pH 6 and so on) on the sketch plan or in a notebook.

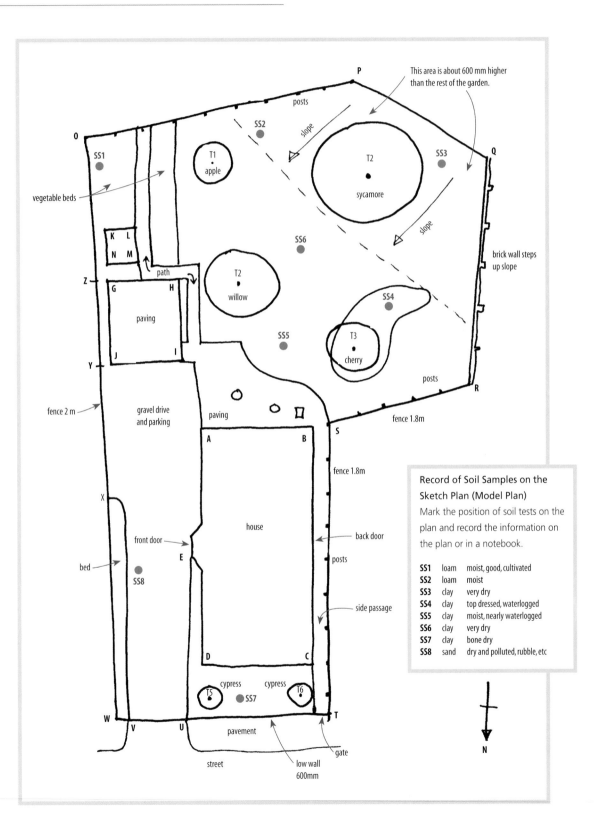

This area is about 600 mm higher than the rest of the garden.

posts

slope

SS2

SS1

T1
apple

vegetable beds

SS3

T2
sycamore

slope

Q

brick wall steps up slope

K L
N M

path

G H

Z

paving

T2
willow

SS6

SS4

T3
cherry

posts

R

J I

Y

SS5

fence 2 m

gravel drive and parking

paving

S

fence 1.8m

A B

fence 1.8m

Record of Soil Samples on the Sketch Plan (Model Plan)

Mark the position of soil tests on the plan and record the information on the plan or in a notebook.

X

house

front door

back door

posts

bed

SS8

E

side passage

SS1	loam	moist, good, cultivated
SS2	loam	moist
SS3	clay	very dry
SS4	clay	top dressed, waterlogged
SS5	clay	moist, nearly waterlogged
SS6	clay	very dry
SS7	clay	bone dry
SS8	sand	dry and polluted, rubble, etc

D C

cypress   cypress

T5   SS7   T6

W V U

pavement

T

gate

street

low wall 600mm

N

Basic Drawing Skills

Once you have collected all the information you require about a site, you will need to draw up the site survey to scale, creating an accurate representation of the garden that concentrates on the ground plane. Although the garden is rarely seen from this "overhead" view, this survey drawing provides a base plan in which spaces and objects can be rearranged.

You will need some basic drawing skills for this stage of the design process. The plan is drawn on a sheet of tracing paper, the size of which will depend on the size of the garden and the scale to which you draw the plan.

You may produce your work in pencil, or you may wish to use ink drawing pens, which can give a more professional effect despite a tendency for nibs to clog and lines to smudge. Your work should be kept as clean as possible. Use an eraser to remove lead smears, and a duster, small brush or cloth to remove eraser rubbings. If the sheet is overworked, some lines may become fuzzy, blurred or indistinct. In this case, overlay a second sheet of tracing paper and draw in only the lines that you want to keep. All horizontal lines should be drawn against a T-square or parallel motion rule, and all vertical lines against a set square, held firmly against the horizontal rule. Always keep pencils well sharpened and draw firmly and accurately.

Preparing to Draw the Plan

Set up a drawing board at a comfortable angle. As a backing sheet for your work use a large sheet of graph paper, A1 (22 × 34 in.) or A2 (17 × 22 in.), depending on the size of your drawing board. Use a T-square or parallel motion rule to check that lines are straight, and stick it down with masking tape, depending on the size of the board. On top of the graph paper, tape down a sheet of tracing paper for your plan drawing.

The drawing board is too steep

Too flat

Here the drawing board is set at a comfortable angle

Check that the graph paper squares are lined up with the T-square or parallel motion rule and then stick down with masking tape.

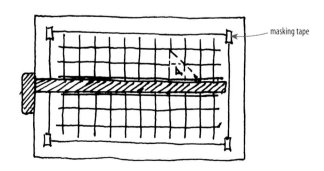

masking tape

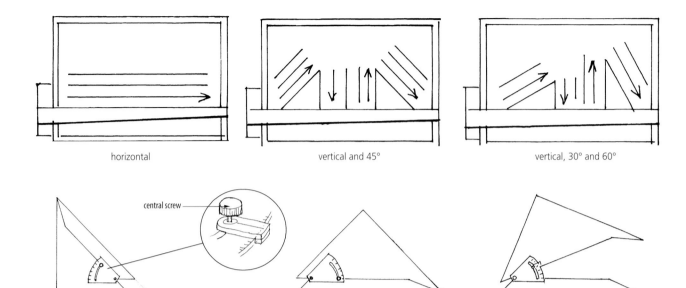

horizontal   vertical and 45°   vertical, 30° and 60°

An adjustable set square can be set at any
pair of angles adding up to 90°.
The central screw that loosens to allow
adjustment doubles as a useful handle.

Paper size

A2 (17 × 22 in.) and A3 (11 × 17 in.) papers are a
convenient size to work with because they are easier
to have printed (as photocopies or dyeline prints)
than A1 paper. However, paper size will depend on
the size of the site and the scale at which it is to be
reproduced.

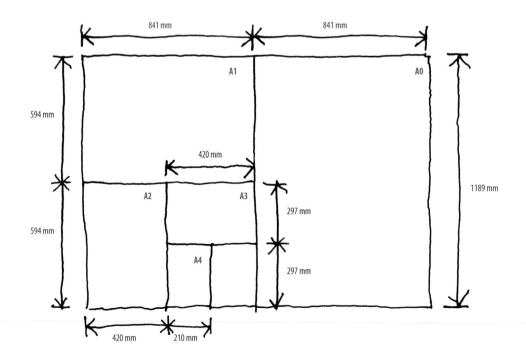

ISO	mm	inches	United States	inches
A8	53 × 74	2.07 × 2.91	Business card	2 × 3.5
A7	74 × 105	2.91 × 4.13	3 × 5	3 × 5
A6	105 × 148	4.13 × 5.83	Microfiche	4.13 × 5.83
A5	148 × 210	5.83 × 8.27	5 × 8	5 × 8
A4	210 × 297	8.27 × 11.69	A	8.5 × 11
A3	297 × 420	11.69 × 16.54	B	11 × 17
A2	420 × 594	16.54 × 23.39	C	17 × 22
A1	594 × 841	23.39 × 33.11	D	22 × 34
A0	841 × 1189	33.11 × 46.81	E	34 × 44

Paper size equivalents
The ISO paper size system is used everywhere except for Canada and the United States. The metric measurements of a range of these "A" sizes are given in the table. A translation of these measurements into decimal inches is also given, together with equivalent paper sizes that are available in the United States.

Working to Scale

If you have never drawn to scale before, this may seem complicated, but it is really quite simple. A scale rule will do the conversion for you. There are two types: one is triangular in section, while the other looks rather like a normal ruler. Both are marked with a range of scales to denote measurements at different proportions, such as 1:1, 1:10, 1:20, 1:50 and so on, which represent different scales. The largest, 1:1, represents a reproduction at the same size as the original (that is, one unit represents one unit of the same size). A ratio of 1:10 (where one unit represents ten units) will give a drawing that is ten times smaller than the actual measurements. The illustrations on this page show how (and why) different scales are appropriate for different situations.

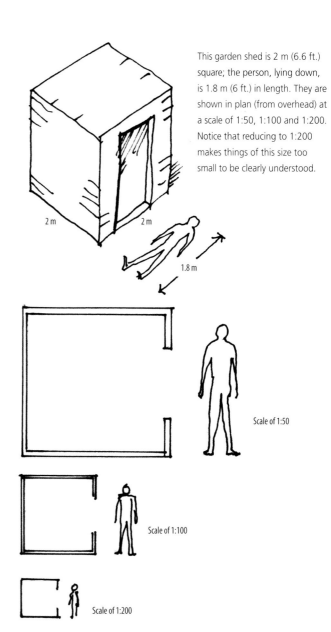

This garden shed is 2 m (6.6 ft.) square; the person, lying down, is 1.8 m (6 ft.) in length. They are shown in plan (from overhead) at a scale of 1:50, 1:100 and 1:200. Notice that reducing to 1:200 makes things of this size too small to be clearly understood.

2 m   2 m

1.8 m

Scale of 1:50

Scale of 1:100

Scale of 1:200

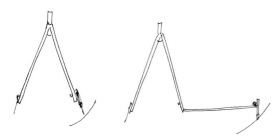

The stretch of a pair of compasses can be extended with a beam attachment arm.

Makeshift compasses can be improvised with a drawing pin, a piece of string and a pencil.

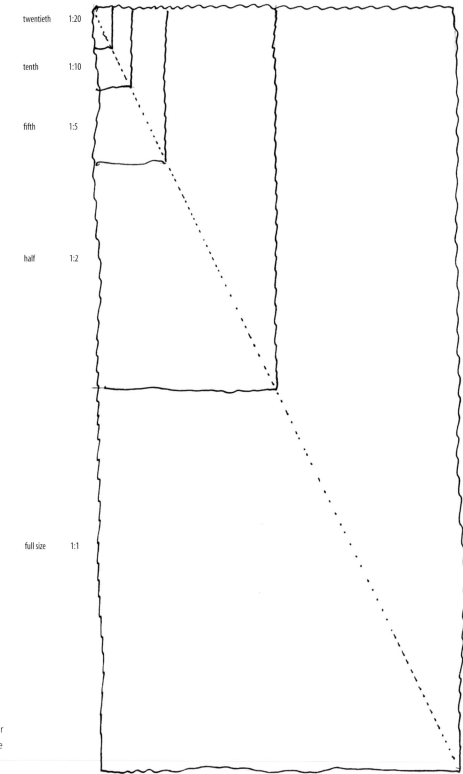

twentieth   1:20

tenth   1:10

fifth   1:5

half   1:2

full size   1:1

At a later stage, when you begin to develop the garden scheme, you may wish to make more detailed drawings of features such as steps, a seat or part of a wall. The outline of a building brick is shown here at different scales.

A full-size drawing (1:1) might occasionally be useful for a detail such as an edge of a step, a moulding or a pool edge.

A half-size drawing (1:2) is a dangerous scale to use as it can easily be confused with a full-size drawing.

A one-fifth (1:5) scale is handy for all sorts of details.

One-tenth (1:10) and one-twentieth (1:20) scales are useful for drawing detailed plans of things like patios, garden rooms or paving.

Practising Drawing to Scale

Before drawing up the plan, practise scaling down the measurements of one room in your house. Select a room that has as many doors or windows along a stretch of wall as possible. You will need drawing equipment (including a scale rule and a pencil) and two measuring tapes.

1. Use a brick to anchor the long tape at one end, and stretch it along the wall, making sure that it lies flat and is not twisted.
2. Record the running dimensions of this baseline, as shown earlier (page 20) to record door and window openings. Mark the starting point as A and the finishing point as B, so that you will know in which direction you are working.
3. Leaving the tape laid down, use the shorter tape to measure the heights of windows and doors and the dimensions of any protruding features, such as bookcases.
4. Set up the drawing board with a parallel motion rule or a T-square and a sheet of tracing paper. Look on the scale rule for the 1:50 scaled measurements and draw in the full length (A–B) of the baseline (and mark the running dimensions). The line you draw will be fifty times smaller than the actual measurement.
5. Repeat at a scale of 1:100.
6. Repeat at a scale of 1:20, provided that it will fit onto the sheet of tracing paper!

In the model garden plan that we are using, the measurements of the site are 17.5 × 26 m (19 × 28 yd.). At a ratio of 1:50, that gives a measurement of 350 × 520 mm (1.2 × 1.7 ft.). This is a useful starting point for working out the scale of the plan.

Choosing an Appropriate Scale for the Plan

Before you begin to draw up the survey you need to decide what scale you are going to use. The scale should be one that will represent the plan clearly on the sheet of tracing paper you have chosen, at a ratio that will reduce the actual measurements to a size that will make a plan that is is easy to handle yet legible. In garden design this is usually either 1:50 or 1:100, or for very large sites, 1:200. A scale of 1:20 might be used for a site such as a small roof garden or terrace. (Later on, as you develop your plan, you may wish to make highly detailed drawings of features and will find that a scale of 1:5 is useful.)

Using the overall measurements of the length and breadth of the site, start with a scale of 1:50, and find the corresponding measurements on the scale rule. Draw up the outline and decide whether it fits the paper you want to use. If not, reduce the scale, perhaps to 1:100. The plan can be orientated in any way to fit onto the sheet, but usually the best way is to place the plan so that it reflects the direction from which the garden is normally viewed.

If at a scale of 1:50 or 1:100 the garden will not fit on a sheet of A2 paper and requires A1 size, there is a danger that the site is too ambitious for a first attempt at garden design.

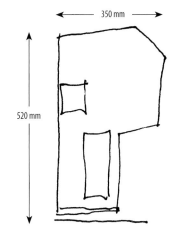

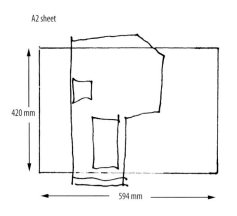

A2 sheet

420 mm

594 mm

At a scale of 1:50 the survey, when placed vertically, will not fit onto an A2 sheet.

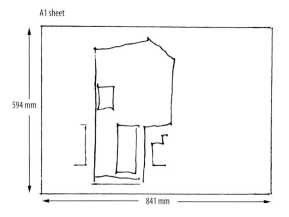

A1 sheet

594 mm

841 mm

On a larger paper size, A1, the survey is slightly cramped and there is not adequate space for a border or notes at the top and bottom of the page.

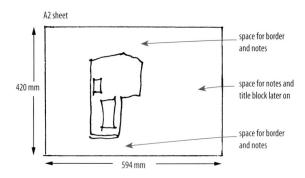

A2 sheet

420 mm

594 mm

space for border and notes

space for notes and title block later on

space for border and notes

Left: By reducing the scale to 1:100, there is adequate space for the plan on a sheet of A2 (17 × 22 in.) paper, as well as for information that will be added at a later stage.

Here the plan is drawn on a horizontal axis. The garden owner finds it hard to relate to this plan because he is not used to viewing the garden sideways on.

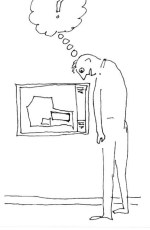

This is the view that is normally seen from the back of the house, and it is easier to understand as a plan when oriented in this way.

Drawing up the Site Survey to Scale

Watching the site take shape on paper is always an exciting stage in the design process, even if it exposes a few inaccuracies of measurement. It is difficult to be completely accurate when surveying, and a small amount of artistic licence is forgivable! But if your measurements do not seem to work, you may need to return to the site to check the suspect ones. If you are inexperienced, it is very easy to make a mistake in reading dimensions off the tape, and you may not notice the error until you come to draw up the survey to scale. For this, you will need your drawing equipment, together with the sketch plan of the site survey and all your supporting notes and plans.

1. Start by deciding on the size of tracing paper you will use and the scale you will work at. Try a scale of 1:50 or 1:100 to start with and a paper size of A2 or A1. If the garden is very large, you could try a scale of 1:200; if very small, a scale of 1:20. The plan should sit comfortably on the sheet, with enough (but not too much) space for information around it, for labelling and for an information panel on the right-hand side.

2. Decide on the orientation of your plan, and then, using masking tape, stick down a large sheet of tracing paper on the board.

3. Using the sketch site plan and your notes for reference, start to draw up the plan (in pencil) in the same order as you surveyed the site, starting with the house and then the other buildings. As you plot the dimensions, tick them off in your notebook to avoid missing a crucial measurement, which will throw out the whole drawing. (If you want to approach things more gradually, draw up the buildings separately at first.)

4. Now work outwards from the buildings to the boundaries and other more distant features. For points that you triangulated you will need to use compasses (with a beam attachment arm for large dimensions). Refer to page 22 if you need to be reminded of how to plot these measurements.

5. Continue plotting all your measurements until you have covered every dimension.

6. Indicate the various site elements with the appropriate symbols. For trees, show the position of the trunk and the spread of the canopy, and note on the plan the name of the tree and its approximate height.

7. For vertical elements, such as fences, walls and steps, write in their height as well as any relevant design details. Add any useful details to the outlines of the buildings, including door and window openings.

8. When you have finished the drawing, put an arrow in the bottom right-hand corner to indicate the north point direction. In the same corner make a note of the scale to which the plan is drawn. Add any other notes to the plan.

9. The site survey will be used as a basis for the next stage of the garden plan, so keep it safely stored.

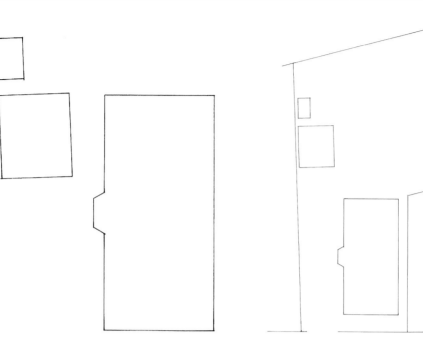

Above: Start with the house, and then draw any other buildings accurately to scale. Their position can be established later.

Above right: Establish the position of the buildings in relation to one another, and then plot the boundaries of the site.

Right: Once you have established the boundaries and main buildings, other large features, such as trees, paths and planting beds, can be plotted.

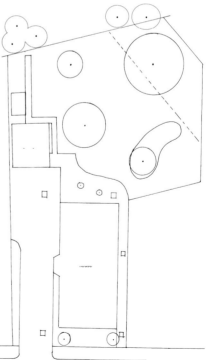

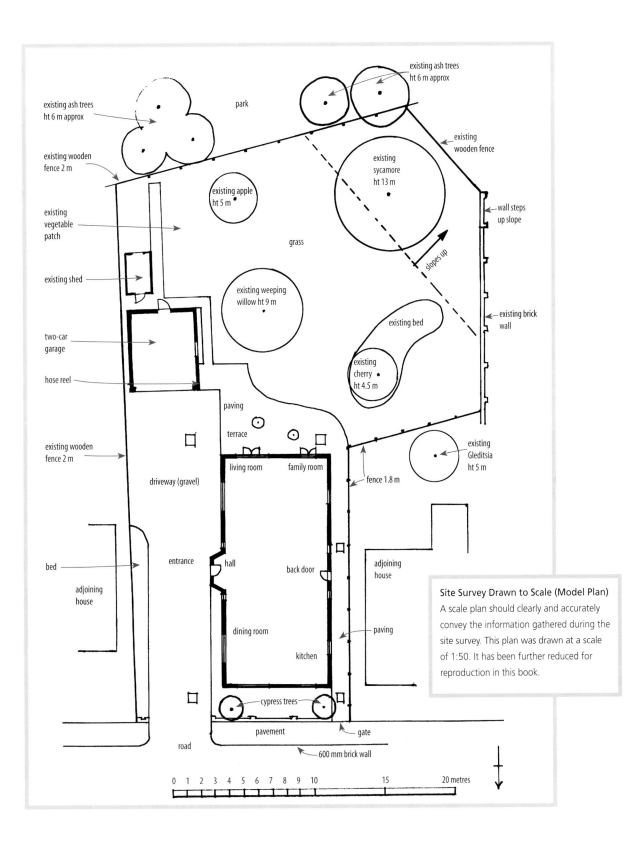

existing ash trees
ht 6 m approx

park

existing ash trees
ht 6 m approx

existing wooden fence

existing wooden
fence 2 m

existing
sycamore
ht 13 m

existing apple
ht 5 m

wall steps
up slope

existing
vegetable
patch

grass

existing shed

slopes up

existing
bed

existing brick
wall

existing weeping
willow ht 9 m

two-car
garage

existing
cherry
ht 4.5 m

hose reel

paving

terrace

existing
Gleditsia
ht 5 m

existing wooden
fence 2 m

living room   family room

fence 1.8 m

driveway (gravel)

entrance   hall   back door

adjoining
house

bed

adjoining
house

dining room   paving

kitchen

Site Survey Drawn to Scale (Model Plan)
A scale plan should clearly and accurately
convey the information gathered during the
site survey. This plan was drawn at a scale
of 1:50. It has been further reduced for
reproduction in this book.

cypress trees

pavement   gate

road

600 mm brick wall

0 1 2 3 4 5 6 7 8 9 10   15   20 metres

Site Inventory Checklist

1. Approach to house
Size of street? Wide - but only local traffic
Traffic intensity? V. Low

2. House
Style and age? 1970's detached single family home.
Condition? Good
Façade materials? Brick and wood siding

3. Outside Services
Location of downpipes? Front left of Garage and front side (right)
Outside lights? (2) - garage 1 at front door
Electric meter? in back garden
Gas meter? same
Taps? Front side right adjacent to down pipe.

4. Hard Landscaping
Condition and materials of paths? Cement - excellent but generic
Steps? cement
Walls? N/A
Other structures? Wood fence w/ gate to back garden.

5. Views from house
To front lhs? Neighbours front garden - open
To front rhs? Obstructed by garage
To front boundary? bound by side walk
To back lhs? Obstructed by trees
To back rhs? Elevated so can see over privacy fence to neighbours patio
To back boundary? Fence (privacy)

6. Sounds or smells? Neighbours dog barking

7. Microclimate
Orientation? North - west
Areas of shade in mid-winter Entire back garden shaded
  a.m.? all day shade
  p.m.?
Areas of shade in the mid-summer All edges near fences shaded
  a.m.? much of the day
  p.m.? Patio gets full afternoon sun
Prevailing wind direction? From East

8. Level changes
Sloping ground? Slopes away from house in front + back.
Areas showing erosion? Tree Roots above ground in front.
Areas showing poor drainage? None
Wall heights? 6 foot privacy fence around entire back garden.
Heights of steps? 6 steps up to front door

9. Soil
Type? Sandy - needs improvement
Depth of topsoil? 3 inches

10. Existing Plants
Location? All trees stay. 3 Aspens + 1 maple in front.
Condition? Good except maple roots exposed in lawn

Recording Information for the Site Inventory: The Checklist

When you have completed drawing up the site survey, the next step is to record the state of the site and make suggestions for improving it. There is so much information to be gathered in this research and preparation phase of the design process that certain points can be easily overlooked. It is helpful, therefore, to refer to a written checklist, or inventory, of existing site conditions such as the one shown here.

The site inventory plan (see page 61) is a factual assessment of everything on the site, from the condition of structures to climatic features, and is prepared as an overlay on the site survey. There will be many reasons, such as cost or lack of access, that will govern what you remove, retain or repair. The site inventory is the first stage in making these decisions.

Photographing the Garden

In addition to surveying and noting facts about the site on your rough sketch plan and scale site survey, there are other steps to be taken before you begin considering the new design. Photographing the garden will allow you to look at its features from a distance, where you can be more practical and dispassionate in your feelings towards the site. Photographs also tend to turn up features often overlooked when on site, such as an unattractive light fitting or a badly rendered wall.

Photography provides the most accurate way of recording views (the camera never lies!). Whether you use a digital camera or a film camera, it is very useful to mount prints of the photographs on card (cardboard) and fix them on the wall in your workplace, providing you with a constant aide-mémoire to help you as you work on the project.

The photographs can also be used later as a basis for "before" and "after" sketches to show how your intentions will alter the garden (see page 254). This is often an easier way of getting your ideas across than doing a thumbnail or perspective sketch.

As has already been seen earlier in this chapter, a photograph can also be useful in estimating the height of features in the garden.

Making a Photographic Record of the Site

1. Standing in a central position, with your back to the house, pivot round from extreme left to extreme right, taking overlapping shots of the site and its surroundings as viewed from the house (see next page). A camera that can take wide panoramic shots would be particularly useful for this exercise. You may find that you can get the best views of a small site from an upstairs window.
2. Stand at the opposite end of the garden, and, moving along a line parallel to the house, take overlapping shots of the house.
3. Take photographs of views from and to carefully selected areas of the garden—for instance, where you may site an important feature, or views from a place where you might want to sit.
4. Take close-up photos of any items that you particularly want to record, such as walls, statues, trees, and pergolas, to show their general condition.
5. Have these photographs printed, mount them on card (cardboard), and study them when you need to be reminded of the site.

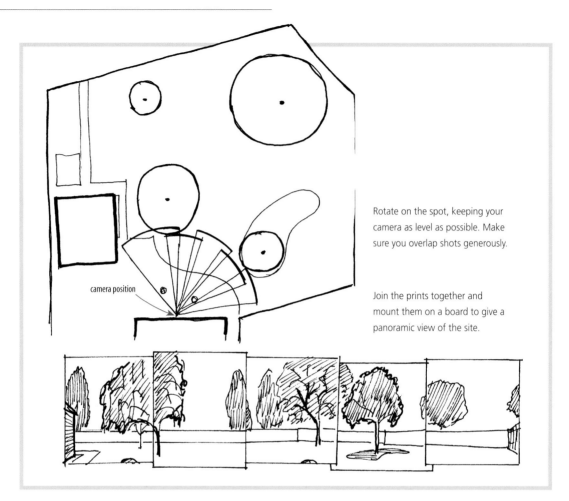

Rotate on the spot, keeping your camera as level as possible. Make sure you overlap shots generously.

Join the prints together and mount them on a board to give a panoramic view of the site.

camera position

The Garden and Its Setting

Planning a garden has much in common with interior decorating and furnishing. There is one subtle difference, however, in that the outdoor room (the garden) is much more influenced by its setting or by what lies immediately beyond its boundary. Just as the surrounding landscape is often visible from the garden, so too will the garden itself exert an influence on its surroundings, sometimes referred to as the Zone of Visual Influence or ZVI. When designing a garden you will need to consider not only what you can see from the site but also how your plans will affect the surroundings and the people passing through. Allow yourself plenty of time to walk around inside and outside the garden to consider how your ideas will affect and relate to the surroundings.

Always consider the safety aspect of your proposals— vigorous thorny climbers, for instance, can be a hazard when overhanging a narrow sidewalk.

Views

First of all, look closely at all the outward views from the garden. Observe and consider the following:

- What are the quality and character of the surroundings?
- Is the pattern of forms, colours and textures created by the combination of man-made features and vegetation?
- Do you like what you see, or is the outlook less than perfect?

If the garden is overlooked, you may want to disguise the boundaries of the garden and create a plan that holds the eye and attention within the site (an "introvert" garden).

Examine each aspect very carefully. Even in the centre of busy, built-up cities there are often glimpses of pleasant views, such as an interesting tree, a cluster of chimney pots or a dramatic skyline, which you can "borrow" to extend the apparent size of your garden (an "extrovert" garden). Every garden appears bigger if the eye is drawn to a viewpoint beyond its boundaries.

An attractive surrounding landscape can be used as a backdrop or inspiration for your new design. You may achieve this by repeating some of the trees, shrubs and materials found in the surrounding landscape, or by echoing the shape of distant features, such as a church spire or roof gable, in your plantings or with clipped topiary. In any outward view it is the shape of the skyline that you will appreciate first. Can you use this line in any way, perhaps by repeating the outline of a curving hill in the shape of a bed or a path? If you can relate your garden to features beyond the boundary, the garden's setting will become part of its overall design.

In most gardens there will be good views to be emphasized or framed up, and less attractive views that require screening. Occasionally, however, a

Make a note of all good and bad views from your garden, as well as the points from which you may be overlooked.

Your notes on views will help you to decide which to screen and which to frame up or emphasize.

Topiary shapes are inspired by the dominant backdrop of the church and its spire.

The design of a window
can greatly influence
the views of the garden
from the house. An
unobstructed picture
window (right) provides
a full view of the garden
from inside the house.
With a shorter window,
(far right) the view is
slightly reduced, creating
a larger "blind area" just
beneath the window
along the house wall.

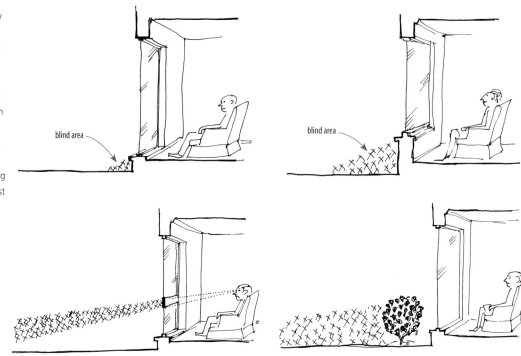

Thick glazing bars or cross-pieces
(above) may affect the view from
the house, particularly from a seated
position. Existing planting around the
house (right) may also block views.

A garden surrounded
by extensive views (left)
is often improved if the
views are broken down
into smaller pictures
(below). Repeating the
curves of distant hills in
the shape of the planting
beds helps to relate the
garden to its setting.

site may be surrounded by extensive pleasant views
which, interestingly, provide too much of a good
thing. They will dominate the eye and reduce the
garden to the status of a viewing platform. In these
situations it is wise to break down the view into a
number of carefully composed pictures, framed
by plantings.

Surroundings

From a distance, the colour of roses or the species of shrubs you plant within the garden may not affect the general view. However, a badly placed tree of the wrong type—a purple beech or a striking golden conifer in a very rural setting, for instance—may seriously damage the view over a considerable distance. On the other hand, tree planting of the right type can bring enormous benefits. For example, the rounded shapes of most deciduous trees, and the shadows which they cast, can break up the hard outlines of buildings, reduce the reflected light from cars, windows or pale surfaces and create a woodland impression from a distance, even when the trees are widely spaced.

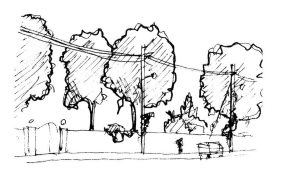

The view from the street has been improved by "losing" the wires against garden trees.

Consider how you can make a positive contribution to the general scene by giving pleasure to those passing by your garden. Even one small tree, cunningly placed, can help to break the monotony of a long treeless street, providing interest as it changes with the seasons and matures over the years.

Trees can soften the hard outlines of buildings, reduce the reflected light from cars, and create a woodland impression from a distance.

The presence of a single tree helps to relieve the monotony of a long row of houses.

When using plants to conceal unattractive features, avoid using unnatural shapes and colour; these will draw attention to themselves and therefore to whatever you are trying to hide. Instead, try to use natural, local plants to harmonize with your surroundings and to blend with, rather than totally obscure, what you are trying to hide. This technique applies equally to town and suburban situations where there are frequently eyesores such as television aerials, drainpipes, fire escapes and ugly buildings from which you would like to distract attention.

Try to think of ways of giving pleasure to people passing by your garden.

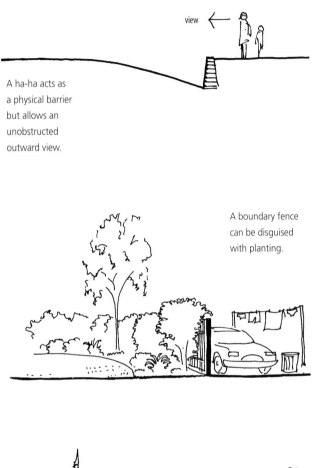

view ←

A ha-ha acts as a physical barrier but allows an unobstructed outward view.

A boundary fence can be disguised with planting.

Boundaries

Generally the boundaries of a garden are fixed and need to be maintained, either for legal reasons, to keep out straying animals or to retain straying children. However, the boundaries do not necessarily need to be seen. They can be concealed with plantings, or they can be sunk, like the eighteenth-century ha-ha (see page 167), to permit an uninterrupted outward view.

If, on the other hand, you wish to emphasize your boundary, then the material used and the general shape must relate to the adjoining house and surroundings so that it is seen as an integral part of the design.

In the country, where the zone of visual influence may extend to the surrounding countryside, boundary planting must be handled very sensitively. Often, the shape and position of the plot is at odds with the general pattern of hills and valleys, woods and fields. By emphasizing these boundaries unduly—for example, with a line of Lombardy poplars or tall conifers—you may create an ugly block that can be seen for miles around.

Left: A garden can be seen from a surprising number of viewpoints.

Right: If you plant your boundaries inappropriately you may spoil the view for miles around.

Sometimes, in order to improve the proportions of an area, an apparent boundary can be built within it while the real boundary line is hidden beyond. Even a small garden can be made to appear more spacious by careful subdivision.

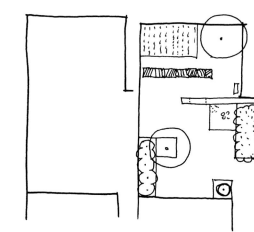

Plan of the existing site   Plan showing proposed design

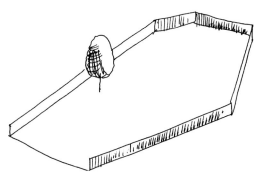

An awkwardly shaped site

Perspective of proposed design

A semi-formal solution

An informal solution

The proportions of awkwardly shaped sites can be improved by disguising the actual boundary and creating apparent boundaries within the space.

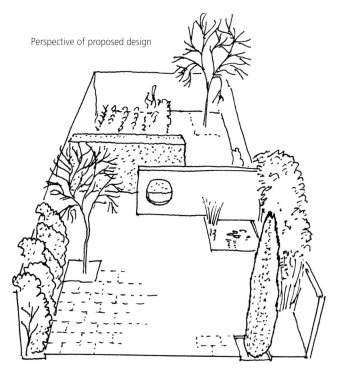

An abstract, asymmetric design illustrating the use of artificial boundaries—one of concrete and one of hedging—to subdivide a garden and make it appear larger. Obscuring parts of the side walls with planting further helps the illusion.

Recording Existing Conditions

Weather, orientation and the condition of the land are important factors that influence what can and cannot be achieved in the garden.

Aspect

Aspect, or the orientation of the garden, refers to the direction—north, south, east or west—in which the house or garden faces, which determines how the sun falls on the garden. You will be able to ascertain aspect with a compass or by using a detailed map or street plan on which you can locate the site, and you should mark the north point in the lower right-hand corner of your drawings.

If your garden is in a cool region you will want to make the most of the sunny areas, but the height of the sun will vary according to the seasons and to what is in its path. Estate agents, when showing houses in the depths of winter, will naturally try to emphasize the appeal of any light and sunny rooms. Beware, however, of tall neighbouring trees—you may find quite a changed atmosphere in midsummer when the trees are in leaf.

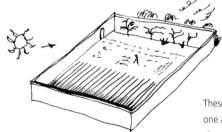

Even in cold climates, many tender Mediterranean plants can flourish on south-facing brick walls in full sun.

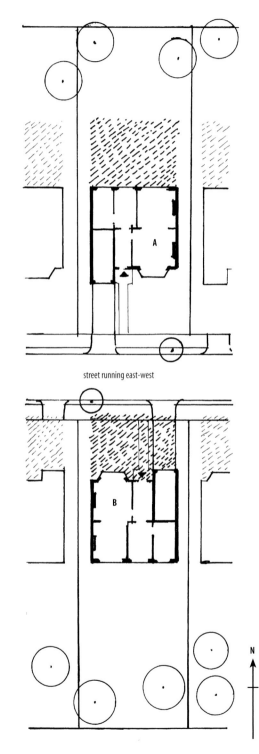

street running east-west

These low-built houses, facing one another across a street, are almost identical. However, because of their orientation, the gardens will feel very different. House A is south facing. This will have a sunny front garden, but the back garden will be shady where adjacent to the house. In contrast, house B will have a shady front garden—but the area adjacent to the house in the back garden will be sunny.

The orientation of a garden
will affect the kinds of
plants that will thrive in it.

Shade

Shade can be beneficial. Most of us now know
about the potential danger of long exposure to
blazing sunshine, and the dappled shade cast by
trees can often provide relief. Shadows can also
create a variety of interesting effects, dependent on
the quality of light. For instance, the Italian cypress
can be used dramatically in warmer climates such as
Italy, where it grows so well, whereas in the variable
British climate the bluish light dilutes the shadows
and lessens the contrast between light and shade.

In warmer or sun-baked areas, creating shade may
be vital to how the garden is used. Man-made shade
structures are easily assembled, but tree planting may

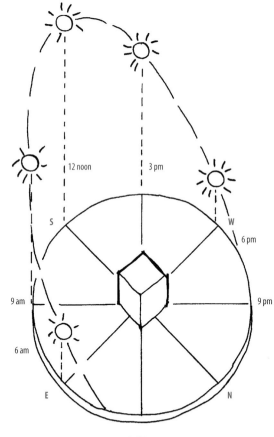

The varied path of the sun
in summer and winter.

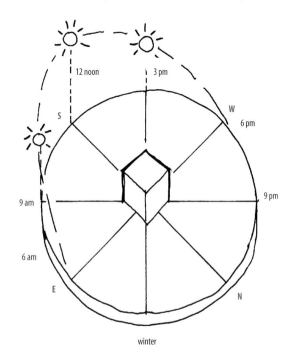

summer

winter

53

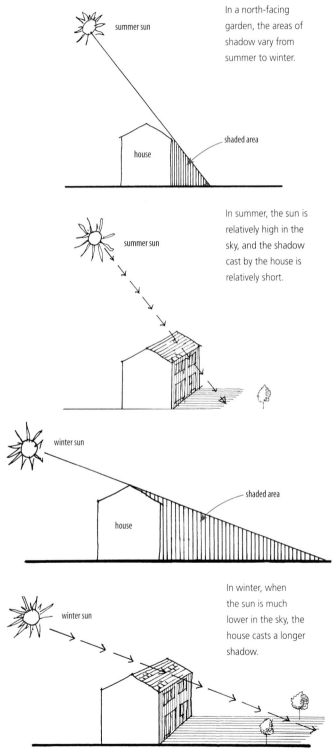

In a north-facing garden, the areas of shadow vary from summer to winter.

summer sun

house

shaded area

In summer, the sun is relatively high in the sky, and the shadow cast by the house is relatively short.

summer sun

winter sun

house

shaded area

In winter, when the sun is much lower in the sky, the house casts a longer shadow.

winter sun

be a wiser long-term investment, bringing wildlife and other natural attributes into the garden. Record your garden's areas of sun and shade on your site plan, as these might affect your design proposals.

Climate

Climate has a major influence on the character of a site and the way in which a garden is used, and must be borne in mind when planning any new design.

The United States as a whole has a highly variable climate. The hardiness-zone system is based on the average annual minimum temperatures and enables North American gardeners to work out the zone in which they live and then select plants that carry the zone rating of their own region or higher. If you know your microclimate, you have an excellent chance of growing plants rated with a lower zone than your region by planting them in the warmer places in your garden. Heat, wind, rainfall and humidity are other factors affecting the hardiness of plants. If your area tends to hold a snow cover from mid-December until mid-March, you can usually grow plants rated for one zone warmer than is indicated for your region.

In much of Britain, the temperate, maritime climate with occasional extremes such as harsh winters or dry summers makes it possible to grow plants introduced from many parts of the world. Under these cool, damp conditions, grass grows especially well, lawns being recognized as an integral part of the English landscape. However, in Britain and the rest of Europe as well as the United States, the regional climate can vary enormously.

Recently climate change has made conditions more extreme. The climate generally has become increasingly erratic, with higher temperatures, violent storms and longer periods of rain or drought. In urban situations these changes may be less noticeable, although rooftop gardens may be affected. It is important to ensure that you choose the right plants for your garden's conditions, and placing them in parts of the garden where they will thrive. Having the right plant in the right place minimizes the need for watering and other techniques, which in addition to being demanding can also be a drain on natural resources.

The climate has an influence not only on the plants that can be grown but also on the materials that are used locally, and this in turn may influence the style or architecture of the houses in the area. In northern or windswept areas of Europe, stone is readily available, and the houses built of it are able to withstand strong winds. In Scandinavian countries, where wood is readily available, brightly painted houses often stand on stilts. Further south, where the climate is less harsh, brick, timber, glass and Perspex (arcrylic plastic) are more frequently used.

Altitude has a bearing on the climate—higher areas are colder and often exposed to strong winds, while lower areas may be subject to prolonged frost pockets. The topography of the locality will also affect the amount of rainfall received. Coastal areas may suffer from salt spray but will have a good quality of light and are rarely are affected by frost.

Wind is among the most damaging factors in a garden, making both plants and people uncomfortable. Exposure to wind can desiccate many plants, in extreme cases tearing foliage from branches. The hasty removal of an established tree or hedge can alter the microclimate, leaving the area exposed to the elements. In Britain the prevailing wind normally comes from the southwest, but it can be unpredictable and may vary according to the surroundings. The most reliable way to work out your own individual microclimate, or local prevailing weather patterns, is to observe the conditions that occur during an entire year, although even then it is possible to encounter sudden unexpected changes.

Wind Tunnels

In cities, particularly, a garden may be affected by wind tunnels channelling the air through the spaces between high buildings. Building a wall to shield an area from wind is expensive and not necessarily effective: although it may offer some protection on the immediate leeward side, on hitting the ground again wind tends to eddy or swirl around in unexpected directions. An alternative is to plant a shelterbelt, windbreak or even a hedge to filter

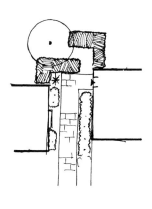

In this typical situation, the wind is channelled through the gap between neighbouring houses, creating an unpleasant wind tunnel effect.

Here, the wind tunnel has been counteracted by the judicious planting of overlapping hedges and a single tree, which work together to filter the wind, reducing its velocity.

A solid barrier, such as a wall, provides some protection from wind on the immediate leeward side, although a lot of pressure is exerted on the barrier on the windward side. Further on, where the wind hits the ground again, it tends to swirl around unexpectedly.

When planting a shelter belt of trees and shrubs, choose a varied mixture of species and heights. The length of the shelter produced on the leeward side will be approximately three times the height of the shelter belt.

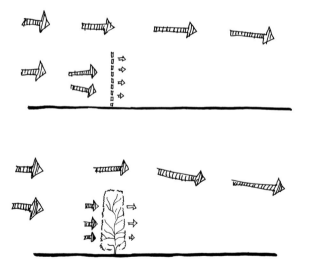

Structures that allow some air to pass through them, such as hedges, trellis or open-slatted fences, tend to provide more effective windbreaks than solid structures. As shown here, these structures act as filters, allowing some wind to pass through, but greatly reducing its velocity.

the wind and reduce its velocity. Use small plants in preference to larger ones so that their roots can get a firm grip in the soil before becoming taller when they may be severely rocked by the wind.

Cold air always flows downhill and onto low ground. On a winter morning you can see the effects of this—higher areas may be frost-free while lower levels are still gripped by frost. Buildings, lawns and terraces interrupt the downward flow of air, creating frost pockets, which remain cold for many hours—as uncomfortable for the roots of plants as for people.

Drainage

Drainage will also have an effect on the site. On sloping sites the rain will drain naturally, whereas on a flat site it may remain for some days, particularly if the soil is compacted or there is no cross-fall to a drainage channel or gulley. A trial pit can be dug to check how quickly the soil drains water away (see page 33). If waterlogging is a serious problem, a drainage system may be necessary.

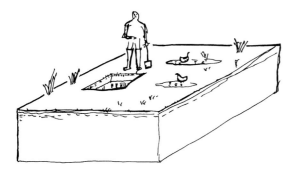

If you suspect poor drainage and/or waterlogging, dig a trial pit.

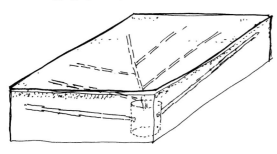

You may need to consider underground soil drainage and a soakaway.

For areas with poor drainage, slope the ground away from the house and away from the centre of the garden into ditches dug either side of the site. Very often the perimeter of the garden will be planted so that any excess water draining into these areas will be absorbed by the soil and plants.

Assessing the Soil

You have already taken soil samples from the garden (page 32), and you now need to assess what can or cannot be grown according to the results of the soil tests. As these may well affect the design of your garden, it is important that you understand the advantages or restrictions that the existing soil pH value, the soil structure and the water table may impose.

Rushes and reeds indicate wet, poor soil.

Thistles spring up on waste ground and poor soil.

Rhododendrons thrive on acid soil.

The type of soil in a garden is conditioned by the underlying geology. Both the texture and mineral content of the surface topsoil are derived from the substrata of gravel, clay or rock. The substrata also determine the relative acidity or alkalinity of the soil. The pH factor governs the type of plants that will thrive in your garden. The pH factor under which the widest range of plants can thrive is a fairly neutral pH of 5.7–6.7, but in very acid areas you may find a reading of pH 4.4 or in very alkaline areas a reading of pH 7.5.

The soil type or pH can often also be recognized by looking at the natural vegetation and identifying "soil indicators", as certain types of plant are known to flourish only on particular types of soil. Rhododendrons and heathers, for instance, will thrive on acid soil, while forms of viburnum or spindle (*Euonymus europaeus*) prefer chalky, alkaline conditions. Extreme degrees of acidity or alkalinity will limit the type of plants that can be grown.

Sandy or peaty soils are often acidic, while heavy clay soil is usually alkaline. Many soils fall between the two and can be classified as neutral.

Soil structure is determined by the size of the particles that make up the soil and by the quantity of accumulated organic matter present in the soil. The layer of soil overlying chalk is often only 75 mm (3 in.) thick. Chalky subsoil is unable to retain moisture and nutrients, so that only shallow-rooted plants that favour a well-drained soil can thrive. Clay soil, often cold and wet, consists of very small, tightly packed particles that stick together and retain moisture for most of the year, only drying out and cracking in prolonged, very hot weather. Sandy or peaty soils, usually warm, are composed of much larger particles, so drainage is quicker and the soil warms up faster. The ideal soil for growing most garden plants is a loam, which consists of a mixture of slightly more sand than clay particles, with a high organic content.

Some useful soil indicators:

Viburnum, spindle—chalky, alkaline soil

Heather, lingonberry—dry, acid or peaty soil

Nettle, chickweed—potentially fertile soil

Canterbury bells, catnip (catmint)—chalky or alkaline soil

Sheep's sorrel—poor, light, dry, acid soil

Foxglove, sandwort—dry, sandy or gravely soil

Paleseed plantain or hoary plantain—dry, hard, stony, alkaline soil

Barren strawberry or wild strawberry—dry, stony, barren soil

Furze or gorse or broom—poor, infertile soil

Heath bedstraw—dry, light, acid soil

Silverweed or silvery cinquefoil or goose tansy, coltsfoot—damp, clay soil

Wild thyme—dry soil

Brooklime, marsh foxtail or water foxtail—wet, fertile soil

Common butterwort, lesser spearwort—wet, infertile soil

Goldenrod—wet sand

Legal Considerations

In most countries, active measures are now taken to protect the countryside and the enjoyment of it. There are certain legal factors that may affect, or be affected by, your proposals. These factors, which include the siting of water points and the removal of existing trees, must be kept in mind from the outset to avoid later confusion and expense. You should always consult the local governing body to confirm which, if any, of these issues may affect your project.

Conservation Areas or Historic Districts

If the property is in a conservation area, there will be strict regulations on what you are allowed to do, including severe pruning or removal of any trees. For advice, consult your local conservation officer or county official.

Tree Preservation Orders

In the United Kingdom, a tree preservation order (TPO) prohibits the removal or cutting down of trees, and there may be an order on certain trees within the garden. The local planning authority will have copies of these TPOs ready for inspection in the district to which they relate, and they are required to send copies of these orders to the owners or occupiers of affected land. Any person who contravenes a TPO is liable to be prosecuted, and the High Court may take out an injunction to stop further disobedience. The authority may also give consent to the cutting down, topping or lopping of trees or groups of trees, but this takes time and may be subject to certain conditions.

In the United States and many other countries, similar restrictions may apply so be sure to keep abreast of the regulations governing the removal of trees in your local area.

Neighbours

The most frequent problems involving neighbours have to do with overhanging and dangerous trees, invasive weeds and the right to light.

When tree branches spread over and roots travel under neighbouring properties, they infringe the right of the owners to the unrestricted use of their land, so the neighbour is entitled, as far as the law is concerned, to cut off the intruding part without notice, even though this may kill the tree. The owners or occupiers of the land are also liable to neighbours and to the public for injuries caused by trees on their land, only escaping liability if they did not know that the tree that caused the injury was dangerous. When it comes to planting, you must ensure that trees will not outgrow their position and cause problems in future.

Landowners are not liable to their neighbours if they allow weeds to grow and the wind to spread their seeds unless these are "injurious weeds", which include thistles, dock and ragwort. In this case, the occupiers of the land may be required to take action within a definite time to stop the weeds spreading, or else be prosecuted.

In the United Kingdom the right to light is a complex issue, the general rule being that nobody is entitled to daylight through their windows unless the landowners or their predecessors have had daylight through their windows for twenty years or more, in which case they will have acquired a right to continue to have a reasonable amount of light as long as the house stands. However, this is a delicate question, and should you envisage interfering with your neighbour's right to light, by building a wall or erecting a building, it would be wise to seek legal advice in your particular region before carrying out any work.

Boundary Ownership

Normally, walls or fences separate small town or village gardens from each other. It is important to establish which boundary is your responsibility—if in doubt, consult your local authority. Disputes regarding dilapidated fences and crumbling walls can easily arise with neighbours, and it is wise to know who is legally responsible for their repair.

Covenant Communities

Covenant communities typically have strict rules about what homeowners in the community can do to the exterior of their homes. When a homeowner buys in an area with a covenant in place, typically all changes to the exterior need to be reviewed by the homeowners association. It is best to find out what is allowed in the community before putting together your design so that you avoid having to change it later.

Pre-excavation Responsibilities

In the United States and Australia, it is illegal in most areas to do any excavation without contacting the county or a "call-before-you-dig" clearinghouse service. Services typically include on-site marking of all underground gas, water and electricity pipes and wires as well as providing you with underground network plans. Neglecting to call before excavating can lead to costly disruption to essential services, injury or death to workers or the general public and heavy financial and legal penalties.

Drawing up the Site Inventory Plan

1. Lay a fresh sheet of tracing paper over the site survey plan.
2. First trace over all the elements shown on the site plan. Referring to your survey notes and the site inventory checklist (see page 44), transfer as much information as you can onto the new drawing using either written descriptions or abstract graphic symbols. Try to use symbols where possible, as they will help to bring your site inventory to life and make it easier to read and refer to later.
3. Make a note of any structural features that you will be retaining, describing the materials used and their general state (for example, worn or newly repaired).
4. Consider existing vegetation, and make a note of any plants that you wish to retain or move in the new design.
5. Using a compass, note the orientation of the site.
6. Observe and note any shadows cast, as well as any sunny areas.
7. Record, if possible, and note the direction of prevailing winds.
8. Note areas of good or poor drainage.
9. Note any areas where frost pockets may occur.
10. Note any other features that will affect comfort in the garden.
11. Establish who owns which boundaries, and record this information.
12. Colour (covered in Chapter 5) can help to enhance the plan. For instance, you may wish to use blue arrows to indicate cold winds and yellow stars to represent sunny spots. However, do not apply colour to the tracing paper, as this will not reproduce when copied; instead, have the plan copied first and then colour up the copy.

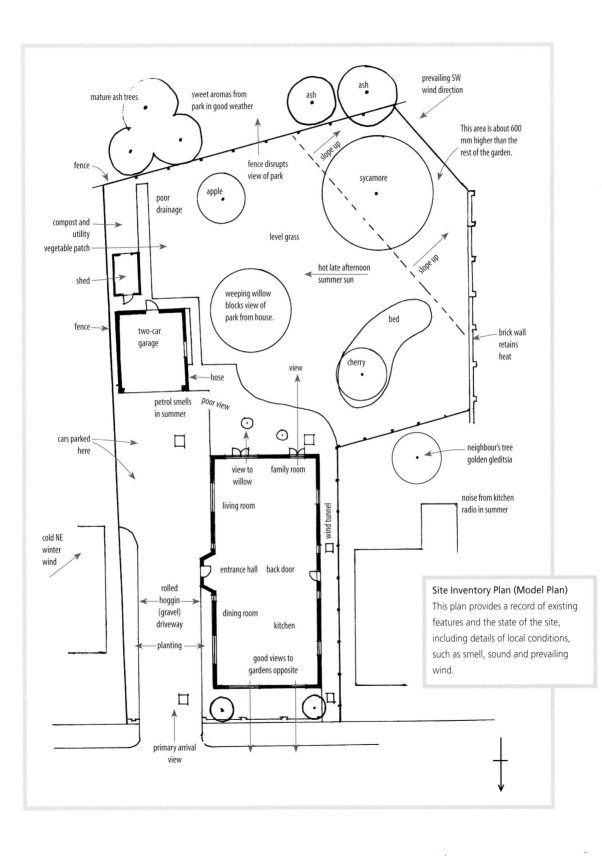

mature ash trees

sweet aromas from park in good weather

ash

ash

prevailing SW wind direction

This area is about 600 mm higher than the rest of the garden.

fence

fence disrupts view of park

slope up

compost and utility

poor drainage

apple

sycamore

vegetable patch

level grass

shed

hot late afternoon summer sun

slope up

weeping willow blocks view of park from house.

fence

bed

brick wall retains heat

two-car garage

cherry

hose

petrol smells in summer

poor view

view

neighbour's tree golden gleditsia

cars parked here

view to willow

family room

noise from kitchen radio in summer

living room

wind tunnel

cold NE winter wind

entrance hall

back door

rolled hoggin (gravel) driveway

dining room

kitchen

planting

good views to gardens opposite

Site Inventory Plan (Model Plan)
This plan provides a record of existing features and the state of the site, including details of local conditions, such as smell, sound and prevailing wind.

primary arrival view

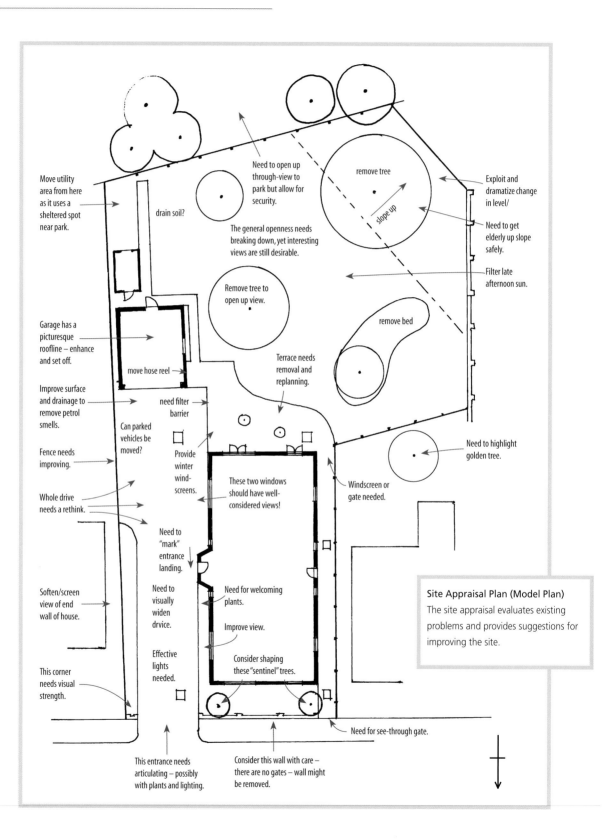

Move utility area from here as it uses a sheltered spot near park.

drain soil?

Need to open up through-view to park but allow for security.

remove tree

slope up

Exploit and dramatize change in level/

Need to get elderly up slope safely.

The general openness needs breaking down, yet interesting views are still desirable.

Filter late afternoon sun.

Garage has a picturesque roofline – enhance and set off.

Remove tree to open up view.

remove bed

move hose reel

Terrace needs removal and replanning.

Improve surface and drainage to remove petrol smells.

need filter barrier

Need to highlight golden tree.

Fence needs improving.

Can parked vehicles be moved?

Provide winter wind-screens.

These two windows should have well-considered views!

Windscreen or gate needed.

Whole drive needs a rethink.

Need to "mark" entrance landing.

Soften/screen view of end wall of house.

Need to visually widen drvice.

Need for welcoming plants.

Improve view.

This corner needs visual strength.

Effective lights needed.

Consider shaping these "sentinel" trees.

Need for see-through gate.

This entrance needs articulating – possibly with plants and lighting.

Consider this wall with care – there are no gates – wall might be removed.

Site Appraisal Plan (Model Plan)
The site appraisal evaluates existing problems and provides suggestions for improving the site.

Drawing up the Site Appraisal

The next stage of the design process involves more thought than the surveying and inventory stages, because, before putting pencil to paper, you will have to take some time to evaluate the importance of the information that you have collected and noted. You will have to ask yourself if the information is relevant and, significantly, whether it presents a problem or offers some potential.

You may, for instance, have recorded on the site inventory the presence of a large tree in the middle of the garden. Now, for the site appraisal, you will have to decide whether the tree presents a problem (for instance, whether it blocks an important view, casts too much shade or is an inappropriate type), or if it offers some potential (it helps to frame the view, provides some privacy or provides a focal point). You will then note down your decision on the site appraisal drawing. For instance, "Large pear tree to remain to provide privacy for new seating area", or simply, "Large pear tree to be integrated into new design".

1. Attach a tracing-paper overlay on the scale drawing of the site survey. Using a pen, work across the plan, annotating it with your well-considered decisions while making the site inventory.
2. Although this overlay is for your own use, practising the habit of writing clearly and evenly will be useful when you are producing later work. Use the T-square or parallel motion rule to keep your remarks running evenly across the sheet.
3. Do not get carried away and lose sight of the particular conditions of the site. Checking back to your appraisal frequently should help you ensure that your design is in keeping with the site conditions.
4. This plan can be used as a tracing-paper overlay on the site survey. If you want to copy it, you will need to trace the outline of the house and boundary and other key features which need to be explained.

Moving Towards the Design Stage

With the research and preparation phase—the site survey, inventory and appraisal—of the design process completed, you should now have a good idea of all the elements that you will need to include in a new design. Referring back to the garden owner's checklist (page 17), you should be able to see at a glance what you have listed as desirable. You may, for instance, have ticked such items as terrace, rose garden, vegetable garden, barbecue area, lawn and shed, all of which will have to be sited somewhere in the design proposals.

At this stage you need to start thinking about where you are going to place each of these items, how much space will be needed to allow for them, and how they are going to function in relation to one another. The site appraisal will help you to decide on positioning, but for every site there will be numerous alternatives.

Where you choose to position various elements will depend both on how you want the items to relate to each other and the constraints of the site. Your site appraisal will be very useful for this. You may, for instance, decide to position a terrace in a particular spot where it is partly shaded by the canopy of an existing tree. Your decision to try out this idea may have been influenced by the comments of the garden users who noted that the terrace, in its existing position, was too hot. With this decision made, you will have to think about what you would like next to the terrace. Would it be suitable to place the lawn here, for the children to play football on, or would this perhaps be an ideal position for a pool, which could also be viewed from the sitting room window? If you decide on the pool you will need to think of what will be suitable to go next to it. In this way, you will gradually fill up all the available space.

There are several different ways of approaching the design process, which are fully explored in the next chapter, and which can be developed through theme plans (see page 89). To help you reach beyond preconceived ideas in your approach to garden design, you may wish to try producing concept diagrams.

Drawing Concept Diagrams

1. Attach a sheet of tracing paper as an overlay on the site survey.
2. Referring back to the garden owner's checklist, use felt-tip pens or a technical drawing pen to draw loose shapes or circles to indicate the most suitable position for each of the desired features, such as the lawn, shed or the position for the barbecue.
3. Remember to allow enough space for each area to function comfortably.
4. If possible, each shape should almost touch the next, so that when you have finished, every area in the garden will be allocated to a particular function.
5. By ticking off each element mentioned on the checklist, you can ensure that nothing has been overlooked.
6. There will be many different alternatives for every design, and you should experiment with these diagrams as much as possible. Keep these drawings to refer to when beginning the preliminary garden plan.

Consolidating the Information

If the many issues that have been covered in this chapter are taken into account at the planning stage, the work will progress more speedily and smoothly later. The site survey, site analysis and site appraisal are vital stages in developing a design. If you are asked to design someone else's garden, they will rarely be shown this information and the

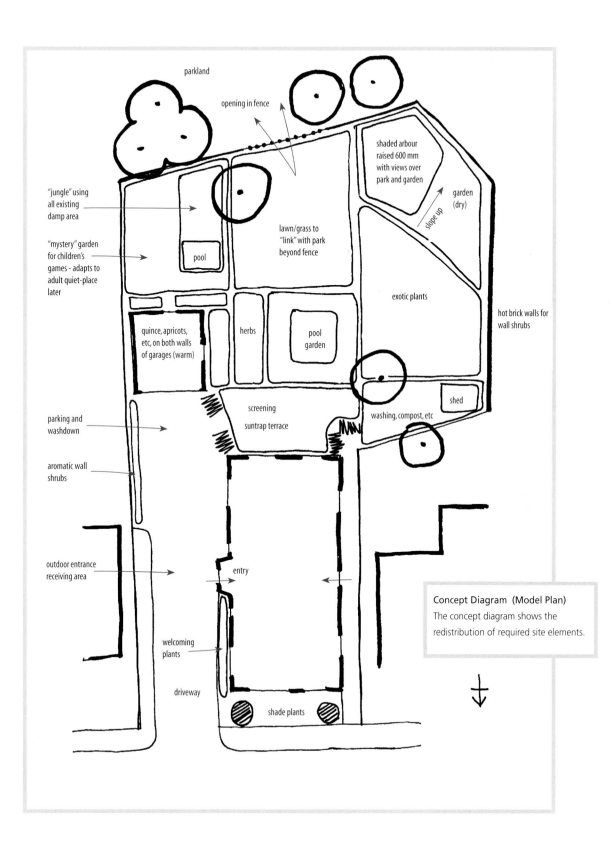

parkland

opening in fence

"jungle" using all existing damp area

"mystery" garden for children's games - adapts to adult quiet-place later

shaded arbour raised 600 mm with views over park and garden

garden (dry)

slope up

lawn/grass to "link" with park beyond fence

pool

exotic plants

hot brick walls for wall shrubs

quince, apricots, etc, on both walls of garages (warm)

herbs

pool garden

shed

parking and washdown

screening

suntrap terrace

washing, compost, etc

aromatic wall shrubs

outdoor entrance receiving area

entry

welcoming plants

driveway

shade plants

Concept Diagram (Model Plan)
The concept diagram shows the redistribution of required site elements.

resulting drawings, but this process should always be undertaken so that you understand the site that you are working with, its limitations and potential. If at a later stage there are queries about how or why you have arrived at your design, you may need to refer back to these notes and drawings.

If you are working for a committee, perhaps for improvements to a communal garden square, or for a public garden, these notes and drawings may be particularly helpful to explain how you have arrived at your solution.

Chapter 2

Developing the Design: Focusing on the Ground Plane

Developing the Design: Focusing on the Ground Plane

With the research and preparation phase completed, you are now ready to start designing. In this chapter you will prepare a preliminary garden layout plan based on the conclusions you reached through the site survey, site inventory and site appraisal, and your initial planning ideas in the concept diagrams.

The graphic language (the ability to put your ideas on paper) is central to the garden design process. It is used to communicate ideas and solutions and to record information. You may have had no experience with drawing and be daunted by the idea of expressing yourself graphically, but the objective is not to produce beautiful pieces of artwork but simply to communicate your ideas. The basic drawing skills that are needed for working plans (covered in Chapter 1) are developed in this chapter to cover those that are needed to create a garden layout plan.

Approaching the Design Process

When thinking of how to start designing a new garden, it is easy to think in terms of playing with the existing features (for example, enlarging the terrace or widening borders). However, this approach does not properly consider the available space and tends to produce predictable results, which do not really constitute a thorough redesign of the garden.

Approaching things in a different way and starting by creating abstract patterns on paper will inspire a variety of alternative designs for your garden, many of which you may not originally have thought of (just as abstract art is open to different interpretations). Once you have experimented and established how to create patterns of different character, you are ready to redesign your site. The patterns can then be combined with a grid structure, which will lead you to create different design themes based on circles, diagonals or rectangles. These themes can then be translated into gardens by imagining each design as three-dimensional and allocating elements, such as a terrace or paths,

to the spaces created by the themes. The three-dimensional implications of your proposals can then be considered, and the way the mood of a space is affected by the quality of light.

Scale and proportion are examined so that you can relate the scale of the human figure to the much greater scale of the outside world. For instance, the dimensions of garden features such as steps need to be more generous than those usually found inside a house. Surfaces and suitable rigid and loose materials for your hard landscaping are also chosen at this stage. As a general guide, the proportions of one-third or two-thirds of hard landscaping to two-thirds or one-third of soft landscaping (lawn, water and planting) are a comfortable ratio to work to.

The presence or absence of water in the garden must be addressed early in the design stage. In areas where water is scarce, your garden layout plan should reflect your concern in both hard landscaping and planting. For practical purposes, the location of the various features should be governed by the type of soil, climate and accessibility. To be aesthetically acceptable, the scale and type of water feature should appear to be a natural part of the design.

Having considered all these factors, you will be ready to examine your previous ideas and refine them, focusing on the horizontal plane of the design (perhaps allowing ample space for a terrace and paths) and enhancing the scheme with some vertical interest, to produce a preliminary garden layout plan.

Drawing Skills for Presentation Plans

The four kinds of plans described in Chapter 1—the site survey, the site inventory, the site appraisal and the concept diagram—are unlikely to be seen by anyone but you, as they are working drawings. However, the next stage—the garden layout plan—should be drawn up on a sheet of tracing paper. This drawing should be neat, clear and well organized so that it can be presented to a client, used by a contractor or simply kept for your own use. This plan will then be reproduced by copying for you to work from at the next stage, and for all subsequent work, giving continuity of the design and the layout of the plan sheet. (Remember that A2 paper is a convenient size to work with, as it is easier to have reproduced as a photocopy, dyeline or blueprint than a larger size.)

The Plan Sheet

Although preprinted architect's plan sheets are available, for a professional finish it is better to design your own master plan sheet. It should contain the following:

— A "title block", containing the name of the garden owner, your name (as the designer), the title of the drawing and the scale to which it is drawn
— An information panel in which to write additional information to supplement the plan
— A north point to denote orientation
— A scale
— The plan
— A border

The title block, north point and scale should always be located in the bottom right-hand corner of your plan so that this information can be seen at a glance when the plan is folded. (It might be difficult to open out the plan outdoors in a high wind!) The plan itself should be positioned centrally in the remaining space, allowing sufficient space around it for any labelling or notes.

Designing a Title Block

The dimensions of the title block will be determined by the organization of the information, the size and style of the lettering and the typeface used. The title block should be in proportion to the sheet size but should not exceed a width of 150 mm (6 in.). The following information should be included:

— Printed details giving your name (or company name) as the designer and your logo if you have one, your address, telephone, fax, mobile number and email address (the design can be printed separately and double up as a visiting card)
— The name and/or address of the client or garden owner
— The title of the drawing (for example, garden layout plan, planting plan, visual)
— The scale or scales used
— The date
— A drawing number (any later revisions should have subsequent numbers)
— Any alterations or revisions, numbered accordingly
— "Drawn by [initials only]" (occasionally different people work on the same drawing)
— A disclaimer
— A statement of copyright

The statement of copyright (for example, © RA) protects you as a designer so that your work cannot be used or copied without your permission. If you are designing a garden for a client it is particularly important to include a disclaimer stating that "all dimensions must be checked on site and not scaled from this drawing". This puts the responsibility

When possible, position your plan so that it reflects your main viewing point of the garden.

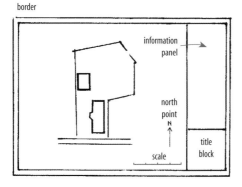

KARENA BATSTONE
——— GARDEN DESIGN ———

21 SOMERSET STREET, KINGSDOWN, BRISTOL BS2 8LZ
TELEPHONE/FACSIMILE: (0117) 9441004

Client:

Title:

Scale: Date:

Drawing no: Revisions: Drawn by:

All dimensions must be checked on site and not scaled from
this drawing.

© Karena Batstone BSc 2009

An example of a title block

for checking dimensions for tendering purposes
or beginning construction on the contractor. This
was necessary before modern drawing reproduction
methods, when drawings were executed on linen,
which could stretch and result in inaccurate
measurements, but it is still in use as a safeguard.

The title block should have your own logo or style.
Choice of lettering or typeface is a personal matter,
but simple, clear styles are usually the most effective.
The title block can be designed as a separate piece of
artwork before being applied to the sheet together
with the information panel and border.

Lettering

The lettering on a title block (and for the labelling
of the plan) can be produced by hand, with stencils
or dry-transfer lettering, (although this is seldom
used nowadays) or by computer. Handwriting is the
quickest method for labelling, but it is only suitable
if your writing is neat and legible, since lettering
is part of the overall visual presentation. Styles of
writing vary enormously, and many different styles
are acceptable.

The important thing is to aim for consistency of
letterform, spacing (between letters, words and lines
of lettering) and style. If you are lettering by hand
or with stencils, it will help if you use lined paper or
lay graph paper under your drawing. Keep the pencil
line weight consistent, and work down from the top
of the page to avoid smudging. A "rolling ruler",
available from most graphic equipment stores, also
helps to improve handwriting.

It is useful to develop a style of lettering that is
comfortable for you. Aim to be clear, consistent and
legible. Try different techniques, particularly when
designing your title block. Practise using stencils,
aiming for even letter and word spacing, holding the
stencil firmly with one hand against the T-square or
parallel motion. It is easier to keep the letters close
together than to space them widely at even intervals.

If you have a computer or typewriter, you may
wish to generate text using this equipment. Where
possible, try out different sizes and typefaces.
Remember that the originals will be copied and that

thin
pencil
guidelines ⟨ ABCDEFGHIJKLMNOPQRRSTUVWXYZ 1234567890
ABCDEFGHIJKLMNOPQRRSTUVWXYZ 1234567890

Above: If you are not using graph paper under the tracing
paper sheet, use pencil guidelines to ensure that the letters are
all the same height.
Right: You can maintain verticals by using a small set square
against your parallel rule.

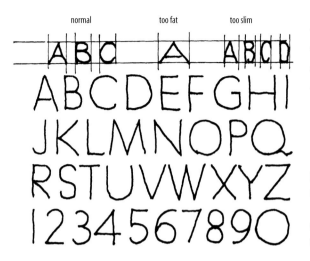

normal   too fat   too slim

ABCDEFGHI
JKLMNOPQ
RSTUVWXYZ
1234567890

typefaces   styles   text sizes
typefaces   *styles*   text sizes
typefaces   **styles**   text sizes
typefaces   STYLES   text sizes
text sizes
text sizes

Left: Oblong proportions result in the most stable lettering.

Above: Computer-generated lettering offers a huge range of styles and sizes.

some typefaces will reproduce better than others. This is a suitable technique to use for designing a title block, but for labelling, the text will need to be printed, cut out and stuck onto your drawing, and this is a time-consuming process.

Information Panel

This area is usually designed as a vertical extension of the title block. It will eventually contain notes (on design intention and hard landscaping or plant numbers, for example) to supplement your drawings.

Border

Your drawings—the garden layout, planting plans and visuals—will look more professional if a border surrounds the sheet on which they are displayed. This will draw attention to the work in the same way as a frame sets off a painting or a photograph.

A border should be drawn in ink with a technical drawing pen in a fairly thick nib size (0.5 mm or 0.7 mm) around the perimeter of the sheet, approximately 10 mm (0.4 in.) from the outside edge.

Borders may consist of a single straight line, a double line (perhaps with the outer line thicker than the inner one) or a pattern. A small detail can be used to

emphasize each corner. Borders may be drawn by hand or on a computer. Experiment with different effects, remembering that you are aiming for a border design that will enhance, rather than distract from, a plan. A simple, clear design is often the most successful and tends to suit the majority of garden styles.

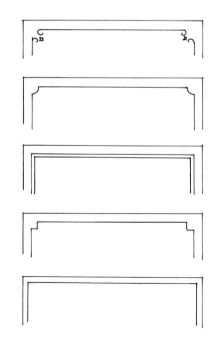

Simple borders are usually the most effective. Fancy or elaborate designs should be used with great care. They may make your design look dated.

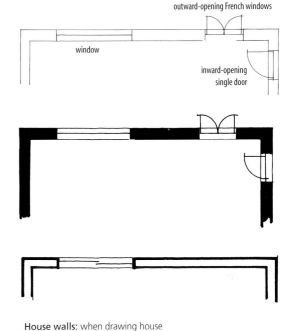

Designing the Master Plan Sheet

1. Fix an A2 (17 × 22 in.) sheet of tracing paper with masking tape on a drawing board, making sure that it is accurately aligned.
2. Draw the border with a 0.5- or 0.7-mm pen about 10 mm (0.4 in.) from the edge of the paper.
3. On a separate sheet of tracing paper, design a title block, with logo if desired. Produce this by hand or on a computer and trim around the edges if necessary.
4. Position the title block at the bottom of the right-hand side of the plan sheet (allowing space below it for the scale and north point), using the border as a guideline, and attach it with glue or invisible tape.
5. The space above the title block is for the information panel. Label it "Notes".
6. If you require more than one master plan sheet, you should copy it onto another sheet of tracing paper.

House walls: when drawing house walls it is important to position doors and windows accurately as these provide key links between the house and garden. House walls have a thickness—usually of around 300 mm (1 ft.)—which should be shown on plan drawings. At a scale of 1:100 or smaller, you can emphasize the house walls by thickening the lines or by filling them in.

Drawing surveys: When drawing a survey, emphasize the house and boundary lines so that these elements are well-defined when the survey is later placed under tracing paper overlays.

Graphic Symbols

Symbols are used on all plan drawings to represent the objects and elements that occur within the site or are intended to feature in the new design. The symbols should be to scale and can be more or less realistic, depending on the time and budget available to complete the plan. The following pages will review some that you have already encountered in Chapter 1 and introduce you to other graphic symbols that are commonly used in garden design.

Look at garden plans from books and magazines to see how other designers have evolved different symbols to indicate features such as hard-landscaping materials and plants.

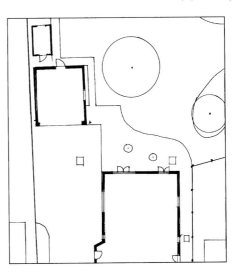

When drawing boundaries such as walls, fences and hedges, always draw the thickness of the boundary to scale.

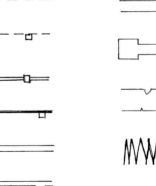

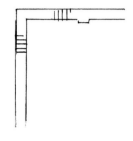

Drawing free-standing walls: The simplest way of drawing a wall is by using a double line and labelling it to indicate the material. If you wish to show more detail, the wall coping for instance, it is only necessary to detail a small section of the wall.

1:50   1:100

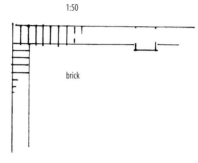

brick

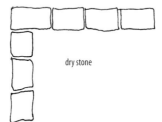

dry stone

concrete casings on walls and piers

220 mm brick wall using well-burnt red facings

Paving and ground surfaces:
When drawing an area of paving it is neither necessary nor possible to show every brick and stone. Provide a separate details sheet (at a larger scale) rather than confuse your plan with too much information. Always label each area to clarify the material used and the layout. You may also distinguish between different surfaces by applying colour.

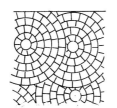
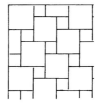

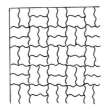

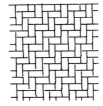

Far left: Water with fountain
Left: Still water

Vertical surfaces: You can give your plan depth—and therefore help the reading of it—if you emphasize all lines representing vertical surfaces, such as those representing tree canopies, free-standing walls, seats, posts, pillars, pergolas and arches (as in the diagram) etc.

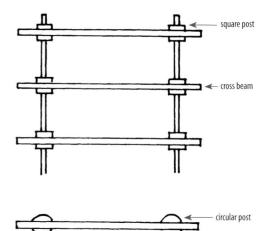

square post

cross beam

circular post

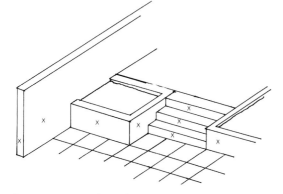

Above: An overview of part of a garden indicating, with crosses, all the vertical surfaces.

Right: A plan drawing of the same part of the garden shows how heavier lines are used to represent all elements with a vertical surface and so clarify the plan. Note how only the outer edge of the retaining wall is emphasized.

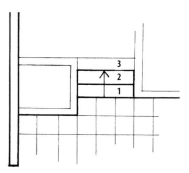

Trees and shrubs: Indicate areas of planting by showing a stylized outline. Plants normally spread out from borders, often overhanging the edge of beds. If you show this overhang (partly concealing the edge of the bed) you will make your plans look more realistic. In Chapter 4, when developing planting plans, you will be shown how to indicate individual plants.

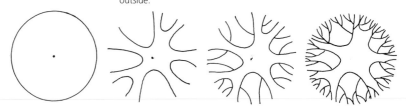

Start with a light guideline circle and locate the centre guideline.

Draw in the main branch structure. Solid branches should taper from thick near the centre to thin near the outside.

Add a few more secondary branches, each one touching the outer circle guideline.

Add many small branches to emphasize the edge.

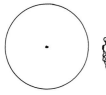    

Simple single circle template outline

Double wavy line

Irregular puffy edge

Bites out of the cookie

The addition of extra lines on one side gives added depth.

Tropical or large-leafed plants

Thin lines may represent leaf ribs.

Always use a circle template guideline for outer edges.

Combine thick and thin lines to provide interest.

Hatch lines to show palm fronds

Loose squiggles with thick and thin lines

Conifers

Begin with a series of circles as light guidelines. Vary their size a little.

A simple heavy outline is the fastest method.

Centres may or may not be located.

Loose wavy lines, double or single, are used for outlines.

Conifers

When the larger tree shadow falls onto the top of shrubs, it should be shortened and made with an irregular edge.

Shrub shadows will be proportionately smaller than tree shadows.

To show pyramid tree form, draw a cone-like guideline. The centre line follows the sun direction.

Draw a loose shadow edge.

A quick outline with an uneven edge for an informal hedge

Box shapes for a trimmed hedge and to define space

Rounded, smooth edges that show two pen sizes overlapping

Designing with Patterns and Shapes

Gardens are essentially made up of hard landscaping and plants, but taken at their most abstract they are composed of lines and shapes that make up a pattern. Before getting into too much detail, you must first become aware of shape, line and pattern and how to use them to create gardens of different character and style.

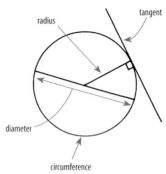

The circle: For designers, the most important parts of a circular shape are its centre, the diameter, the radii, the circumference and the tangent. Each of these is capable of generating different forms.

Experimenting with Shapes

In garden design the two most commonly used geometric shapes are the square and the circle, or parts of these two. When we describe a design theme as circular, what we mean is that the circles, or circular shapes, predominate. Circular themes are rarely composed entirely of circles. Similarly, in a rectilinear theme the rectangles, or parts of a rectangle, predominate. These rectangles may originate from using multiples of a square grid. The diagonal theme also employs mainly squares and rectangles, but these are set at an angle to the house or existing terrace to introduce a strong directional element.

Learning how to use and combine shapes to create patterns is the key to producing positive, strong designs. It is worth looking carefully at different shapes and themes to identify the components that are important in their design use.

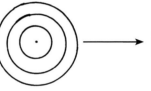

The centre can generate concentric circles

Forms evolved from extended radii

To create strong relationships and avoid awkward angles, lines that meet the circle's circumference should meet it at right angles or tangentially.

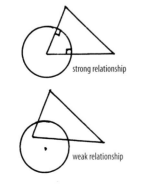

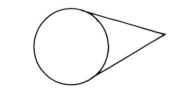

Forms evolved from using tangents

The square: The most important components of a square are the sides, the axes, the diagonals and their extensions.

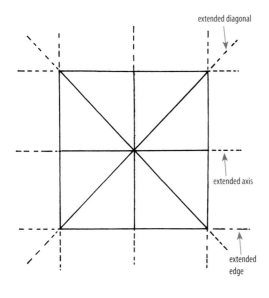

extended diagonal

extended axis

extended edge

Examples of shapes arising from the square

Combining shapes: When combining shapes, try to align the components of one form with those of another (such as a circle combined with a square) to create a strong relationship.

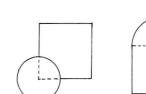

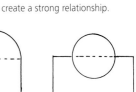

When overlapping circles of different size, try to place the centre points of the smaller circles on the circumference of the larger. If this is not possible, try to ensure that each circle bites substantially into another.

Curvilinear patterns evolve from the outlines of adjoining circles. Often the curved outline of part of one circle will turn, as a reversed curve, into the next circle. Curves should always be generous and appear to flow naturally.

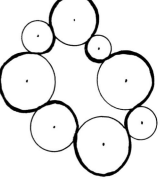

Experimenting with Patterns

A grid is a good starting point for creating patterns. The grid helps to ensure that the shapes created on it relate to one another both in size and through continuity of line. Study the patterns shown here and notice how they differ: some patterns are static, while others are flowing and dynamic. Think about these patterns in relation to a garden—static patterns give a feeling of calm and peacefulness, while dynamic patterns give a sense of drama and excitement. Notice how different shapes have different qualities and how they can be used to give the space a feeling of order, informality or boldness.

Note also how shapes can be directional and used to create optical illusions. For example, lines that run away from the viewer will make an area appear longer, while lines running horizontally will appear to give added breadth.

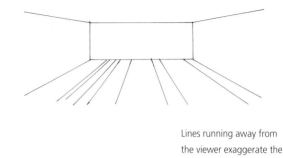

Lines running away from the viewer exaggerate the length of a site.

Lines running across a site exaggerate the width.

A grid is a useful starting point for creating patterns.

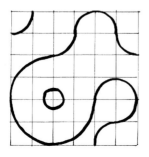

static, symmetrical, ordered

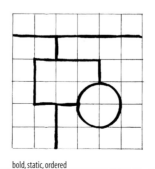

dynamic, asymmetrical

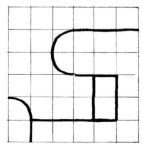

dynamic, combined with a static element (square-shaped area)

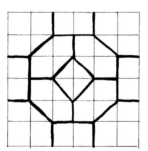

informal, flowing

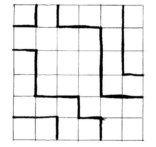

bold, static, ordered

informal

Adding Depth

Shading some areas divides the pattern into positive and negative space, or mass and void. It automatically gives depth to a pattern and should help you to visualize the composition as the ground plan of a garden. Both mass and void are equally important in a design, and it is the interplay between these two that gives a garden its character. Using the informal pattern illustrated here, try to imagine the shaded areas as plantings, for instance, and the areas without shading as grass or paving. Now try reversing the process.

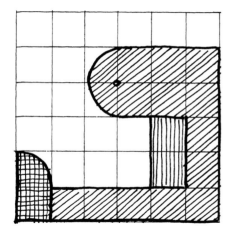

Shading selected areas of a pattern divides it into mass (the shaded part) and void (the unshaded). Experiment with shading different areas of a pattern, then reversing the shading, as shown.

Try to picture the shaded areas as solid objects—planting, benches, raised beds, and so on—and the unshaded areas as representing the garden floor—lawn, paving, or pools, for example.

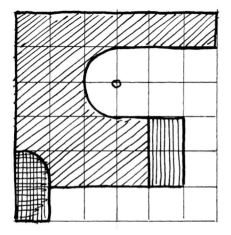

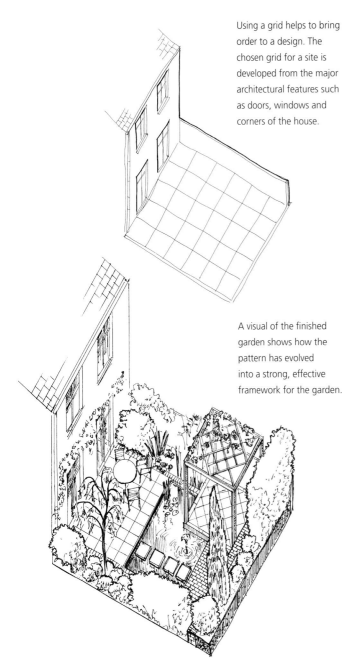

Using a grid helps to bring order to a design. The chosen grid for a site is developed from the major architectural features such as doors, windows and corners of the house.

A visual of the finished garden shows how the pattern has evolved into a strong, effective framework for the garden.

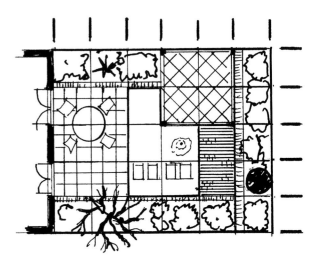

A pattern is drawn up on the grid and developed into a plan

onto the paths and paving, blurring the lines of the pattern, but the underlying framework will still be there, and its presence, even when obscured, will bring a sense of order to the design. Usually, the framework consists mainly of hard landscaping, such as paths, paving, steps and walls. These elements tend to be both more permanent and more expensive than the soft landscaping, or plantings, so the pattern in which the garden is laid out must be effective.

Relating Patterns to Gardens

When designing a garden, you are trying to create interesting patterns within the space or site boundary. The shapes created by the pattern will become the framework of the garden. When the garden has matured, the planting may spill over

Exploring Patterns and Designs

1. Lay a sheet of tracing paper on top of a sheet of graph paper and stick it down with masking tape.
2. Using the bold graph-paper squares as a guide, draw the outline of six squares—use six major graph-paper squares horizontally and vertically for each outline.
3. Consider the examples shown on page 80 and make up your own patterns, using the information about shapes (on pages 78–79) to give you ideas. Shade in some areas.

4. Try reversing the shaded and plain areas.
5. Try to assess the character of each pattern, and decide which you prefer. Decide whether it is static or dynamic, formal or informal, historic or contemporary.
6. Consider these patterns in terms of gardens by thinking of the lighter areas as hard landscaping and the shaded areas as plantings.
7. Take a further sheet of tracing paper, lay it over the first and stick it down.
8. Using coloured pencils or felt-tips, try to translate your patterns into gardens. Show paving, pools, lawns, plantings, beds and so on. Repeat with all six patterns.
9. Try to analyze why you like each of them. What does the pattern do? Do you like the ratio of hard landscaping to soft landscaping, or could it be improved?

Creating Grids for Different Sites

All of the patterns given in this chapter have been developed for an isolated abstract space, but gardens are rarely isolated—they are usually connected to houses or other structures which they should relate to and be developed from. The most effective way of relating house to garden is by using a grid that springs from the dominant house lines or major lines of force. By designing the garden on the grid you will automatically link the spaces in the garden to those of the house, providing a connection which will help the garden sit comfortably in its relationship with the house. The most successful garden layout plans are often those in which the designer has used the proportions of the house—the spaces between doors and windows, for instance—to determine a grid for their design. The garden will then appear to have sprung from the property itself, rather than being superimposed upon it.

Where to Start

The first step in developing a grid is to look closely at the façade of the house, using your site survey and any photographs you may have taken on site. Look at prominent outside walls and corners and any protruding bays or indentations, such as extensions or wall buttresses. Which are the most obvious points? Usually the house corners will be the most dominant lines, and an extension of these across the site will form the starting point for the grid. There may also be regularly spaced windows and doors or an existing terrace whose proportions and materials are perfectly acceptable and which you will want to retain. All of these things may influence your grid.

Dividing up the Space

Now look at the dimensions between the dominant site lines to see if they fall into some sort of module. You may find, for instance, that the distance between the house corner and an extension is 2 m (6.6 ft.), the distance from the extension to the next corner is 4 m (13.12 ft.) and the projection of the extension is 2 m (6.6 ft.). In this case a 2-m (6.6-ft.) grid would fit within all three dimensions.

In deciding where to place the horizontal lines of your grid, re-examine the boundary fences, walls, gates or doorways. You may find that there are some prominent points, such as regularly spaced piers on garden walls, or posts on fences, that could be the starting points for your horizontal grid lines. If the boundary demarcation is totally featureless, you can simply subdivide the overall length of the garden.

The Benefits of a Square Grid

Although existing features in your garden may suggest a grid made up of differently sized and shaped rectangles, you are advised to stick to a square grid. When developing design themes later, the square grid will allow you to use circular shapes that could not be superimposed so easily onto a

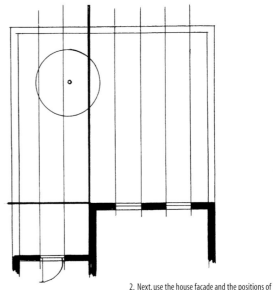

1. Begin the grid by extending the corner lines of the house.

2. Next, use the house facade and the positions of doors, windows or other dominant features to help you divide it into equal divisions, as shown.

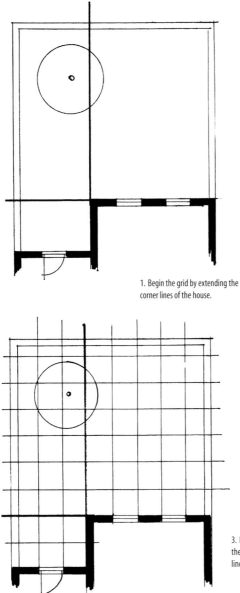
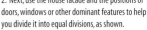

In this example, the developed grid fits perfectly with the dimensions of the house and the position of its doors and windows. If your grid proves difficult to fit, try experimenting with moving it up and down or from side to side across the site. You may then find a stronger relationship between all the different elements.

3. Draw in the horizontal grid lines (spaced the same distance apart as the vertical lines) to complete the grid.

rectangular grid. Do not worry if the house and boundaries do not coincide precisely with your grid lines—the grid is a design tool, not a straitjacket.

Grid Size

Your grid can be as large or small as you like, but the golden rule is that the scale of the grid should derive from the mass of the property, which means that if the house is large, the grid must also be large, and vice versa. Too small a grid often results in a fussy and overdesigned garden. Initially, it is usually better to create a larger grid and then subdivide it.

If the front of the house and garden are large, it may be helpful to use a smaller grid in the vicinity of the

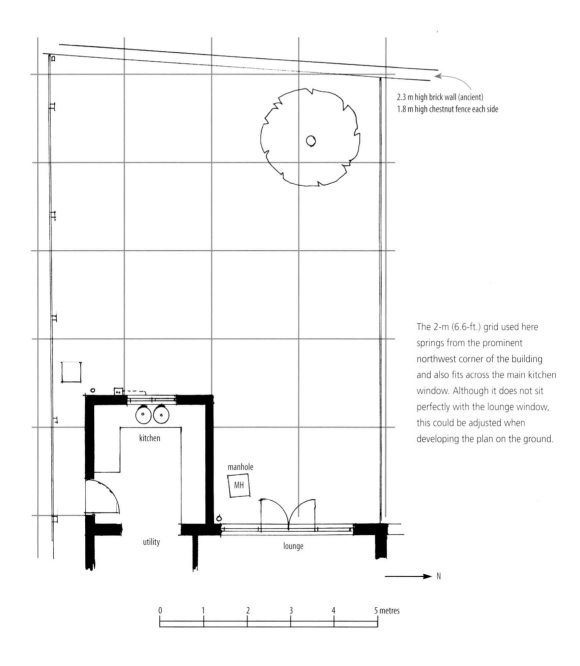

2.3 m high brick wall (ancient)
1.8 m high chestnut fence each side

kitchen

manhole
MH

utility

lounge

The 2-m (6.6-ft.) grid used here springs from the prominent northwest corner of the building and also fits across the main kitchen window. Although it does not sit perfectly with the lounge window, this could be adjusted when developing the plan on the ground.

N

0   1   2   3   4   5 metres

house—to unite building and terrace, for instance, or for a more formal area immediately adjacent to the house. The small grid unit can then be enlarged (doubled or even quadrupled) and used to encompass the larger and more distant part of the garden, where using a small grid would result in a fussy, cluttered effect. Any island beds, woodland trees or even areas of rough grass could be accommodated on this enlarged grid, allowing more generous dimensions while still relating back to the house and the smaller grid.

The examples on pages 88–90 show three different designs for a large country site. In two of them the grid size has been tripled in size; in one, the grid has been doubled.

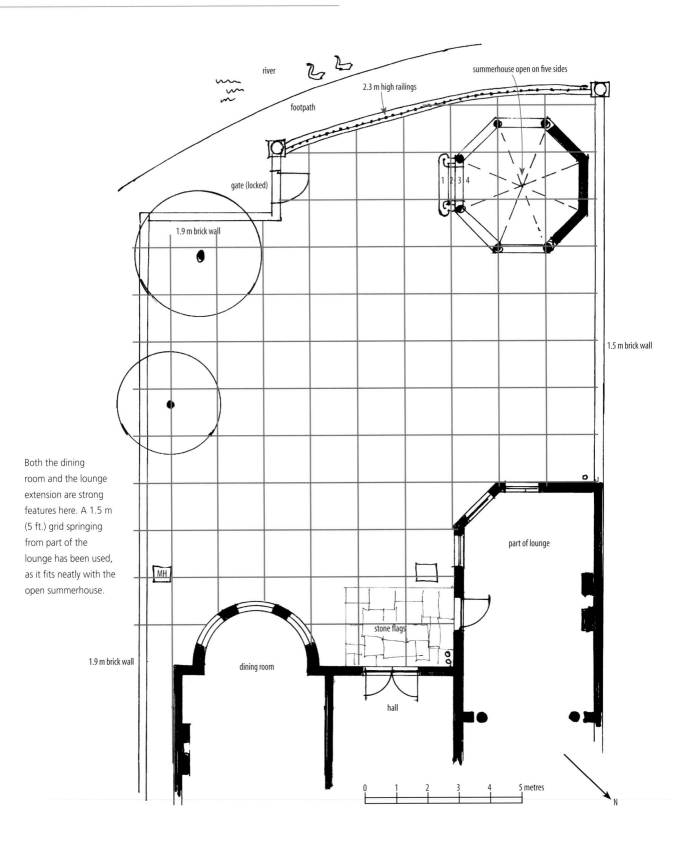

river

2.3 m high railings

summerhouse open on five sides

footpath

gate (locked)

1.9 m brick wall

1 2 3 4

1.5 m brick wall

Both the dining
room and the lounge
extension are strong
features here. A 1.5 m
(5 ft.) grid springing
from part of the
lounge has been used,
as it fits neatly with the
open summerhouse.

MH

part of lounge

1.9 m brick wall

stone flags

dining room

hall

0   1   2   3   4   5 metres

N

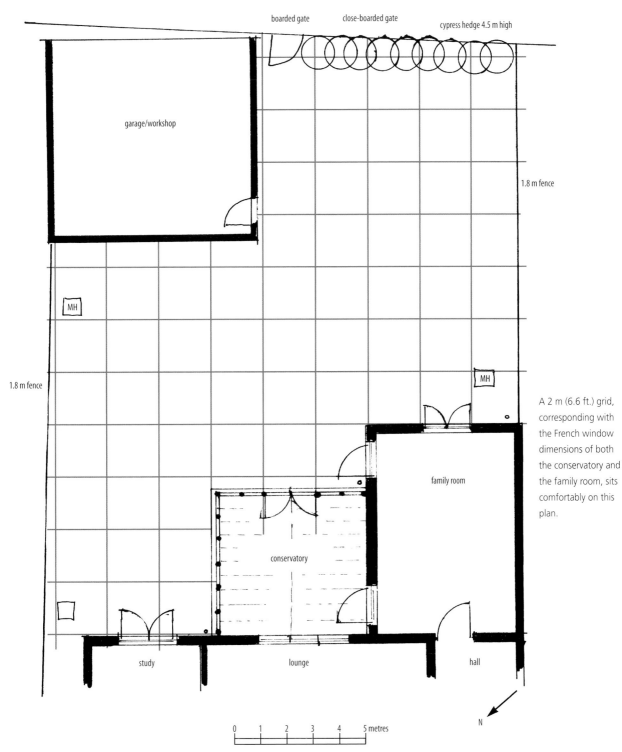

back lane

boarded gate   close-boarded gate

cypress hedge 4.5 m high

garage/workshop

1.8 m fence

MH

MH

1.8 m fence

A 2 m (6.6 ft.) grid, corresponding with the French window dimensions of both the conservatory and the family room, sits comfortably on this plan.

family room

conservatory

study   lounge   hall

N

0   1   2   3   4   5 metres

DEVELOPING THE DESIGN

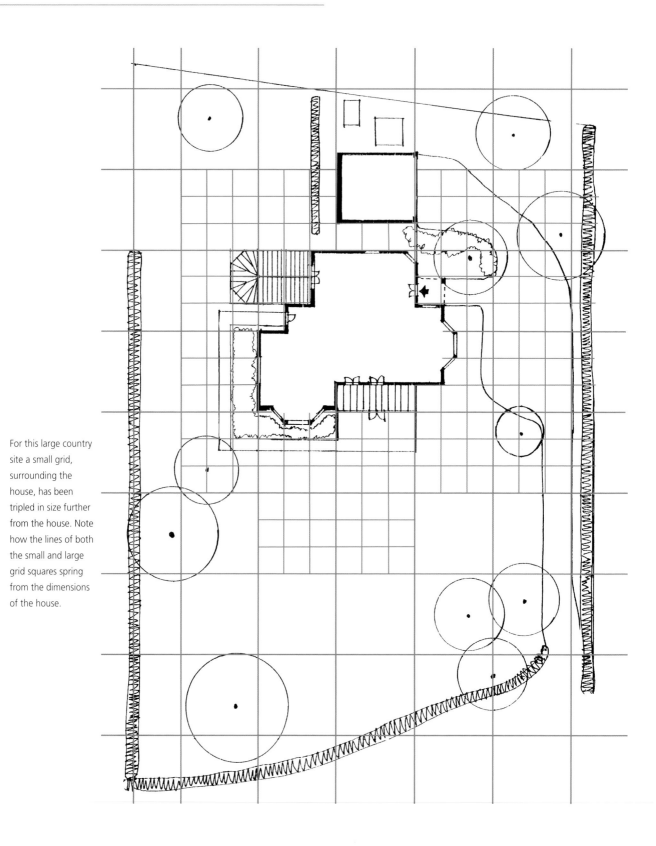

For this large country site a small grid, surrounding the house, has been tripled in size further from the house. Note how the lines of both the small and large grid squares spring from the dimensions of the house.

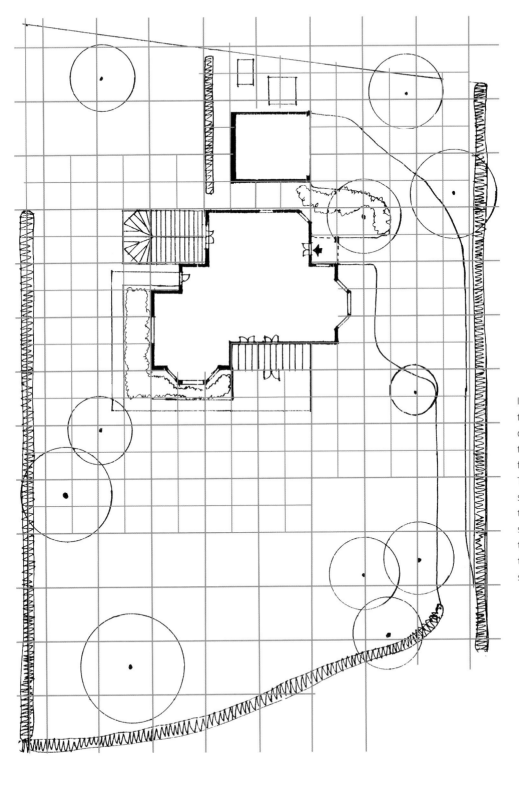

In this example, the grid has been doubled, rather than tripled, in size, further from the house. This solution is less satisfactory because the doubled grid squares do not relate to the dimensions of the house, nor to the scale of existing trees.

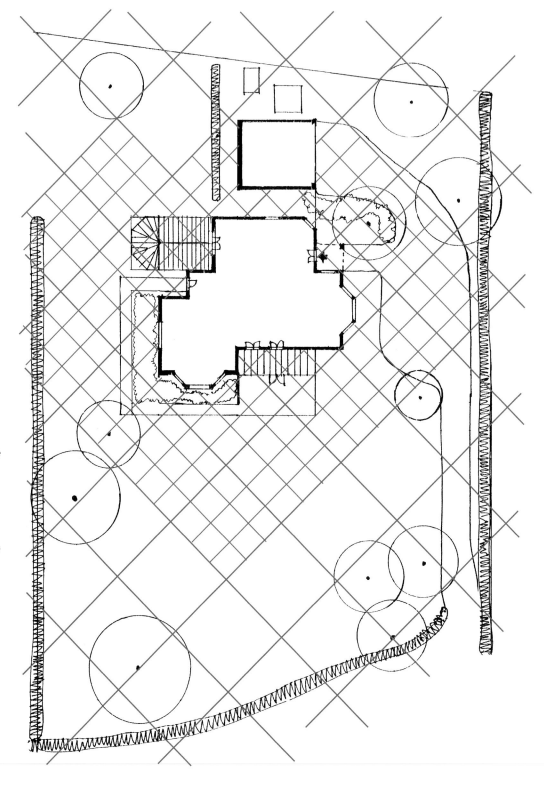

When dividing a garden into different areas, aim for one dominant area on the ground plane, rather than several areas of approximately the same size. By turning the grid, in this diagonal solution, the lawn predominates.

Moving and Turning the Grid

When you are drawing up the grid, extend the lines substantially beyond the site itself so that you can experiment with shifting the grid around and turning it at an angle. You may find that you can create an interesting diagonal effect or a more obvious link between different features.

Once you have become accustomed to designing with this grid system, you will find it easy to work out the grid, and it should prevent such design faults as paths, pergolas or even garden seats not being properly aligned with windows or doorways. When your eye has been trained to observe these alignments, anything out of line or wrongly placed will be a constant source of irritation.

Devising Grids for the Site

1. Stick down a sheet of tracing paper over the site survey. You will draw your grid onto this. A graph-paper backing sheet may be useful as a guide for ruling lines, but do not use this as your grid. The size of the grid will vary with each plan and should stem from the size or proportions of the house and garden.
2. Using the main lines of either house, buildings, doors or windows as a starting point, draw, with your set square and T-square or parallel motion, one vertical and one horizontal line to extend beyond the entire width or length of the site. Try to choose the most prominent points of the building, such as the corners of the house or a protruding bay window.
3. Then, using your scale rule, on the line that offers the most obvious divisions (determined by the features of the house), mark off equal divisions across and beyond the site. Draw these with the T-square, or parallel motion, and set square. Extending

the lines beyond the boundaries of the site itself will allow you to move the grid around later.

4. Again using the scale rule and your drawing equipment, draw equally spaced lines, perpendicular to the first lines, across the site to create your grid.
5. Try turning the grid and translating it into areas of hard and soft landscaping by experimenting with moving the grid around first at an angle of, say, forty-five degrees to the house, then at about thirty-three degrees. Try to line up the turned grid lines with something such as the edge of a window or door, or the corner of the house. Does this work better for this particular site?
6. Stick down another sheet of tracing paper, with masking tape, as an overlay on top of the first.
7. Trace over the new grid, drawn at an angle.
8. Now try to work up each plan into areas of hard landscaping (man-made structures) and soft landscaping (plants).
9. Evaluate what you have done. Have you created a formal or informal pattern? Is the pattern balanced and ordered? Is it directional? What illusions, if any, have your lines created? If you crouch down and put your eyes at the same level as your plan, you may see this more easily. You may now have the basis of an exciting new layout.

Theme Plans

There is usually one particular way in which the grid works best and one angle that will work better than others. To help you decide, try experimenting with a design on a rectilinear theme, a circular theme, and a diagonal theme for your garden site. All of these relate back to the shapes and patterns considered

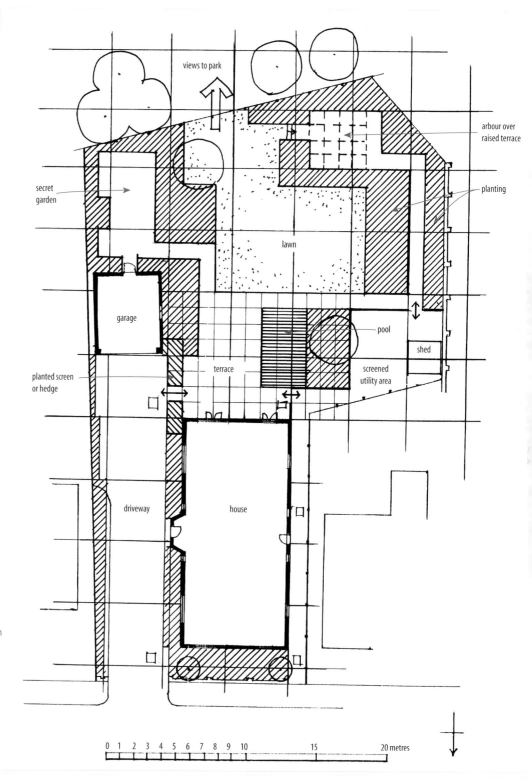

views to park

arbour over
raised terrace

secret
garden

planting

lawn

garage

pool

shed

planted screen
or hedge

terrace

screened
utility area

driveway

house

Theme Plan 1: A small-scale grid has been used near the house in this model garden plan. Further from the house the grid has been quadrupled in size. In this rectilinear theme plan, the areas have been divided up into rectangles (rather than squares), which give direction to the plan, leading people around a site, as well as directing views through it to the parkland beyond.

0 1 2 3 4 5 6 7 8 9 10   15   20 metres

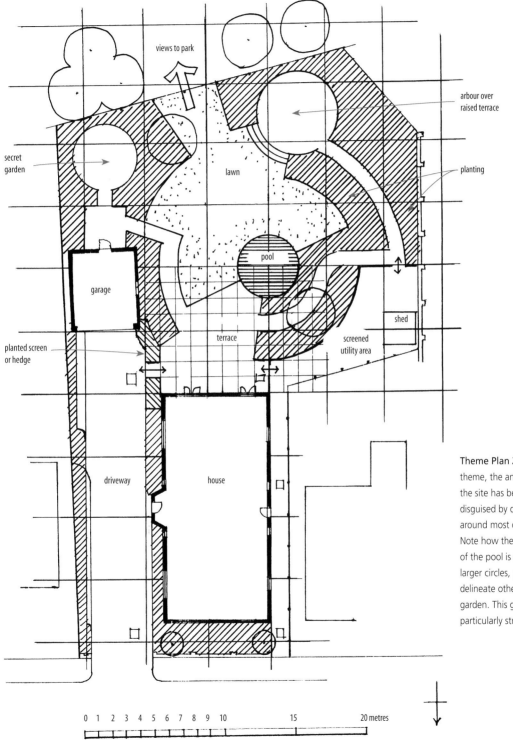

views to park

arbour over
raised terrace

secret
garden

planting

lawn

pool

garage

shed

planted screen
or hedge

terrace

screened
utility area

Theme Plan 2: In this circular
theme, the angular shape of
the site has been completely
disguised by dense planting
around most of the perimeter.
Note how the centre point
of the pool is shared by
larger circles, parts of which
delineate other features in the
garden. This gives the pool a
particularly strong focus.

driveway

house

0 1 2 3 4 5 6 7 8 9 10   15   20 metres

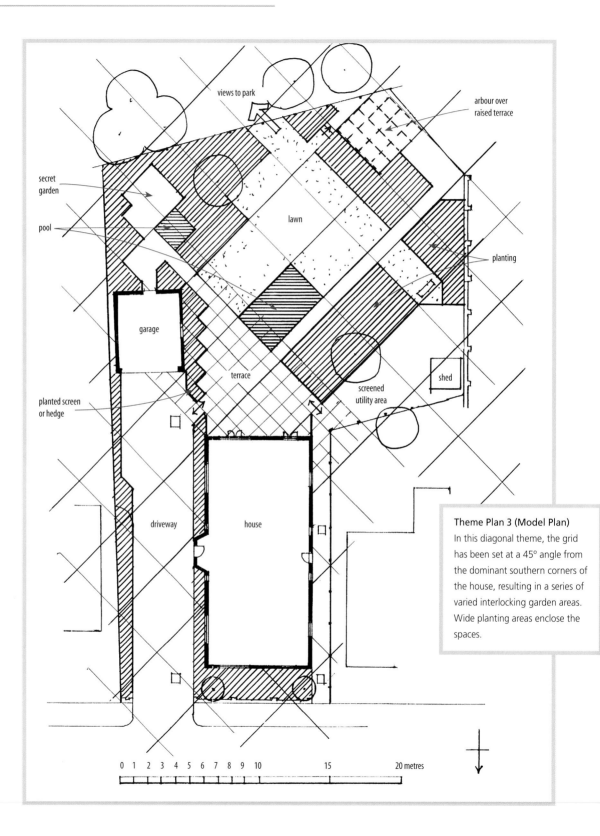

views to park

arbour over
raised terrace

secret
garden

pool

lawn

planting

garage

terrace

screened
utility area

shed

planted screen
or hedge

driveway

house

Theme Plan 3 (Model Plan)
In this diagonal theme, the grid
has been set at a 45° angle from
the dominant southern corners of
the house, resulting in a series of
varied interlocking garden areas.
Wide planting areas enclose the
spaces.

0 1 2 3 4 5 6 7 8 9 10   15   20 metres

earlier in this chapter. Developing these themes will help you break down any preconceived ideas for the space that you are redesigning and should give rise to completely original concepts for what may previously have been a boring and predictable layout.

It is important to stress that this stage of designing is experimental, and you should allow yourself numerous sheets of tracing paper, stuck down over your survey and grid, to test out different ideas. Do make sure that you have indicated any major existing trees as circles on your survey. Trees may well influence your design, as they cannot be moved, but this also should have shown up on your site inventory and appraisal.

The examples on the previous pages show three different design solutions for the large suburban garden that is the model site for this book. All of the plans suit the outline shape of the site and the style and mass of the house. Each of the design solutions was developed from the same grid. The grid was turned at forty-five degrees for the diagonal design (opposite), and it was this theme that was chosen to be developed into the garden layout plan.

Using the Grid to Direct the Ground Plane

By using the grid to direct your lines, the garden design should work as a balanced whole, mass balancing void, with no leftover corners or weak, wiggly lines. To avoid sharp corners, lines should ideally meet at right angles.

Avoid awkward angles or leftover spaces by ensuring that lines meet at right angles.

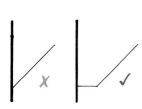
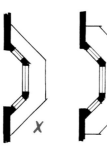
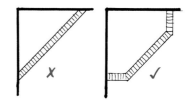

Drawing up Experimental Theme Plans

1. On your drawing board stick down the site survey plan with masking tape and then place the tracing-paper grid sheet over the plan.
2. Experiment with turning the grid at different angles.
3. Use a further sheet of tracing paper and, with a pencil, trace off any grids that you think may be suitable. (You will probably need to use several sheets of tracing paper until you have achieved setting the grid at an angle that you like.)
4. Now develop your design by using tracing-paper overlays with your chosen grid, and work up (in pencil) the various themes—circular, diagonal and rectilinear.
5. Keep these rough pencil theme plans carefully. You will need to refer to them when you draw up the preliminary garden layout plan (see page 143).

Perhaps the theme you choose might spring from the house itself—a circular theme taken from a curved window, for instance. In general, circles require more space than rectangles, and if the house is obviously rectangular, with straight walls giving a boxed-in effect, it may be overambitious (and alien to the site) to superimpose a circular theme. Examples of successful and unsuccessful designs based on circular and curvilinear shapes for a small rectangular site are shown on the next page.

DEVELOPING THE DESIGN

Unsuccessful theme plans:
In this circular design (right),
there is insufficient space to
make the transition between
the rectangular house and the
circles. Each shape seems to
collide with the next rather
than leading naturally into it.
Although the intention is to
disguise the rectangular shape
of the plot with planting, there
is insufficient space around the
larger circle to achieve this.
In this small space, the free
form curvilinear design (far
right) is at odds with the parallel
surrounding walls.

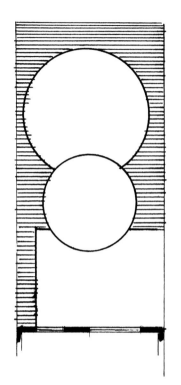

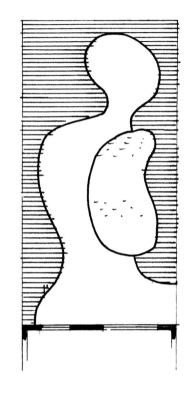

Successful theme plans: In this
example (right) a geometry of
squares is used. The circle fits
into square 1 and although the
square disappears, it is strongly
implied. Square 2 provides a link
between the two main garden
rooms, like an ante-room or
vestibule.

The strong curve of this design
(far right) will be softened as the
planting matures, and the sense
of space will increase as the
walls become obscured. Note
how the position of the trees
emphasizes the design.

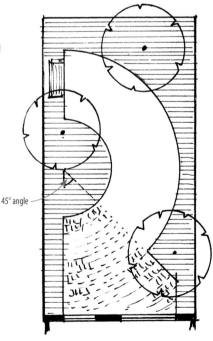

45° angle

To increase the apparent length of a site, slant the plan using the angle formed by the longest diagonal.

Before making your decision on which theme to adopt, do try turning the grid through forty-five degrees or slanting the plan, perhaps from one corner to the distant opposite corner. This is a very effective method of exploiting the maximum length of the site, as shown in the example on this page, and it was the chosen solution for the model plan (see page 94).

Planning an Outdoor Space

If you find the concept of outdoor space hard to envisage, it may be helpful to think of it as an outdoor room. Just as an indoor room is enclosed by the floor, walls and ceiling, so are outdoor rooms defined by the ground plane (the garden floor), the vertical plane (walls, fences and so on) and the overhead plane (tree canopies, pergolas or anything that interrupts the view of the sky). Within this context, perhaps it is easier to develop an awareness of the three-dimensional aspects of mass and void and to consider the effects of light and water in the garden.

Space

It is wrong to think of space, or void, as nothingness: space has character and mood. An enclosed space, for instance, may afford a garden privacy or intimacy, in contrast to an open space, which is essentially outward-looking and may feel insecure.

A garden dominated by mass is enclosed and secluded.

DEVELOPING THE DESIGN

The interplay between mass and void creates the structure of the garden. When void predominates, a garden feels more open and exposed.

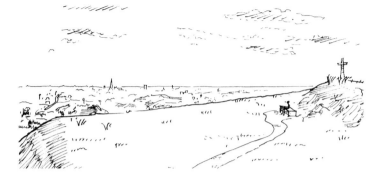

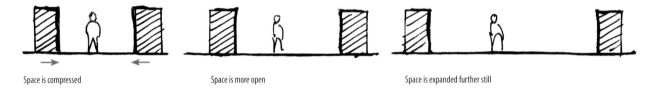

Space is compressed

Space is more open

Space is expanded further still

Above: Using bricks or children's wooden blocks, vary the width between them, as shown, to see how the space is affected when viewed at eye level.

Right: The movement of space is conditioned by the placing of the masses.

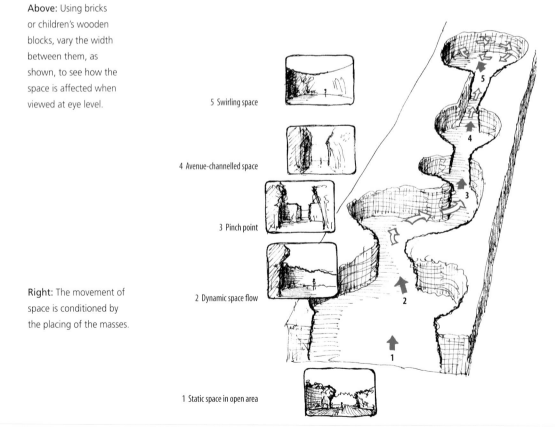

5 Swirling space

4 Avenue-channelled space

3 Pinch point

2 Dynamic space flow

1 Static space in open area

Space is not necessarily static but can be made to flow like water. The speed at which it flows can be altered, too. It can move slowly (down a broad drive or around shrub beds to fill a void of lawn) or swiftly (forced down through a narrow path). This apparent movement of space, created by the placing of the masses between which it flows, creates far more excitement and stimulus in the garden than any number of rare plants or bright colours.

Light

The mood of a space is affected by light, and the amount and quality of light entering a garden is affected by the elements placed within or existing close to it. For example, in the growing season a mature tree may completely block sunlight from entering a small garden.

Light Quality and Intensity

We are so used to the presence of daylight that we take it for granted, quite forgetting that its quality and quantity totally control the way in which everything is seen and, therefore, how it should be designed.

The quality of the light varies with latitude. In Britain, even on a bright day, the near distance is tinged with blue and the shadows have no clear definition, while on a sunless day the whole scene lacks clarity, as though it were a slightly smudged pencil sketch. In hotter countries, stronger sunlight makes shadows appear more defined. Temperate gardens tend to need a larger proportion of void to mass, so that enough light can enter the composition. If your garden is in a country where the light is hard and clear, the ratio can be reversed so that there is more dark mass to offset small, brightly lit voids.

In temperate climates, the sun is relatively weak and casts soft, hazy shadows. The low angle of the sun results in long shadows for much of the year.

Lower planting around the perimeter allows more light into the garden.

In tropical climates, on or near to the equator, the sun is strong and bright, casting dense, well-defined shadows. The sun is high in the sky all the year round, producing relatively short shadows.

To increase the amount of shade in the garden, the relative mass is increased by introducing a tall hedge on one boundary and planting umbrella-shaped trees within the garden.

Objects with a well-defined shape or form look most effective when silhouetted by being lit from behind.

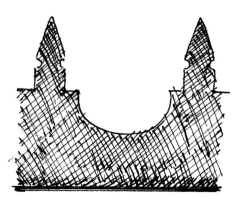

Creating Special Effects

When designing a garden it is important to consider the effects that you want to create with light by arranging the masses in a suitable way. The shape of an object (the detail of a wrought-iron gate, for instance) can be emphasized by being silhouetted against a light background. If, on the other hand, the texture of something (such as smooth rocks or gnarled tree trunks) needs emphasizing, the object should be lit from the front, or it should be in sun as opposed to shade.

Looking from dark to light—or, even better, from light through dark to light beyond—adds drama and depth to the view. In temperate climates, where the light conditions may be rather diffuse, it is still possible to create striking effects. The rays of low-level afternoon sun playing through sparsely foliaged trees can cast moving dappled shadows, for instance, and shafts of light can be used to highlight a carefully sited statue.

The direction from which an object is lit affects how it is perceived.

Reducing the amount of light before a vista accentuates the scene.

Looking through dark to light   Looking from light through to light beyond

Interior and exterior scales differ. External proportions need to be more generous. Indoors, the height of this door looks fine—it is in scale with the interior. Outdoors, the height and the width will be inadequate and out of scale. Note how cramped the door and pergola have become. You need to "scale up" when outdoors.

Scale and Proportion

Scale and proportion are also important factors to bear in mind when thinking about spaces, as without them there can be no harmony of design. Within a built environment, architects create interior living and working spaces that are in scale with the human figure. However, outside, where the sky is the limit, these interior proportions feel meagre and uncomfortable. Outside, the garden designer has to relate the scale of the human figure to the limitless expanse of horizon and sky, requiring the tall verticals of trees or buildings to help balance the horizon. Also, gardens are places for leisure, and they need more ample proportions.

To relate to external scale, steps, paths and openings must be more generous than those found within a building. A useful exercise is to take your flexible tape and measure the steps of your own interior staircase, and then go out to a nearby garden or park and compare these interior measurements with a comfortable flight of outdoor steps. You should find that the stairs indoors—even though they look and feel perfectly comfortable in their more intimate indoor setting—are narrower and steeper than the garden steps.

However, gardens must also relate to the human scale, keeping the human frame and the space it

may take up as an integral part of the design. Paths, steps, arbours and sitting areas should be sufficiently generous to be comfortable and intimate, not overgenerous, daunting and empty. Good proportions are the real foundation of the garden.

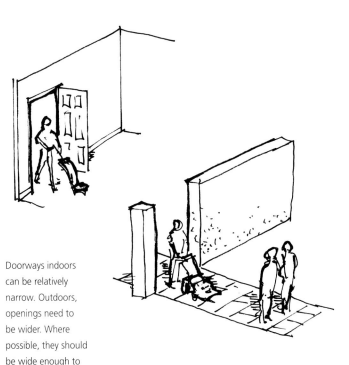

Doorways indoors can be relatively narrow. Outdoors, openings need to be wider. Where possible, they should be wide enough to allow two people to walk through side by side.

Indoors, people adjust to the space they are in and can feel perfectly comfortable sitting very close to one another. Outdoors, if space allows, you may need to double the size of an area used for a similar function to prevent people feeling restricted.

Designing steps for exterior use: Steps based on typical domestic indoor dimensions are inappropriate for outdoor use. Not only will they feel cramped in scale, but they could also be dangerous.

Always scale up steps outdoors by creating wider and deeper treads and reducing the riser height.

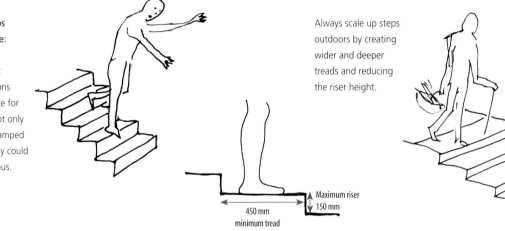

450 mm minimum tread

Maximum riser 150 mm

Staircases should have plenty of room and frequent generous landings. Above all else, design for safety.

For all sorts of reasons, consider using ramps as an alternative or substitute for steps.

Water

If water is available and you would like a water feature in your garden, begin by considering the different options before deciding on the form it will take. Water has a seductive, elusive quality that can greatly enhance any setting and, when used effectively, it can command more attention than any other garden feature. It has the attribute of reflecting light and makes a strong impact on the garden layout.

If well designed and integrated, a water feature can be a great asset to a garden, but, if used badly, it can be a depressing mistake. Water should be used with discretion, becoming part of the structure of your design. In small gardens, water is best used formally, either in conjunction with a building or as a sculptural feature or fountain. Using water informally, in free-form shapes imitating natural ponds, requires more space. Once you have determined which type of water feature you want, decide whether it should flow or be static. The safety aspect, particularly for children, is of prime concern—being caged in as a precaution does not enhance any water feature.

Once you have decided on your concept, it may be advisable to call in a water specialist who should be able to foresee any potential problems.

Historical Use of Water

Water has been prized in the design of gardens since ancient times. It was used as an integral part of many early Mogul, Persian and Islamic gardens, cooling down the atmosphere, soothing the spirits and giving an additional dimension to a flat landscape.

In Europe during the Renaissance a renewed interest in hydraulics led to a proliferation of water devices, particularly in Italian and French gardens. Fountains had huge jets of water that soared into the air; grottoes had trick water features, which, to the amusement of the host, soaked unsuspecting visitors; cascades tumbled down water staircases; and a series of spouts and rills emitted sounds that imitated music. It was the height of fashion to include an unusual water feature in a garden setting, and wealthy landowners who took pride in their gardens engaged designers with knowledge of modern hydraulics to turn their fantasies into reality.

Although today we accept hydraulic systems, such as pumps, as part of everyday life, there is still huge scope for the imagination when it comes to using water in a garden.

The Qualities of Water

Water awakens the senses. Its movement and reflection provide a feast for the eyes; the range of sounds it produces, from gentle dripping to loud crashing, has the ability to calm or invigorate; and its tactile quality, whether liquid or in the form of ice, is fascinating. When used in a garden it can provide a home for plants and wildlife, colourful swirls of fish and water plants adding to its visual appeal. Water can also enhance the quality of other materials, deepening the colours of mosaic tiles, for instance, or highlighting the smooth surface of river pebbles.

Still water and reflection
The most striking attribute of still water is its power to reflect, thereby doubling the value of any

A sheet of water used to bring light into a garden.

image that falls on its surface. This can be used to great effect in a garden. It can unify a design by bringing together the ground plane, the vertical plane and the overhead plane, and it can create a feeling of space by bringing light into the garden.

To bring out the best of water's reflective quality, it is important to contain the water in a material that is as dark as possible. The reflections on the surface of a swimming pool are usually poor or nonexistent during the day, because the floor and walls are generally pale in colour and can be clearly seen. If, on the other hand, the pool were painted black, the reflected images would be clear, even in cloudy weather, and the interior would be invisible. Of course, this would only apply to ornamental pools— a black swimming pool would be most uninviting.

Being unable to judge the depth of a pool or pond adds a sense of mystery to the feature and has practical advantages as well. Not only does the darkness obscure functional items, such as plant containers and supports for stepping stones, but it also allows the designer to construct a relatively shallow pool, thereby saving on construction expenses.

When thinking about reflections, consider the importance of the water level. As the side of the

pool will be reflected in the water, the water level will appear to be lower than it is, reducing the apparent surface area. To maximize the reflective area, you will need to raise the water level as high as possible. In formal pools it should be kept just below the level of the coping stones or edging. You can experiment with the effect of reflections by placing small objects on a hand mirror.

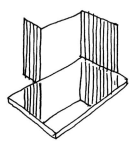

Fold some stiff paper or card and stand it up against the edge of a mirror. Try a variety of different shapes.

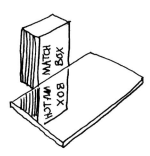

Place a match box against the edge of the mirror and note how its height is doubled.

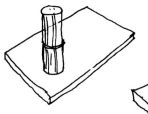

A salt cellar placed on the mirror becomes a long cylinder.

Use an ordinary bristle brush to understand how rushes or reeds will reflect in still water.

Colour

If the sun does not fall directly on the surface of the water, the reflected sky appears a more intense blue. This fact can be used to advantage in small town courtyards, where the enhanced colour and light reflected back from the surface of the water can turn a gloomy, dull space into one with vibrant interest.

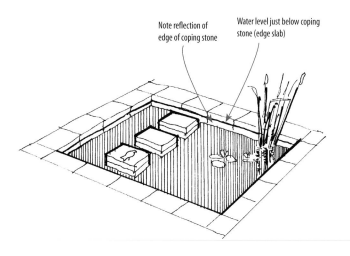

Note reflection of edge of coping stone

Water level just below coping stone (edge slab)

To increase the darkness or depth of colour of the water, dramatize the effect by using dark large-leaved evergreens in the background.

Fountains look most effective when situated in full sun, against a dark background.

Water as the main feature of a small courtyard enhances the feeling of light and colour.

Catalogues may show you perfect spray effects produced by different nozzles but in reality, the tiny holes are easily clogged and the wind can also spoil the effect.

Left: Simple jets are often more effective—the height of the fountain can be easily adjusted at the pump.

Movement

Moving water shimmers and sparkles in the light and adds a refreshing quality of sound which is much appreciated in hot countries. Because of the way light dances on moving water, it works best when it is positioned in full sun. Fountains, for instance, are particularly effective when positioned in full sun with a shady background, preferably of dark green plants.

One way in which moving water differs from still water is by the sounds it creates. A small amount—trickling onto rocks in a pool, for instance—can be delicate and musical, whereas a large volume, forced up through the jet of a powerful fountain or cascading over rocks into a pool far below, can produce loud hissing or burbling sounds that bring a sense of excitement to a garden. In an urban setting these sounds can help to reduce outside noise, particularly the distant sounds of traffic or people.

Designing with Water

Remember that if you decide to include water in your garden, it is essential that the particular water feature be properly integrated into the design as a whole, complementing existing features as well as proposed hard landscaping and plantings. This applies whether you are creating a new feature or adapting an existing water source, such as a stream or pond.

The need for water and the way it should or should not be used varies considerably by region.

Stylistically, some water features would be more in keeping with the natural surroundings than others. In Maine, for example, much of the coastal landscape is broken up by the natural effects of rocks and trees, and as a result coastal waters lap gently against the shore. Reflecting this, the design of the Asticou Azalea Garden in Northeast Harbor uses large pieces of granite as stepping stones to continue a path across a stream. In Arizona, mirror-like reflecting pools complement the bold shapes and textures of desert plantings.

Reflections of illuminated foliage near a pool add interest at night.

In several areas of the United Kingdom, such as Cornwall and the south and west coast of Scotland, where the sea is less threatening, the natural landscape is also used to enhance and soften humankind's intervention. Stone from local quarries is often used for stepping stones used to cross water, giving children the enjoyment of the potential danger of getting wet.

Water in the landscape can also become something of a cultural phenomenon. In the certain parts of the United States, because of high summer temperatures, it is common to have a swimming pool; current trends also include hot tubs as well as lap pools (long, narrow pools for serious swimmers) naturalized by adding waterfalls or streams. In cooler areas, however, pools are often considered a luxury that few people can afford. Pools often take up large portions of the garden and can pose many design challenges.

Climate should be considered when designing any garden water feature. In very hot areas, small amounts of water may be impractical because frequent refilling is required owing to rapid evaporation. Similarly, in very cold winter areas, features should be designed either to accommodate freezing water or to be easy to drain down annually.

National and local water restrictions should also be considered. Pools and water features use a great deal of water, and although they may benefit wildlife, they can also use up precious supplies. Investigate filling pools with harvested rainwater and, ideally, use solar-powered features.

Solar-Powered Water Features

To maintain the oxygen levels of the water in a pool or a pond, a "greener" option is to use an oxygenation system that is powered by the sun's rays. A solar-powered oxygenator generally includes a panel made of a photovoltaic material that converts solar energy into electricity without using the mains supply.

These days, there are many solar-powered options from which to choose. While some panels must be kept close to the water feature, some units include panels that can be moved around the garden as long as they are facing the sun. If your area is generally overcast, it is possible to find units with inbuilt batteries that will allow operation in variable weather or at night, while others can be programmed with a time switch to work at set intervals. Some solar-powered oxygenators are supplied with "airstones" that diffuse oxygen into the water, keeping the pool or pond water clear.

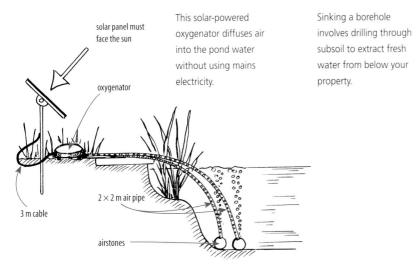

solar panel must face the sun

oxygenator

3 m cable

2 × 2 m air pipe

airstones

This solar-powered oxygenator diffuses air into the pond water without using mains electricity.

Sinking a borehole involves drilling through subsoil to extract fresh water from below your property.

well cap and inspection cover

sloping ground

outlet pipe and cable

well casing

water table

casing bottom

submersible pump

well screen

Boreholes

For some properties the most effective and reliable water source can come from sinking a borehole which will provide fresh water for pools, the garden and even drinking. This involves drilling down through the subsoil into the aquifers below, lining the hole, installing a submersible pump to draw the water, and finally capping the hole to leave only a small inspection cover visible. Drilling depths can vary enormously, from 20 m to 150 m (6 to 46 ft.) which will have an impact on costs and viability. In Britain, the extraction of up to twenty thousand litres per day is allowed without requiring a licence from Defra (the Department for Environment, Food and Rural Affairs) but it is important to check local restrictions before drilling.

The uncomplicated drilling process typically takes one to two weeks, and is usually best done when the garden is being constructed. Given the uncertainty of future water supplies, sinking a borehole may be viewed as a long-term asset.

Broadly speaking, water features can be divided into those that are formal (and obviously artificial) and those that are informal (either natural or naturalistic and imitating nature). Generally, formal features look better in small urban gardens or positioned close to the house in larger gardens; informal water features are more in keeping with natural landscapes and gardens in rural settings.

Formal water features

The size, shape and location of a formal water feature should be determined by existing features. The water feature will be part of the grid so that it relates strongly to all other elements and is an integral part of the design. Unlike informal water features, often elusive or partly concealed, water used in a formal setting tends to make a strong statement.

Formal pools, rills and canals are geometric in shape and do not pretend to look natural. They are constructed of rigid materials, such as concrete (used alone or with a flexible butyl liner) or premoulded resin. Resin pools, although widely available, are rarely satisfactory because you are unlikely to find the exact dimensions of pool that you need. In any case, most of these have overshaped, irregular outlines that emphasize artificiality and do not lend themselves well to formal situations.

DEVELOPING THE DESIGN

Site survey: A new pool was an important feature for this garden design, and a way had to be found to integrate it successfully on this rectilinear grid. The clients required:

- a pool for reflection and tranquillity
- the garden to look wider
- no steps—they have elderly parents
- space for shrubs
- an existing tree to be retained
- outdoor seating areas.

The garden layout plan (right) shows the solution that was reached, and a visual (opposite page) illustrates the simple, placid oriental mood of the proposed pool.

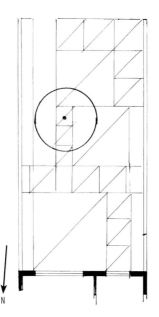

N

Garden layout plan: The pool runs almost across the width of the garden and separates the terrace from the garden emphatically. It creates a sense of "here"—the terrace—and "there"—the garden beyond.

Linking the two areas is a flat bridge set level and without any steps. It is built of standard "off-the-shelf" precast concrete window lintels. These are thin, inexpensive, and robust. Such lintels are available in a variety of standard lengths. For safety, a handrail with two posts at each end is added.

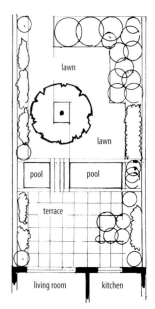

lawn

lawn

pool   pool

terrace

living room   kitchen

In this example, note how the pool has been made deliberately long and set almost flush with the paving to reduce the foreshortening effect of perspective. Although the pool appears considerably shorter when seen from indoors, the surface of the water will be visible enough to allow a view of the reflection of the statue. The carefully placed water lilies do not obscure the reflection.

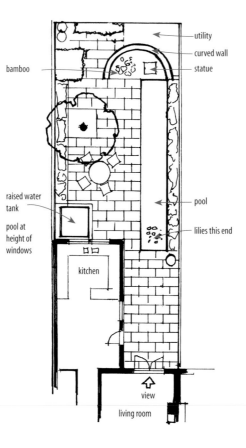

bamboo

utility

curved wall

statue

raised water tank

pool at height of windows

kitchen

pool

lilies this end

view

living room

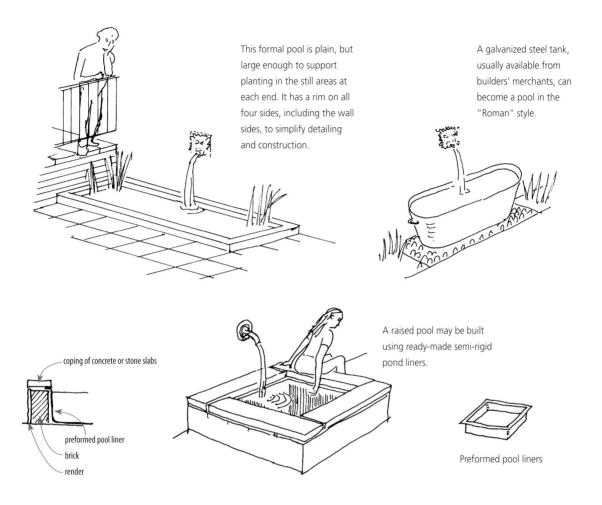

This formal pool is plain, but large enough to support planting in the still areas at each end. It has a rim on all four sides, including the wall sides, to simplify detailing and construction.

A galvanized steel tank, usually available from builders' merchants, can become a pool in the "Roman" style.

coping of concrete or stone slabs

preformed pool liner

brick

render

A raised pool may be built using ready-made semi-rigid pond liners.

Preformed pool liners

If left to its own devices, water will form single-celled algae, quickly followed by blanket weed. Counteracting this involves either establishing a delicately balanced ecosystem, or resorting to regular doses of a chemical to prevent algae or any other plant from growing. The chemical is normally supplied as a slow-dissolving tablet administered by hand or through a simple dosing unit installed in a small service chamber.

Informal water features

If you already have a natural water feature in your garden, you may want to emphasize it and include it in your design. This may involve designing a bridge to cross from one side of a stream to another, changing the direction and movement of the water or providing some waterside plantings. However, a natural water source can also be used to feed a formal water feature, if this style is more appropriate.

When creating a new naturalistic pond, it is essential that you study ponds and lakes in their natural setting. What you are trying to achieve is a pond that looks as if it has always been there. Examine how natural water features have occurred and their effect on the surrounding land, particularly during flooding or drought. A natural source of water may not remain constant. Normally water occupies the lowest part of any site, its surface creating a datum level to which everything else relates. The effect is seldom convincing if ponds are deliberately placed high up or on sloping ground, unless in a natural hollow.

Generally, pools on hills, unless in convincing hollows, can look most unnatural.

A naturalistic water feature can be modelled on a flat site by excavating the soil and mounding it up on each side of a "valley" (above). Planting on the mounds can emphasize height. Edge planting and detailing need care for a convincing natural effect (below).

A water course may broaden into a pool. Here the pool sits in a shallow hollow which is formed in the way described above.

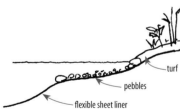

turf

pebbles

flexible sheet liner

Obscure the liner at the edge of a naturalistic water feature with turf and pebbles. To secure the plants, place them in plastic perforated baskets lined with soil and upturned turves, then sink these into position.

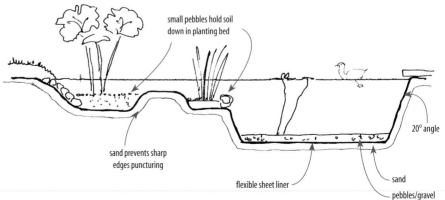

small pebbles hold soil down in planting bed

sand prevents sharp edges puncturing

20° angle

flexible sheet liner

sand

pebbles/gravel

It is essential that any pool or water feature should hold water, and the romantic idea of using puddled clay, to a minimum depth of 450 mm (1.5 ft.), is ill-advised as it is not totally impermeable, may shrink and crack in dry weather and can be damaged by plant roots or burrowing animals. Flexible sheet liners are more reliable; they should be guaranteed against water loss, are supplied in roll form, are usually viable for up to twenty years and are less expensive to install. To be convincing, the waterproof membrane needs to be hidden beneath the edging material which can be stone, brick, timber or soil.

The surrounding contours, too, must be carefully considered, since the edge of the water is in itself a contour line, and if this (or the reflection of the adjoining landform) looks unnatural, the whole feature will be exposed as a fraud. Pay particular attention to the shapes formed by the water, how it flows around or over obstacles and exactly what happens at the water's edge.

With an artificial pond it is generally the point where land meets water that is most difficult to resolve, resulting in unconvincing shorelines of concrete or butyl liner. Generally, the material from which the pond is made should be carried up well beyond the visible edge of the water, at a shallow angle that will allow a marshy zone merging into a shingle beach. The shingle will only be revealed when the water level drops.

Moving water can add excitement and drama, or it can be subtle and subdued. Either way, it should mimic the natural landscape as it streams and cascades, falling naturally over stone rather than machined slabs. In addition to a pipe to transport the water, a pump will be needed to carry water around, and this pump may either be submerged in the water feature's lowest pool, or kept in a ventilated dry housing below the level of the lowest pool.

Using Grey Water

Reusing cleaned "grey" water, or waste water from any household source excluding the toilet, is an eco-friendly option for providing irrigation in the garden, and it may be used in certain water features as well.

If you have enough space and the inclination to really "go green", a specially constructed reed bed can do the hard work of cleaning the water with the help of bacteria, removing harmful chemicals and pollutants that can otherwise build up over time if untreated grey water is used in the garden. The reed bed may form a feature in itself, formal or informal depending on the outline shape. The bed consists of an excavated waterproof pit measuring about 600–750 mm (2–2.5 ft.) deep, backfilled with layers of loose stone, gravel or pea shingle and sand. The top layer is usually fine, washed sand into which the reeds, such as *Phragmites communis* or *P. australis*, are planted at a density of about four per square metre. The reed bed should cover at least one square metre for every occupant in the house.

A harvesting system must be installed to collect and store the water that is filtered before use. The filtration system can be installed in a garage or garden shed, but space for clean water storage will also be needed (see page 193). Storage tanks should not be installed within 5 m (16.4 ft.) of a house or other property. Most systems use energy for pumps and filters, and the set-up and running costs can be expensive, but this may be redeemed over the long term.

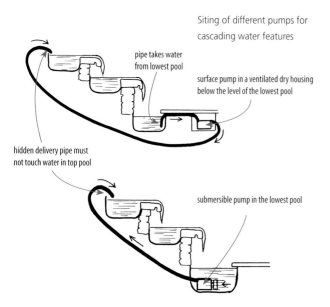

Siting of different pumps for cascading water features

pipe takes water from lowest pool

surface pump in a ventilated dry housing below the level of the lowest pool

hidden delivery pipe must not touch water in top pool

submersible pump in the lowest pool

If ornamental water is beyond your budget, unavailable or considered unsafe, a dry stream- or river-like effect can be created by arranging small stones or broken pieces of slate or crushed glass to "flow" through part of the garden. In areas that are prone to flash flooding, similar stones can be arranged in specially constructed "rills" that will conduct surplus water away from vulnerable terraces or seating areas, but will still look attractive when dry.

You can simulate the effect of moving water in the garden by arranging small pebbles or slate pieces in a stream- or river-like pattern.

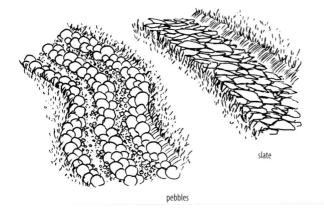

slate

pebbles

Size

Water features should be treated in a similar way to other features in a garden with respect to size. If the garden is very large, the water feature should also be generous. If small, the feature will need to be smaller, reflecting the proportions of the site. However, a pool needs space in which to express itself, and anything under about 2.5 m (8.2 ft.) in length or width may look more like a conspicuous puddle!

From a practical point of view, a small pool is subject to more temperature variation, particularly if shallow, and is more ecologically unstable than a larger body of water, affecting the water clarity and the balance of plant and animal life. The depth of a pool should be proportionate to its surface area—the greater the surface area, the greater the depth required to produce stability. Generally, the minimum depth is about 1 m (3.3 ft.), sufficient to hide the planting baskets of both aquatic and marginal plants placed below the surface, and to allow fish to survive.

An important point to consider when determining the size of a pool is that planting either in or close to the pool will tend to encroach upon the water area and may reduce it considerably if you are using invasive marginal plants.

If space will not allow for a large pool, there are other options. Where ground space is limited, you can use a wall-mounted fountain. Elaborate lions, dolphin heads or simple metal spouts spill water to into a pool or, if the feature is required to double as a birdbath, first into a shallow bowl. Circular millstones can have a spout that allows water to run over and around them, and lush effects can be achieved by planting moisture-loving plants in deep, damp soil nearby.

Location

The success of a water feature may depend on where it is sited. The position of trees and the aspect and orientation of the site have a bearing on this.

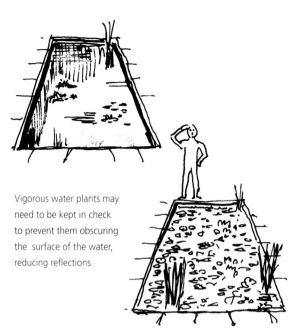

Vigorous water plants may need to be kept in check to prevent them obscuring the surface of the water, reducing reflections.

A small water feature can double as a bird bath.

Overhanging trees

Generally it is advisable to site water features away from overhanging trees. In a formal setting, leaves can make the pool look unkempt, and if the pool is not very deep, vegetation collecting at the bottom may turn the water black and result in a proliferation of duck weed over the surface. If a formal pool is to be surrounded by plantings, and particularly if the area is windswept, it is advisable to raise it above ground level to reduce the amount of vegetation blown into the water.

If you intend your pool to provide a home to plant and animal life, beware of siting it near trees with poisonous leaves, berries or seeds, such as yew, holly and laburnum.

Sun and shade

Most plants and animals thrive better in pools that receive sun for at least half a day, preferably more in temperate regions. In hot countries, less would be

acceptable. If you only have a shady site, you will not be able to grow water lilies, but mosses and ferns will thrive.

A few species of fish, such as golden orfe, are happy in cold water. However, fish will consume tadpoles and other water creatures, disrupting the fragile ecological balance.

Directing circulation

Having dwelt on the aesthetic qualities of water, it is worth remembering that water can be used to direct the circulation of people through a garden. Unless stones or planks are used as crossing points, most people will walk around, rather than through, a stretch of water!

Using reflection

Still water can be used to bring light into a garden, but if water is to be used in this way, the pool must be sited so that it catches the available sunshine and reflects it back to an intended part of the garden or house. To achieve this, the level of the water may have to be lowered or raised.

If your intention in using still water is to reflect the surroundings of a garden, consider the angle of the sun. Ideally, as you view the water, the sun should be shining from behind you. If it is shining towards you, the glare it produces may prevent you from seeing any reflections.

Reflected light from this large raised pool brightens a downstairs room. As the surface of the water is blown by breezes, ripples are reflected onto the ceiling.

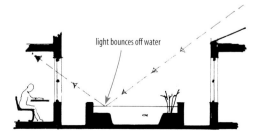

light bounces off water

Practical Problems

A badly designed water feature may detract from the enjoyment of a garden. Ponds constructed without an overflow pipe may flood and ruin large areas of lawn or plantings, and the entire structure of a pool can be damaged, if not suitably constructed, by harsh weather conditions, such as frost or ice.

In hot countries in particular, a shallow pool of water that is not circulated may attract breeding colonies of mosquitoes or other insects and become smelly and stagnant.

A 45° slope is extremely dangerous—from inside the water it is hard to reach the edge of the pool or to get a foothold from which to get out.

Sheer sides are safer than sloping ones, particularly if they contain a ledge. The ledge can also be used as a shelf for the planting baskets of marginal plants.

A gradually sloping "beach" is the safest construction for a pool.

Safety Considerations

Undoubtedly, one of the most important issues in designing a water feature is whether children are likely to use the garden. A young child can drown in as little as 2 cm (1 in.) of water, and all non-swimmers are at risk with deep pools. Ways of increasing safety include covering a formal pool with black-painted metal bars or a steel mesh that can support the weight of an adult, or fencing off a pond or stream. The fence need not be exposed but can be cleverly disguised with plantings. When designing pools, a sheer side is far safer than one with sloping sides at forty-five degrees. At this angle anyone in the water would find it hard to reach and grasp hold of the edge of the pool or to get a foothold from which to exit.

So, when children are young, it is advisable to avoid stretches of water. But if you or the garden owner would like a water feature in the future, do consider how an existing feature may later be adapted inexpensively. A large sandpit, for instance, may be sited and designed for easy conversion. There are many ways of introducing water into a garden without risk to children. You could, for example, create a jet of water that splashes over pebbles. The water would then trickle back through to an underground reservoir and be re-circulated with a pump.

A fountain over cobbles provides a child-friendly water feature.

Refining Ideas for the Preliminary Garden Layout Plan

When preparing the first stages of the garden layout plan you will be focusing on the ground plane and will need to consider how you will be combining hard landscaping (anything that is man-made, such as paving, paths, walls, arches or buildings) with soft landscaping (soil, grass, water or plant material). At this point it may be wise to refer back to your completed site appraisal and concept diagram (see Chapter 1) and reconsider the following:

– How do your proposals satisfy the recommendations of your appraisal?
– Have you allowed enough space for different activities?
– Are the spaces large enough for people to move about in?
– Have you sited them in appropriate places?
– Have you considered the environmental effect of your proposals?

You will probably need to readjust some of your earlier ideas before moving on to make decisions about the horizontal (and later some of the vertical) elements of your layout. The success of your design will depend on how you divide up the garden into these different hard and soft areas and how you link one area with another.

The fashion in twentieth-century gardens was the creation of garden rooms, dividing up the site into a series of interlocking spaces, each with an individual character or style of plantings. Division gives an opportunity for several different types of garden within the whole garden and can relate well to the interior proportions of modern houses. Current trends are influenced by television makeovers and the media, and materials such as acrylics, aluminium, glass, Perspex and galvanized steel have become fashionable. Hedging can also be used as an environmentally-friendly alternative to hard landscaping.

When refining your ideas for the preliminary garden layout plan, keep referring back to your site appraisal.

The Ground Plane or Garden Floor: Horizontal Elements in the Design

The garden floor is perhaps the most important single element in the design. It is the link between house and garden, can be divided up into the appropriate proportions for mass and void and is also usually the most expensive part of the garden to construct. There is a huge and often bewildering choice of materials available, but you must consider whether the material you use will be in keeping with the site and the surroundings. The material must also be suited to the purpose. For instance, heavy and thick stone paving would be inappropriate for the scale of a small circular paved area, and the cost of labour to cut each stone to fit the space would be prohibitive. Consider using permeable materials that allow water to pass through to the soil below; avoid covering the ground with too much unnecessary hard landscaping which will hinder absorption of rainfall and lead to runoff problems. To keep costs reasonable, and transport and labour charges down, the material you choose should be sourced locally and suited to the role it is to perform.

Paved Areas and Terraces

It is often easiest to begin with the paved areas, as this is usually the terrace adjacent to the house, although if the main rooms of the house face away

DEVELOPING THE DESIGN

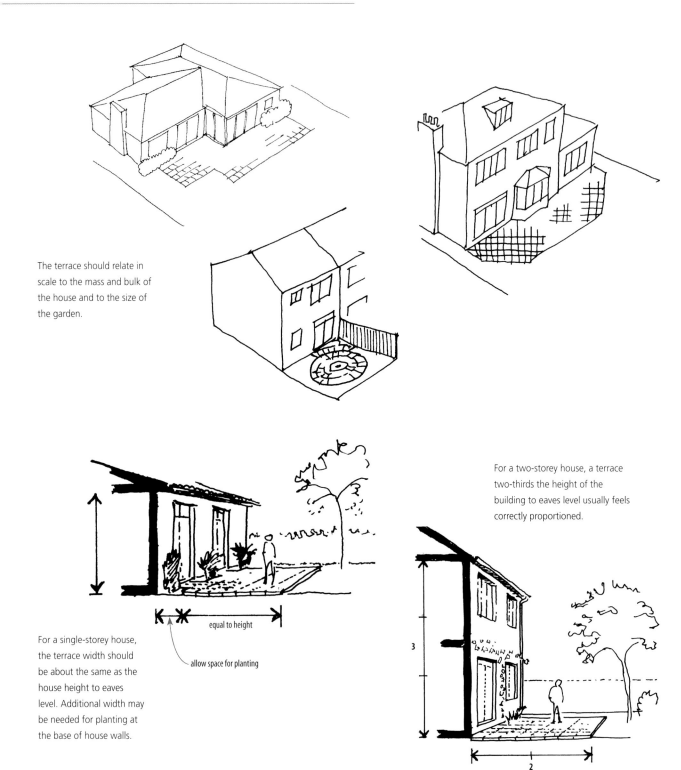

The terrace should relate in scale to the mass and bulk of the house and to the size of the garden.

For a two-storey house, a terrace two-thirds the height of the building to eaves level usually feels correctly proportioned.

equal to height

allow space for planting

For a single-storey house, the terrace width should be about the same as the house height to eaves level. Additional width may be needed for planting at the base of house walls.

3

2

The DPC is usually about 150 mm (6 in) above ground level.

150 mm

The damp proof course is a horizontal layer of impervious material laid in a wall to prevent the damp from rising. Soil piled up above the DPC effectively bridges it, allowing damp to seep inside.

To create a terrace level with the floor indoors without bridging the DPC use a slatted timber deck supported on bricks, with an accessible and ventilated space beneath. This bridges the "trench" between window and terrace.

If a raised terrace is unavoidable, then ample transition space and careful design is essential.

generous space

from the direction of the sun it may be necessary to have the terrace, or sitting area, some distance from the house. Permeable surfaces are now an essential consideration in any design, especially where front gardens and driveways are concerned, and in Britain legislation now requires the issue of permeability to encompass private front gardens, with planning permission required for the use of non-permeable paving.

The terrace usually provides the major horizontal link between house and garden, the width being at a minimum two-thirds of the height of the house to the level of the eaves. With low buildings, the full height of the house will produce a better proportion. Narrow or small terraces often look meagre, as if there were insufficient paving stones available. They also restrict the amount of seating. Mixing local materials, such as brick and timber, gives a natural appearance and may help to blend in with the surroundings. Where possible, leave open joints between the paving material so that water can permeate. Try to leave some space for planting at the foot of the house wall, softening the hard right-angle

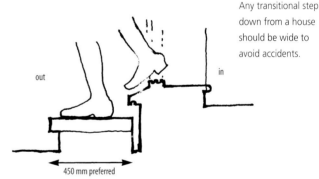

Any transitional step down from a house should be wide to avoid accidents.

out

in

450 mm preferred

junction between wall and terrace. Leave enough room for generous planting, rather than having a thin line of plants trying to survive in builders' leftover rubble. Make sure that the soil remains clear of the damp-proof course (DPC).

The terrace should, if possible, be on the same level as the interior floor of the house, but this will depend on the height of the DPC or foundation. Usually the DPC or foundation is at least 150 mm (6 in.) above ground level and can be stepped with the fall of the ground. Ignoring this level (where moisture cannot permeate) by building or banking up soil can lead to problems such as rising damp or flooding. Bugs or termites can also cause premature deterioration of the house structure.

If the finished terrace level is below the interior floor level of the house, try to ensure that the transitional step (or steps) are wide enough to allow a person to stand and adjust to the change of level. If the terrace is above the interior floor level, the steps that lead up to it should be wide and shallow for easy going. There may even need to be a change of level in the terrace itself, and, if so, you should make this as obvious as possible to avoid accidents. Any terraces or areas of paving in other parts of the garden should be dealt with in the same way as the main terrace.

Most gardens require a space for car parking. The tyres of the car need hard standing beneath them, while the ground underneath the main body of the vehicle can be filled in with easily drained loose gravel or stone, low-growing plants or a combination of these materials.

A "porous" driveway consists of two strips of brick paving for car wheels with gravel and low planting between.

When designing to a grid, remember that this grid can be carried through in the paving pattern, albeit at a smaller scale. This can be particularly effective if your design is on the diagonal, the paving being laid at the same diagonal angle, following the lines of the grid.

Paths

Paths are the arteries of a garden and often lead off and out from the terrace, following grid lines that flow from gateways, doors or windows. Before considering a path, it is important to decide on its exact purpose, since paths leading nowhere (often in a roundabout fashion) always appear ridiculous. Path proportions should relate in scale to other garden features and to the adjoining house.

It is important to think carefully about who will be using the path. Main paths, perhaps designed to draw people through the garden and allow them to examine views or details of plantings, should, if there is room, be about 1.2–1.5 m (4–5 ft.) in width, to allow two people to stroll in comfort. Paths that lead up to the front door of a house should also be generous, as there will often be a group of people approaching or leaving a house together. Consider constructing an overhang or porch in the area immediately adjacent to the front door to protect people from rain or sun while waiting for the door to open.

Main paths should allow two people to stroll together in comfort.

1.2–1.5 m

When designing paths always consider who is going to use them.

2 m

Allow a generous width for entrance paths, where people tend to congregate.

Service paths need not be wide but they should avoid sharp bends and be designed for ease of use.

When designing a path it is vital that it clearly contributes to the overall layout of the garden. A path that appears to have been put in as an afterthought to save wear on the grass always looks out of place. As the main function of a path is to allow access from one point to another, most people will try to take the shortest route, called a "desire line". Consider other options, such as gentle curves, which will appear more exaggerated in perspective than they do on plan. The maximum extent to which a path can be curved without corner-cutting is known as the "critical curve". Raised edges, such as cobblestones set on edge, will act as a psychological deterrent to cutting corners. Planting can also act as a barrier, particularly if a prickly plant such as a low-growing berberis is used. Staggered edges, usually using large flagstones, can add interest to a straight path.

Subsidiary and service paths need be only 1 m (3.3 ft.) or less in width but must avoid sharp curves or right angles which would be inconvenient for wheelbarrows. A service path between a border and hedge needs to take the base of a stepladder safely and should only be about the width of the ladder.

All paths should be laid to a camber, or a slightly arched surface, to allow water to drain away quickly. Occasional gulleys at path edges may be needed to drain away excess water during flooding. Avoid using materials that may become slippery in wet or damp weather, especially in shady areas where moss and lichen may accumulate.

A curved path may tempt people to take the shortest route—known as a desire line—but strategic planting can stop this.

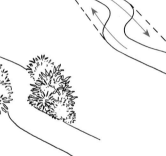

Setting the path on a slightly arched surface, using a cross fall or leaving gaps or gulleys at the lower edging can help to deflect excess rainwater.

camber

cross fall, or slope to a gulley

gaps in the lower edging allow water to drain away and avoid flooding

fall

DEVELOPING THE DESIGN

Planting Areas

As a general rule, these should be as wide as possible, for as plants mature, they tend to take up more space than originally envisaged. Climbers, shrubs, herbaceous plants and bulbs, and perhaps annuals, cannot be effectively combined in a narrow strip at the base of a wall, where the soil is generally dry and unproductive. An absolute minimum width is usually 1 m (3.3 ft.), but this will only allow space for the spread of one fairly small or upright shrub. A more generous dimension of 2–3 m (6.6–9.8 ft.) will allow you more scope in designing plant groupings.

If the planting area is backed by a hedge, extra space must be allowed not only for the hedge to grow outwards but also for clipping. An additional 1 m (3.3 ft.) may be needed and will allow for a service path along the rear of the border.

Avoid wiggly lines as an edge to your borders. If curves are an integral part of your design, ensure that they are generously shaped. Planting outlines, which are generally soft and irregular, are set off best by strong shapes—a straight line is usually the best foil.

Materials

When developing your preliminary garden layout plan you will need to state where your garden surfaces, structures, ornaments, furniture and so on are to be located. Now you need to be more specific, and for each element you will need to decide on the type of material required and how much space it will take up as well as considering the sustainability of the materials chosen, This means that the materials should not be produced or be able to degrade in a way that affects the environment. It must be able to be extracted, transported and used so that it does not cause environmental degradation, including the transport cost in terms of pollution. This may mean seeking out local products that are also more likely to be in keeping with the surroundings.

Cement and gravel are two widely used but dubious products. Cement (eventually to become concrete) begins with the mining of limestone and sand—a process that destroys local habitats and makes irreparable changes to the environment. Transport to the processing plant, the energy used in manufacture, the high levels of noxious material released into the atmosphere and the water used in washing out cement plants, mixers and tools, plus the corrosive and alkaline runoff that can cause serious pollution in watercourses, means that alternatives should be considered.

Although some gravel comes from land sources, most is dredged from the sea floor, changing it fundamentally and affecting already-depleted fish stocks. It may be difficult to plan a garden excluding cement and gravel completely, but before you decide, consider dry stone walls, turf banks or recycled materials such as bricks, glass, or broken pipes or tiles.

Most wide borders—particularly mixed or herbaceous borders—need a service path at the back so that the plants at the rear can be easily reached. Where planting is backed by a hedge, leave space for clipping and for the hedge to grow wider.

The service path will not be visible when the plants mature.

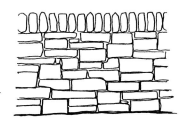

A "natural" wall of broken stone is a more sustainable alternative to cement.

Turves of heather cut and laid upside down on top of one another eventually knit together to form a strong heather wall or bank.

Inspiration and Reference

To help you choose materials, you may want to visit gardens and consult books by leading designers. Perhaps you have read about a garden and admired the detailed construction. Try to identify a style appropriate to your chosen garden and then follow that through with conviction—diluting the idea, to be safe, often shows a lack of confidence that may be apparent in your design. There is no sin in adapting someone else's idea for your own purpose.

Spend some time walking around your locality, looking closely at the materials that have been used and assessing their effect. Notice whether the materials have been used imaginatively, if the workmanship is good and if successful combinations of materials have been used. For future reference, photograph details, make drawings or take measurements.

Visit as many local garden centres and builders' merchants as possible to find out which materials are available in your area. There may be a quarry or timber yard nearby that could provide local or recycled material at reasonable cost. In order to compare quality, design and the long-term effect of these, make a note of the important points: the cost

per unit or per square metre or yard, delivery time and distance, availability, and the dimensions and durability of the materials.

Making Choices

When choosing materials, compare characteristics of appearance, design use and suitability. Ideally the materials should be functional, easy to maintain, affordable and readily available while also being as sustainable as possible. They should complement the overall garden design in style and character and relate to the house and its setting.

Try to restrict yourself to using no more than three different types of hard landscaping material in a design. More than this tends to look like a sponsored demonstration garden at a flower show or garden festival, where the designer is required to use the manufacturer's materials.

Surfacing

The structural materials used for garden surfaces have different characteristics in terms of wear, appearance and cost. All have their own merits and drawbacks. Some are "loose", such as gravel and bark, some "fluid", such as concrete, and some "rigid", such as paving stones or bricks. The choice between permeable and impermeable surfacing is becoming more critical, and the legal restrictions will vary between different countries.

Although each category is considered separately here, different paving elements can be combined to produce interesting variations of colour, texture and pattern. When combining different materials, do ensure that they interlock properly and that any patterns created complement the design of the garden as a whole. From a practical point of view, mixing different materials can help to keep costs down, and from an aesthetic point of view a combination of, say, brick and stone or timber, can relieve an excess of either material.

Loose Surfacing

Loose surfacing consists of aggregate materials such as gravel, shingle, small pebbles, glass chippings and bark that are consolidated but not fixed rigidly into place. They are suitable for areas of any shape. Used for garden surfaces they provide textural interest as well as a weed-suppressing base suitable for walking on. They are comparatively inexpensive and easy to lay, with maintenance consisting only of an occasional raking, weed killing, and replenishing of the top layer. One disadvantage of loose surfacing is that they tend to migrate into neighbouring areas. To prevent this they need to be properly contained, either with a brick-on-edge strip or by preservative-treated ("tanalized") timber boards secured with wooden pegs. These are not necessary, however, where a gravelled or barked area adjoins a hard surface, such as a stone terrace.

Gravel avoids any need to cut to shape.

Use timber edging to contain loose surfacing.

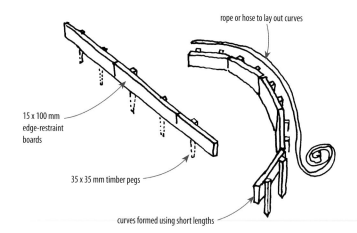

15 x 100 mm edge-restraint boards

rope or hose to lay out curves

35 x 35 mm timber pegs

curves formed using short lengths

Unless very well consolidated, loose surfacing is not ideal for areas where garden furniture will be placed, or where buggies (strollers), wheelchairs and wheelbarrows will need access. In addition to being used for surfaces to walk on, loose materials can be used in conjunction with plantings. Plants grown in gravelled areas create an informal, self-seeded look. Gravel and bark can be applied as a mulch to planting beds. Dry stream beds, composed of light-reflecting gravel, are a good alternative to water streams where real water would be impractical or unsafe.

Design use or suitability

Gravel:
- drives and paths
- terraces, particularly when used in combination with other materials, such as brick, stone or timber
- dry stream beds
- traditional and modern settings
- urban and rural situations

Wood and bark chippings:
- paths in rural settings
- children's play areas
- large areas of plantings where maintenance may be a problem

Gravel

Gravel comes in many different colours and textures, depending on the parent rock that produces the chippings. Gravel sizes vary from 20 mm (0.8 in.) coarse-gauge chippings to 3 mm (0.1 in.) fine grit. It is completely permeable if laid on a compacted base that will allow water to soak through, although weeds can still grow through it. Once a suitably compacted base has been laid, a permeable landscape fabric can be applied before the gravel is put down; this will prevent any deep-rooted weeds from growing through and reduce the likelihood of seeds taking root within the gravel. Where heavier use by bicycles, prams or vehicles is expected, use cellular plastic-moulded honeycomb frames that will hold the gravel in place at an even depth to prevent sinking.

Resin bonded aggregate, available in a wide range of colours, is made by mixing the gravel with a resin during the laying process. When it is set the gravel is bonded together, forming a suitable surface for driveways and paths that appears like conventional gravel but is solid and does not move. If laid correctly, it allows water to drain through; use a qualified contractor to carry out the work.

Self-compacting gravel is a mixture of aggregate and a powdered clay-like dust that is spread and compacted with a vibrating plate, forming a hard surface but allowing water to permeate. The colour choice is at present restricted.

Pea shingle (pea gravel) is dredged from the sea and rivers. More rounded in shape than gravel chippings, it provides a softer surface more suited to decorative areas than those subject to hard wear.

When selecting gravel, always try to match any existing stonework, such as garden walls or the façade of a house.

Wood or bark chippings

Chippings can be made up of any type of wood or bark and are supplied in coarse or fine cuts.

Fluid Paving Materials

Fluid paving materials are those that are initially fluid, or paste-like, but which then harden to form a very solid, durable but impermeable surface. These include in situ or poured concrete and asphalt. Because of their initial fluidity they can be used for areas of any shape.

Fluid paving materials can be used for areas of any shape.

Design use or suitability

In situ concrete:
- paths or drives
- terraces, particularly when combined with natural materials

Asphalt:
- service paths and drives only

In situ concrete

In situ concrete consists of a mixture of cement, the aggregates sharp sand and stones (known together as ballast) and water. When the water is added, the mixture initially forms a fluid paste, which later sets hard. Concrete mixes can be bought in bags, ready for mixing with water, either by hand or in a motorized mixing machine. For large areas, however, it is more economical to mix the ingredients yourself.

In situ concrete is used extensively in gardens as a base for garden structures such as walls and sheds, but it can also be used as a surface in its own right and indeed is a most underestimated material. It has several benefits:

- It is relatively inexpensive to install.
- If properly exploited, it is capable of considerable variation, both in surface treatment and by the inclusion of different aggregates.
- Various forms and shapes can be imprinted or stamped onto the concrete while it is still wet, or the aggregate can be exposed by brushing with water and a stiff broom just before the concrete sets.
- Colours can be varied by adding special colouring powders or different sands to the mix.

Most of the drawbacks of in situ concrete arise from its mix and installation. If you require a textured or imprinted surface it is important to experiment first. Similarly, you should experiment with any colour dyes added to the mix. The final colour always looks different when the concrete has dried.

For large expanses of concrete, over 5 m (16.4 ft.) in any direction, expansion joints must be incorporated into the design to avoid the concrete cracking as it settles. These joints, although necessary, can be made to look attractive using materials such as bricks, setts or pressure-treated timber boards. The expansion joints, which can also allow water to permeate, will form an integral part of the paving design and should be carefully selected to complement the rest of the garden.

Bricks make the necessary expansion joints in in situ concrete.

Asphalt

Asphalt is sold prepacked for direct application to a firm surface, such as concrete or gravel. Preferable in black, it is also available in red and green, and can be textured by adding stone chippings to the surface and rolling them in.

To allow for runoff and to avoid puddles, all in situ concrete or asphalt surface should be laid with a cross fall to carry away excess water. The fall should always be away from the property unless a drainage gulley is installed to protect the property wall.

When placed up against a building, non-porous surfaces like tarmac or concrete must be efficiently drained into permeable material such as gravel or soil.

Small-Scale Rigid Paving Materials

Small-scale rigid paving materials, such as bricks, pavers, setts and cobbles, are available in a wide range of styles, finishes and sizes. Because of their small size they can be laid out in a variety of attractive, interlocking patterns to complement the overall design of a garden.

When set in sand, small rigid materials allow free drainage of water through the joints. They are thus ideal to use around proposed or existing trees.

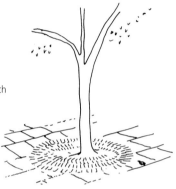

Bricks laid on loose sand allow water and air to reach the tree roots.

The small unit size of all these materials makes them very labour intensive to lay, and because of this, when used alone they tend to be more suitable for paths than for terraces in the garden. For a terrace, a large expanse of bricks or setts can look rather cold and severe. It is far better to combine these small-scale materials with other materials, such as large slabs, timber or areas of gravel or lawn.

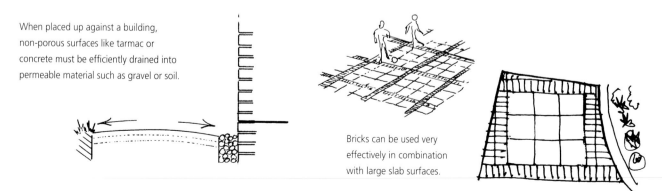

Bricks can be used very effectively in combination with large slab surfaces.

Design use or suitability

All of these small-scale materials can be used to create patterns to break up areas of larger-scale materials.

Bricks and pavers:
– rectangular areas of paving or terrace
– to provide a visual link with other brick structures, such as the house
– as edging for lawns and gravelled areas
– as runners for drainage

Granite (or other stone) setts:
– rectangular and circular shapes
– paths and drives
– to create a natural look

Cobbles:
– ornamental areas, such as surrounding the base of an urn
– areas where walking is discouraged (cobbles are uncomfortable to walk on)

Bricks and pavers

Bricks and pavers, small and usually rectangular in shape, are made from both clay and concrete. Generally, bricks are used for walling and pavers for paving, but certain bricks can also be used to pave areas, provided they are guaranteed to withstand frost in cold climates. Choose a style and colour of brick that complements your house and its surroundings.

Basket weave brick paving can be laid between a frame of railway sleepers.

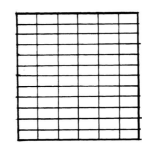

Brick/Block Paving

Stretcher bond: This bond can help draw the eye across a space. It is an excellent bond for pathways. It can also be used for larger areas. When viewed "end on" its character changes. It can be useful used diagonally to "stretch" space.

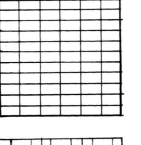

Stack bond: A modern-looking pattern. The bricks or blocks do not bond by interlinking. Any settlement in the ground, or poor workmanship, will show. It can be used in small areas to give a spartan or austere mood.

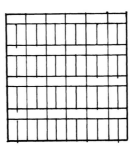

Herringbone: This is a popular bond. It looks good from any angle.

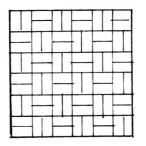

Basket weave and stack bond combination: This has a larger scale. The eye can easily read the bonding. It can be used for paths, terraces and even steps. It requires good setting out.

Basket weave: This bond looks identical from either direction.

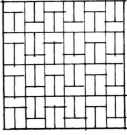

Basket weave variation

Facing or stock bricks are available in a variety of colours but are unable to withstand severe frost.

Engineering bricks, in a dark greyish blue colour, are very hard-wearing. They are most suitable for edging areas, as their smooth surface makes them rather slippery when wet. They tend to be more expensive than ordinary bricks.

Pavers (sometimes called paviours) are thinner than bricks, more hard-wearing and frost-resistant, and are ideal for paving. Clay pavers usually come in shades of red, concrete pavers in shades of beige, grey and blue-grey.

Block paving is often used for driveways because of its load-bearing capacity and low cost. It is now available in a wide range of colours and sizes, and it allows water to drain away because when laid the blocks are filled with a jointing sand. The unified appearance tends to look unnatural so they should be used with discretion.

Blocks laid dry on a sand bed with sand brushed into the joints will allow water to pass through.

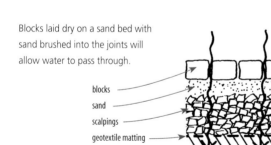

blocks
sand
scalpings
geotextile matting

Cellular paving is provided in a grid system, is made from either plastic or concrete and is laid on a prepared sub-base. With in the cells, grass can be

Cellular concrete or high-density plastic blocks with cells through which grass can grow make for a natural-looking, free-draining driveway surface.

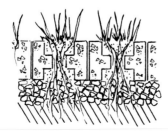

sown in soil or aggregates can be laid. The systems were originally designed for heavily used areas where the wear on grass was a problem.

Granite (or other stone) setts

Setts are small blocks, generally $100 \times 100 \times 100$ mm ($4 \times 4 \times 4$ in.) of granite or other hard stone. They have roughened, uneven surfaces. There are now several concrete versions of setts that have a flat face and provide a smoother surface more suitable for walking on.

granite setts channel
water to trees

cobbles
discourage
walking

stone paving says
"walk here"

Use materials to direct circulation.

Granite setts mark out the private gravel drive from the public street, even without gates.

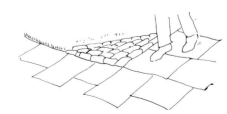

Setts take the wear at an otherwise vulnerable corner of a lawn.

Cobbles

Cobbles are natural waterworn pebbles about the size and shape of a somewhat flattened goose egg. They can be laid in mortar, either loosely or closely packed together, depending on the effect required.

All small-scale paving can be laid on a compacted sand base to allow water to percolate to the subsoil below.

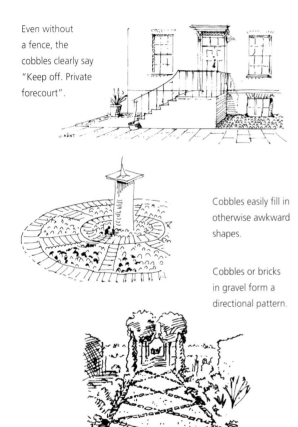

Even without a fence, the cobbles clearly say "Keep off. Private forecourt".

Cobbles easily fill in otherwise awkward shapes.

Cobbles or bricks in gravel form a directional pattern.

Large-Scale Rigid Paving Materials

Large-unit paving materials include stone paving slabs and precast concrete slabs. Both are hard-wearing, easy to lay and are available in a huge variety of colours and surface textures. Generally, a smooth surface is suitable for areas containing furniture, and a rougher, more nonslip surface is suitable for steps or areas surrounding a swimming pool.

Natural stone, even secondhand, is heavy and expensive both to purchase and to install. Try to find a local source to avoid transport costs, and avoid too much cutting as this will drive up labour costs. Many natural stones become very slippery when damp and may be unsuitable for paved areas used by the elderly or children.

Large slabs can be laid out in a variety of patterns to complement the overall garden design. If using natural stone, a random rectangular or similar layout reduces the amount of cutting required. For an informal look, joints can be left open for planting pockets.

Occasionally, in an old or neglected garden, some paving slabs may be unearthed, perhaps even lurking beneath existing paths or lawns. Where possible, try to use these whole, as breaking them up into smaller sizes tends to spoil their effect. Crazy paving (a mix of paving randomly broken into irregular sizes) should be avoided as it tends to look unprofessional and unfinished and is notoriously difficult to lay effectively.

Design use or suitability

Stone and precast slabs:
— terraces, pathways and drives, either alone or combined with other materials
— as "stepping stones" through gravel, brick or lawn
— with plantings growing through joints for an informal look

Imitation paving

If you select imitation paving, it is important to consider the following:
— Does the colour go right through the material, or is it only applied to the surface? If superficial, the colour will fade with time and

exposure, gradually revealing the pure grey
concrete beneath.
— How does the material look after it has been
laid down for several years? Some types
improve with age, perhaps toning down or
acquiring moss or lichen. Others are prone
to chipping and cracking and remain looking
rather crude.
— What does the material look like when wet?
— For paving slabs, is there a wide range of sizes
available? Choosing an appropriate size can
reduce labour costs considerably. If the slabs
are to look natural, perhaps being laid in a
random pattern, the more sizes there are, the
easier it will be to achieve a convincing effect.
— How easy is it to cut?

Stone flags

Stone flags, possibly the most beautiful of paving
materials, come in a wide range of colour tones.
(In the United Kingdom, the best known is York
stone, but many other types of stone are available,
depending on your locality.) All stone takes its colour
from the geological formation of the locality, which
can vary enormously in different areas of a country.
Most of it is heavy to transport, lift and lay.

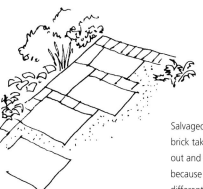

Salvaged stone and
brick takes time to lay
out and time to design
because the slabs are all
different sizes.

Precast slabs

Precast slabs are available in many shapes and sizes,
but all are essentially made of concrete, which is
coloured and given textures, sometimes to imitate
natural materials, such as stone. Precast slabs are often

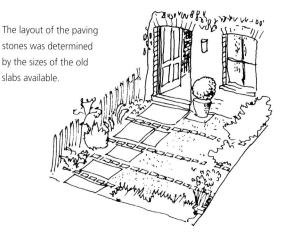

The layout of the paving
stones was determined
by the sizes of the old
slabs available.

used as a cheaper alternative to stone. If you want the
slabs to look as much like real stone as possible, buy
the slabs in a variety of sizes and lay them in a random
rectangular pattern for a natural look. The slabs should
be close together in a compacted sand base. For a
permeable finish, all large-scale rigid paving should be
laid with porous material between the joints.

Cross-section of permeable slab paving

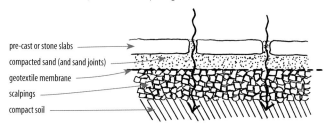

pre-cast or stone slabs
compacted sand (and sand joints)
geotextile membrane
scalpings
compact soil

Timber Decking

Timber decking, or wooden planking, provides an
attractive, hard surface. It is very adaptable and easily
cut, either to fit a particular area or to be made up
into panels. It is suited to both natural and urban
designs. In Europe and other temperate countries,
the damp climate tends to make it slippery. This can
be countered by covering the surface in wire mesh
netting, although this does spoil the appearance.
However, it can be an alternative to stone or brick as
a terrace material and is very comfortable on a warm
sunny day. It can also provide an inexpensive change
of level in a garden.

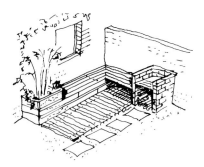

Timber decking is a useful and attractive material which can be used for a wide variety of constructions.

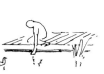

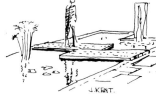

The timber available for outdoor use is cut from a large variety of trees, either hardwood or softwood. Hardwood is derived from broad-leaved trees, such as beech, teak and oak. It is much more expensive than softwood but does not need to be treated against rot as it has a natural resistance. Softwood comes from coniferous trees, such as pine and larch. With the exception of Western red cedar, which is tolerant to moisture and weathers well, all softwoods must be treated with a preservative to guard against rot and insect attack (such woods are "tanalized" or "pressure-impregnated"). Both hardwoods and softwoods can be stained or painted any colour. If left untreated, hardwoods will age naturally to a pleasant silver-grey colour.

Design use or suitability

Decking:

- terraces, particularly in warm, sunny areas or climates
- balconies
- suitable for a modern design
- useful for creating a unified look incorporating such features as a terrace, a pergola, built-in seating and barbecues
- looks good in conjunction with water
- is ecologically sound if locally sourced

Grass, Lawns and Wildflower Meadows

Grass is a versatile element in the garden. While most people think of areas of grass as lawn, there are other options that do not require regular mowing, Longer grass, with the addition of bulbs and wildflowers, perhaps with a curved mown path running through it, needs less maintenance. This should either be straight or of smooth curves, and it is easiest if the width is the same as the cutting blade of the mower. While large areas of the lawn can be left unmown, a close-cut strip on either side of the driveway can give a neat appeareance.

Gently winding paths can be mown through areas of long grass.

While large grassy areas may be left unmown, a closely cut strip on either side of a driveway gives a neat appearance.

The area between trees can often be difficult to mow, so bulbs could be grown in long grass.

If you do wish to have a lawn in your garden, it can provide a unifying base for the surrounding planting. The shape should be kept simple, without being broken up by island beds which will only get in the way of the mower. When planning the lawn, think about the type of mowing machine that may be used for cutting it—will it need an electric cable to run it, or space for a turning circle at the end of each strip? Ideally, your lawn should be the width of multiples of the width of the mower to avoid an unnecessary run. Avoid using small or awkwardly shaped areas of grass as these will be a nuisance and time-consuming to cut or mow.

When planning the dimensions of a mown path, choose a width that corresponds to the width of the lawn mower—the same width or two or three times wider.

Often a lawn forms the largest single area in a design, complementing the rest of the garden by showing off the surrounding plants to their best effect. It can highlight a vista or draw the eye away from something that might be best hidden, and it can act as a "void" in the garden.

The maintenance of a lawn can be very demanding. Although generally inexpensive to install when compared with other surfaces, regular mowing maintenance and lawn treatments drive up costs. To keep a lawn in good condition requires a traditional care programme to include regular mowing, aerating to improve drainage, scarifying (which removes dead grass, moss and weeds known as "thatch") and regular autumn and spring feeding. Some franchise companies offer a good regular lawn care service, providing fertilizers and nutrients at a competitive cost, thus relieving the owner of lawn care responsibility.

Design use or suitability

Mown grass:
– a soft surface to walk and play on
– a foil for flower borders, paved areas and water
– ideal to use for making curved areas

– cools the surrounding air in summer
– attracts bird and insect life
– provides a sustainable, tactile surface that helps reduce water runoff from what might otherwise have been a hard area

Rough grass:
– for wild areas of the garden
– acts as a link with surrounding countryside
– a low-maintenance alternative to mown grass
– provides a natural habitat for wildlife
– requires less mowing and maintenance than mown grass
– can be difficult to establish

Lawns

There are many different qualities of lawn suitable for different purposes. Immaculate velvety lawns, so typical of elegant English gardens, are usually primarily decorative, laid out in bold shapes to complement the overall garden design or to act as a foil for plantings. They have a fine texture. All require moisture to remain green—grass roots are superficial, rarely going deeper than a few centimetres or inches into the soil, so they are prone to drying out during drought. Golf courses, where the fairways must be kept green, use a vast quantity of water, and in a domestic situation a drought-enforced water ban on using hose pipes and sprinklers in gardens can ruin the desired lush effect. However, beneath the soil the roots often remain viable for a long time, and even a badly desiccated lawn can be restored to a lush green with a good downpour.

If traditional grass is to be used for a general utility or play area, imperfections are acceptable and inevitable. Coarser grass will take heavier wear, and there are mixtures suitable for many different needs. The better mixtures avoid rye grass, which has flower heads that are resistant to mowing and which forms clumps rather than knitting together laterally. Seed mixtures are also available for areas of light shade, although if it is to be used in conjunction with another mix, it is important to make sure they will

yield the same shade of green, For best effect, the edges of a lawn should be cut with an edging tool every two or three weeks to give crisply defined outline, which means more labour.

Pristine lawns require a considerable amount of maintenance and are unsuitable if subject to heavy wear. Keeping any type of mown lawn short and uniform requires one or two weekly mowings during the growing season.

With hotter, drier summers becoming the norm in most temperate countries, maintaining a lawn may no longer be a sustainable option unless the turf industry adopts a different approach to the traditional regime. If the amount of fertilizer is reduced, lush spring growth is avoided. If they are not watered at all in spring, the grass plants develop deeper root systems, helping the grass to remain greener for longer. Allowing the clippings to mulch back into the sward reduces the need for water and boosts nutrients. The UK turf industry constantly experiments with new strains of grass, altering seed mixtures to see which are most resistant to drought. In warmer and drier climates, different types of grass seed are used, and although this produces a coarser surface, in times of drought it remains green for longer.

To overcome the sustainability problem, look at alternatives. The first and most obvious is to reduce the size of the lawn. The second is to seek out other plant options by using plants that have a low creeping habit, such as some of the herb and *Sedum* species and that will survive with the minimum of water. Preparation for this type of "lawn" requires a weed-free, level and firm soil surface for the roots to establish themselves. Thereafter the plants can be left to spread naturally.

There are other ways of using grass, too. An eye-catching feature can be created by covering a bank with ground cover plants, or making a flight of steps formed out of grass. A grass roof can be an unusual addition to a garden shed. A modular

DEVELOPING THE DESIGN

A bank which might be difficult to mow could be planted with ground cover plants.

system can be adapted to create a living grass wall, but this will need an inbuilt irrigation system, plus occasional cutting or trimming. A living wall is easily constructed and quick to assemble, consisting of cells in a series of half-metre squares with a couple of plugs in each cell. The squares then slot into a rail system on the wall with built-in irrigation. Many types of grass soon outgrow their small cells, and herbs can be used instead. Because of the necessary irrigation installed, avoid herbs which need dry conditions. Try mint, lemon balm, oregano, parsley and chives, plus perhaps alpine strawberries.

Mowers

The vast array of models offered by different manufacturers is constantly being updated and improved, but the main consideration in buying a mower is to match the garden's requirements to a suitable machine.

Cylinder mowers, often fitted with rollers at the front and rear, have a scissorlike action and can produce the highest-quality cut and the traditional striped pattern. They are quieter than the other types. Ride-on machines operate in a similar way.

Rotary mowers have a disc with one or more blades spinning horizontally at high speed, and are generally fitted with wheels. The cut can be set higher, so they are able to cope with long grass.

Strimmers have an engine mounted at one end of a long pole, driving a high-speed spinning disc fitted with up to four nylon cords at the other. They are versatile and can be used for trimming edges around obstacles and areas where other mowers cannot operate.

In all cases, health and safety are crucial and any operator should be aware of the safety features of the machine as well as its limitations and capabilities.

Rough grass and wildflower meadows

Rough grass is basically grass left to grow long, requiring a cut only two or three times per year. It can be very attractive, providing a suitable medium for growing bulbs and wildflowers, although when in full growth it is difficult to walk through. There are many different species of grass, and the appearance of a grass meadow will depend on the species you grow. If you are growing other plants through it, cutting time is crucial. Bulbs must be left to die down, and wildflowers must be left until after flowering so that their seeds will be distributed. If the ground has been heavily fertilized, the grass, being more aggressive, will grow more quickly and gradually stifle the wildflowers, so choose a recommended non-aggressive grass seed.

Grass is unlikely to thrive in heavily shaded areas and is unsuited to places where mowing would be difficult, but several seed companies provide seed species bred to cope with various difficult conditions, such as shade or pedestrian traffic.

Despite the current interest in wildflower meadows, they are difficult to establish, particularly if the ground has previously been well fertilized. It is not simply a matter of buying some wildflower seed and sprinkling it around. Poor, thin soils are preferable, which can mean scraping off the topsoil to reach subsoil that has not been grazed, and would thus be richer in nutrients as a result of animal droppings. Removal of stones, careful raking and levelling of soil can then be followed by sowing and raking in grass and wildflower seed in the correctly weighed proportions according to the suppliers' instructions. Soil preparation is best carried out in autumn, then left to weather until spring sowing. Try to obtain a local seed source to preserve any genetic variation in local wildflower populations, and never take wild plants from the countryside, which is usually illegal. An alternative is to sow non-aggressive grass seed, adding wildflower plugs once the grass is established.

Edging

Edging is often used decoratively to provide a border around an area, but it also has the important function of providing a separation between two areas that would otherwise tend to mingle, such as a planted area and a gravel path. Most paths require an edging to hold them together and separate them from the soil. If abutting a lawn, the finished level of the edging needs to be below the level of the lawn to allow the mower to skim over unimpeded.

Pressure-treated timber cut into short strips can follow the curves of a lawn, separating two areas.

saw cuts make bending easier

wooden edging

turf laid over the top of edging

supporting pegs

There are many materials that are suitable to use for edging—pressure-treated timber, bricks laid on edge, cobbles, stone or purpose-made Victorian "rope" tiles. Timber, which soon weathers and becomes unnoticeable, may need to be cut into shorter strips to follow the lines of a curved path. The unnatural appearance of metal and plastic edging should be avoided.

Design use or suitability
Edging:
— to repeat a material used elsewhere and help relate one area to another
— to separate two areas that would otherwise mingle
— to provide a mowing strip, eliminating the need to edge a lawn
— to disguise the edge of a pool liner

Vertical and Overhead Elements

When you have allocated the ground plane surfaces on your preliminary garden layout plan, try lining up the plan at your own eye level, either by crouching down or by bringing the plan up to your eye level. Apart from the areas that you visualize as plantings, the space will still look flat and probably rather boring. Study the three-dimensional aspect of the garden and try to imagine how it might look, then consider how you might interrupt the flatness of the ground plane by introducing vertical and overhead features. Some examples of features you might consider are steps, walls, buildings, arbours, arches, pergolas, statues, pots or urns, seats, trees and large specimen shrubs.

Again, at this stage there is no need to decide exactly what shape or form these features will take, or of what material they will be built. Simply indicate where they will be by writing them in on your plan, trying to keep their proportions on the grid, or on a subdivision of it. Now try again putting yourself on the same eye level as your plan. Can you imagine the difference the verticals make? Even a slight change of level, such as two steps down or up and then back again, can make a garden more interesting. Low retaining walls for planting areas can give, in addition to visual appeal, an area raised up to a sunnier aspect with improved drainage, with the retaining walls sometimes doubling as extra seating, with or without cushions.

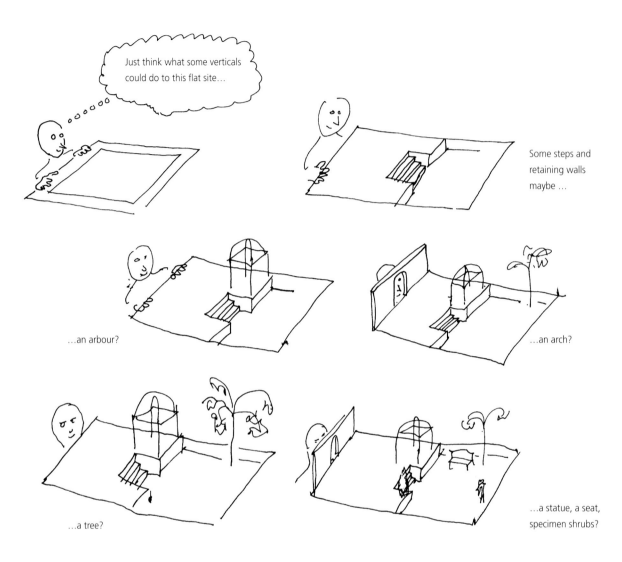

Just think what some verticals could do to this flat site…

Some steps and retaining walls maybe …

…an arbour?

…an arch?

…a tree?

…a statue, a seat, specimen shrubs?

A low retaining wall can provide better drainage for a range of plants, informal "built-in" seating, and easier gardening for the elderly.

Levels

Very few gardens are absolutely flat, although they often appear to be so, and even slight changes of level, necessitating no more than one or two steps, can be used to create interest and variety. Although your garden may be relatively level, there may be the possibility of steps up or down from the terrace and a couple more partway along the length of the garden. If this is the case, try to avoid making the break halfway along the garden, since 50:50 is not a comfortable proportion. Dividing the garden up into thirds is often a better solution.

Steps and Ramps

Steps

Remember that, compared with interiors, the scale outdoors is greatly increased, and the width of treads and heights of risers should be as generous as possible. The location of the level change will influence the step layout. When designing steps, keep them low, with the risers at best 100 mm (4 in.) and certainly no more than 150 mm (6 in.). The treads should be as wide as possible—450 mm (1.5 ft.), if practicable. Your steps may need an edging, such as a balustrade or retaining wall, parts of which can double as a plinth for pots and containers.

Planning permission in the UK now requires ramps to give level access to all domestic new buildings and extensions, and similar consideration should be given to level changes in gardens. Be sure to check restrictions of level changes in your area.

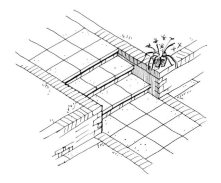

A sunken area with ample steps provides a conversation area and a protected place for a sand pit.

These well-designed steps have a retaining wall which doubles as a plinth for a pot.

Ramps

Ramps can provide useful access to the garden for those using buggies (strollers) and wheelchairs, and they are also invaluable for wheelbarrows and mowers.

Ramps built alongside steps offer access for disabled visitors.

When installing wheelchair ramps the following need to be considered:
– Width. The surface width of the ramp should be at least 1200 mm (3 ft. 4 in.).
– Gradient. A gradient of 1 in 20 is preferred but where space is limited keep to a maximum of 1 in 12.
– Landings. If the gradient is 1 in 15, level landings 1.5 m (5 ft.) long should be provided at 5 m (16 ft.) intervals.

Sloping Ground and Sculpting the Land

A level change within a garden should be treated as an opportunity to add interest, possibly through the use of hard landscape materials to create steps, walls and ramps. Severe changes in level and wall construction should be overseen by a qualified surveyor especially if the soil is sandy and liable to erosion in wet weather.

If there is a slope across the width of the garden, you must try to correct this, since looking out over a cross fall gives a very uneasy feeling, as though the whole place were sliding downhill. If the fall is slight, you may be able to correct it by "cut and fill", or reducing the level on the upper side and filling in the lower level with soil removed from that upper level (see page 29), or just by filling the lower area with tall, dense plantings.

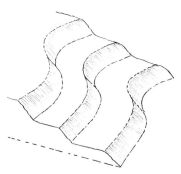

Land, especially on a slope, can be sculpted to create terraces that can be grassed over, provided that the slope is not too steep to be mown.

Land sculpting, very effective even in small gardens, requires more expertise and expert advice should be sought before the necessary JCB diggers are employed.

Slope Construction and Maintenance Principles

1. JCB operation. Use a skilled operator who can understand the shapes you wish to create.
2. Compaction and water retention. The slopes need to be properly compacted in layers to avoid slump and settlement. Use biodegradable materials such as a geotextile to improve soil stability and to prevent soil erosion. Slopes need to be well drained to avoid boggy pockets, and well irrigated to prevent turf from drying out.
3. Working the slopes. Only work in dry weather, and handle the soil as little as possible.
4. Soil storage. Store turf, topsoil and subsoil separately and for as short a time as possible.
5. Soil structure. This is vital in keeping the soil well aerated and to establish and maintain planting.

6. Maintenance. If slopes are to be mown, the slope should be less than 1 in 2. Mowers such as hover mowers can be used on one to one slopes but electric ones are often too heavy to operate safely and can flood.
7. Laying turf. On steep slopes turf should be laid vertically, rather than horizontally which can allow the turf to slip.
8. Grass seed and wildflowers. An appropriate seed mix should be sown shallowly in early spring and must kept moist.

Sheds, Ancillary Buildings and Play Equipment

Most gardens contain, or at least require, a certain number of ancillary buildings. Firstly there is the garage, which is frequently already present but may well require concealment or linking back to the house by a wall or hedge. There may also be a garden shed, and perhaps a greenhouse, summerhouse, children's playhouse, jacuzzi or outdoor spa, but all these should be carefully sited and selected as design elements to be incorporated into the final garden plan. Sheds are generally allowed under planning legislation, but in the UK,

A multi-activity children's area has a swing, climbing frame and castle all in a large, ship-shaped sand pit. When designing children's play equipment safety is the priority.

they must not exceed fifty percent of the garden space. In conservation areas, planning permission is required if they exceed 10 m^3 (33 ft.^{3}) in volume, flat roof sheds should not exceed 3 m (10 ft.) in height and ridged roofs must be no taller than 4 m (13 ft.). Storage sheds are rarely permitted in front gardens and should be sited at least 20 m (65 ft.) away from the highway.

Completing the garden owner's checklist in Chapter 1 will have helped you to decide if there is a need for any structures that are not already present. Try to group them in a logical way—shed, greenhouse, garage and bin store might well fit together—and allow plenty of working space adjacent to them. Often the rear wall of one building can double for another, saving on space and cost.

Garden shed size will depend on its intended function; sheds are often only used as additional storage areas for mowers and bicycles, but if possible allow for more space than necessary—it will soon be filled. Some sheds can double as workshops or additional office space. Incorporating a damp-proofing membrane into the base will help protect stored materials. If easy access with a path or ramp is important, this should be worked into the plan.

Most sheds are made of timber sold as prefabricated panels that bolt together. Security may be an issue, so if the contents are valuable, take adequate precautions as most household insurance companies will not cover equipment stored in a shed as locks are easily broken or removed. The roof is usually covered with waterproof asphalt sheets or roofing felt, but there are other roofing options. Corrugated Perspex, for instance, will allow light into the shed, which is useful for potting up seedlings and other chores. Garage roofs, outhouses, flat roof extensions, and porches can all be candidates for the "living" roof treatment.

Painting or staining a fairly mundane shed can make it appear to recede into the background (if painted

Clear, corrugated plastic roofing can be worked into the roof structure to let light in.

a dark colour), or stand out as a garden feature (if painted or stained a bright colour). Staining has the advantage over painting as a further coat of wood stain may only be needed every three of four years, while paint needs to be renewed more often.

The recent trend for "green" or "living" roofs has given sheds a new dimension. Covering a roof with low-maintenance plants can transform an ordinary structure into a central focal point that benefits wildlife, increases biodiversity and will keep the shed cooler in summer and warmer in winter, in addition to giving it some sound insulation. It also provides an opportunity for growing a wide range of plants, both native and non-native. When viewed from above, a green roof can disguise the building. In these water-conscious times, any vegetation that covers impermeable surfaces, such as roofs or paths, has the advantage of trapping rainfall, preventing it from being shed and lost to drains.

Making a green roof consists of building up a series of layers that differ mainly in the depth of growing medium and therefore the type of plant life they can support. They can be obtained from and installed by a commercial company, or constructed on a do-it-yourself basis (or a combination of both).

A typical "living" roof consists of:
— Waterproof layer. This should also be "root-proof" and commercial companies usually provide a twenty-five year guarantee against leakage.
— Drainage layer. Placed on top of the waterproof layer, the drainage layer removes excess water from the roof, avoiding waterlogging which many plants will not tolerate. The drainage layer

is usually made of small-scale aggregates or plastic cellular layers.

— Filter mat. A geotextile material placed between the drainage layer and the soil to prevent detritus from clogging the drainage layer.

— Soil or growing medium layer. Usually consisting of an artificial soil that is lightweight, such as clay granules, perlite, vermiculite, recycled crushed bricks or tiles, mixed with a small proportion (ten to twenty percent volume) of organic matter or lightweight compost.

style of roof	average depth of materials	type of vegetation	approximate load in kg/m^2
extensive green roof	5 cm	mainly sedums/mosses	70–80
	5–10 cm	wildflowers and drought-resistant planting	80–150
semi-extensive green roof	10–20 cm	drought-resistant plants and hardy sub shrubs	150–200
	20–50 cm	medium shrubs, perennials and grasses	200 +

All manner of garden buildings could have living roofs, as long as the roof is capable of supporting the extra weight.

free drainage is important

A shallow growing medium allows cultivation of sedums en masse, for a carpet-like effect.

sedum

2 cm of growing medium

geotextile mat or blanket to retain some moisture

drainage

roof structure —could be a strong shed roof

A deeper growing medium can support perennials, grasses and subshrubs.

growing medium for grass or other suitable plants

geotextile mat or blanket

drainage material

insulation

roof structure —suitably strong for supporting the above, especially in very wet weather or heavy snow

— Planting. The living elements of the roof. As the chart above shows, the depth of growing medium (or soil) will determine the type of plants to be grown.

Green roof plantings

Commercial companies often supply sedum species as pre-grown mats to be placed on top of the drainage layer, but there are also other options such as wildflower meadows or alpine plants. It is not difficult to undertake the planting yourself onto a ready-supplied base, using either potted or plug plants, a seed mix or a combination of both. Irrigation should be installed if the living roof is to remain green and healthy during drought. It is important to choose a planting style that suits your climate, as well as the amount of maintenance you are prepared to devote.

The two most important factors when deciding whether to install a green roof are structural loading and waterproofing. It is important to check whether the roof can take the additional weight to be imposed on it, perhaps by using a reliable roofing contractor to oversee the construction work.

Pivots, Focal Points and Garden Art

Arbours, statues or urns and garden seats can be used to subtly turn a corner, acting as a pivot, or as a focal point to be seen through an arch or pergola. Trees or specimen shrubs, even topiary, can also act

Traditional focal points include statuary and furniture.

This garden statue is too small for its surroundings.

A larger statue is much better proportioned.

Too many, poorly coordinated ornaments can make a garden look more like a garden centre.

A simple, thoughtfully placed ornament is often far more effective.

as a pivot. The shape of a tree canopy can echo the shape of a pool or provide a positive shape or mass to complement a void.

The increase in the popularity of art for gardens can result in indiscriminate and unsuitable choices. Many garden centres offer mass-produced items strangely out of context and scale with nature, so seek out an artist's gallery or sculpture park where genuine artwork is displayed or can be built to commission.

Overcrowding can demean some well-chosen items. Careful siting will make or break the connection between landscape and art, and space will need to be allowed for comfortable viewing. Use planting as a backdrop, considering the subsequent seasonal effects in winter as well as summer, when garden art and sculpture are often being viewed from within the house. Use simplicity and restraint—plus occasionally a sense of humour.

DEVELOPING THE DESIGN

The enclosing wall or hedge must act as a backdrop or foil for whatever is to be seen against it. The various boundaries illustrated here suit many different styles of planting.

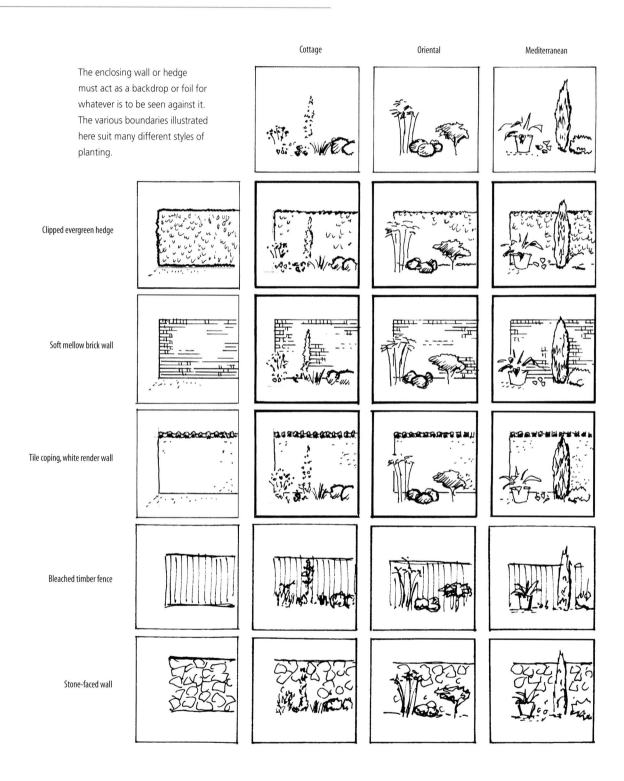

Cottage Oriental Mediterranean

Clipped evergreen hedge

Soft mellow brick wall

Tile coping, white render wall

Bleached timber fence

Stone-faced wall

Boundaries

At this stage in developing the preliminary garden layout plan, the garden boundaries should be considered. In Britain, gardeners tend to enclose their land, to set it physically apart from neighbouring land by constructing or planting a barrier that must be crossed before admission is granted into what is deemed a private area. This custom probably dates from medieval times when protection against a hostile force was necessary, but the habit continues today. In the United States the boundaries are often less defined; sometimes open landscape is marked by a simple and visually unobtrusive fence.

There are many ways to enclose a property, and walls, fences and hedges perform virtually the same function. As the chosen enclosure will often act as a backdrop or foil to the design or planting of the garden, it must be selected to set off whatever is to be seen against it; this is why boundaries need to be considered at this stage.

Boundaries constructed of horizontal wire, or wire mesh, will allow views through them. For best results supporting fence posts should be carefully positioned and obscured where possible.

Gates and Entrances

Access will be required through the enclosure, so a suitable gateway, wide enough for people or for vehicles, will need to be included. Often the most obvious or direct route may not be the best. Offsetting a gate or entrance to gradually reveal, upon approaching, the objective (such as garage or garden shed) is subtle and intriguing, but once again, keep to the grid and do not think about the type or material of the enclosure or entrance at this stage.

When designing the entrances, allow wide enough access for vehicles as well as people.

The Preliminary Garden Layout Plan

The time has come to choose one of the theme plans and to develop your design and commit your ideas to paper. This stage will concentrate on organizing the horizontal plane; the next stage will focus on the vertical and overhead planes.

The garden layout plan is still in an embryo state. In the next chapter, almost inevitably, you will need to adjust your preliminary dimensions to fit all the desired elements and materials into the space.

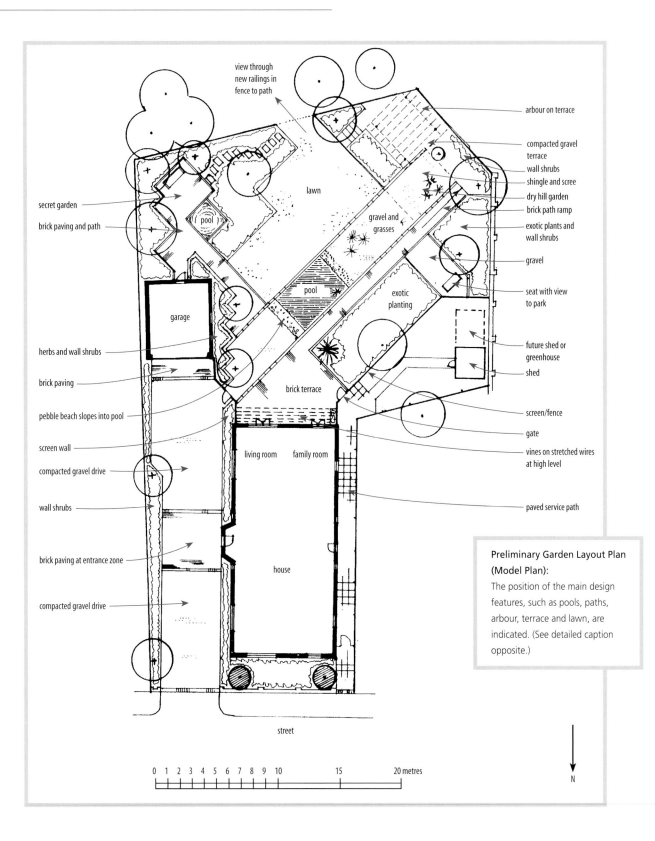

view through
new railings in
fence to path

arbour on terrace

compacted gravel
terrace

wall shrubs

shingle and scree

dry hill garden

brick path ramp

exotic plants and
wall shrubs

gravel

seat with view
to park

future shed or
greenhouse

shed

screen/fence

gate

vines on stretched wires
at high level

paved service path

lawn

gravel and
grasses

pool

exotic
planting

pool

brick terrace

secret garden

brick paving and path

herbs and wall shrubs

brick paving

pebble beach slopes into pool

screen wall

compacted gravel drive

wall shrubs

brick paving at entrance zone

compacted gravel drive

garage

living room   family room

house

street

0 1 2 3 4 5 6 7 8 9 10   15   20 metres

N

Preliminary Garden Layout Plan (Model Plan):

The position of the main design features, such as pools, paths, arbour, terrace and lawn, are indicated. (See detailed caption opposite.)

Preliminary Garden Layout Plan (Model Plan)

With reference to the garden owner's brief and site appraisal, the following developments have been made:

1. More space has been allowed for planting, and the lawn has been reduced in size.
2. A hill garden runs down the slope into a gravel garden, planted with grasses to give movement and a focus to the centre of the garden.
3. An overhead vine-covered wire arbour has been introduced to provide shade, shelter and intimacy on the south-facing terrace.
4. A path has been infiltrated through the "jungle" shrub belt to lead into the secret garden.
5. The area in front of the French windows has doors "in the wings" to left and right. It can be used as an outdoor theatre for children's shows or musical events at parties.
6. Important trees have been located to improve vistas, provide focal points and give enclosure.

Drawing up the Preliminary Garden Layout Plan

1. Choose your preferred theme plan—circular, diagonal or rectilinear. Stick it down onto your drawing board with masking tape.
2. Over this plan, stick down a further sheet of tracing paper.
3. Draw in the outline of your chosen theme plan in pencil, and trace over the house outline and the site boundary. It may also be useful to draw in the grid in pencil as a guide for working it up at a later stage.
4. If necessary, using a sharp pencil, adjust the spaces from your themed plan to ensure that they are correctly sized and located and that the design works when considered in three dimensions. You will be able to see this more easily if you look at your plan at eye level and try to imagine how it will look when built.
5. When you are satisfied that the design could work, state by writing on the plan which areas are designated for hard landscape and which for plantings (for example, label the lawn, paving, path, pool, planting and so on).
6. Set out your sheet carefully and pay attention to the clarity of your graphics and lettering.
7. Now draw in the north point, either freehand or by using your computer (and cutting and pasting it on the plan). The north point should always be located in the bottom right-hand corner. Remember also to note here the scale to which you are drawing.
8. When you are happy with this draft preliminary plan, lay one of your tracing-paper master plan sheets of an appropriate size over the plan and stick it down with masking tape. Ensure that the draft preliminary garden layout plan is positioned centrally within the area devoted to plans and that it does not encroach on the right-hand area that is reserved for notes and title block.
9. Now start to draw up the finished preliminary plan. Trace off (with a sharp pencil or ink drawing pens) all the horizontal lines on plan, using a T-square or parallel motion, and use a sheet of graph

paper as a backing guide. Varying the width of the lines used will make your drawn plan more realistic. Trace the heavier lines first, then the finer lines. If using a pen, decide which pen nib sizes you will use for each feature and write this down. Use the largest nib (0.5 mm or 0.7 mm) for the largest features: house, boundary wall, tree canopy and so on; use a smaller nib (0.35 mm or 0.5 mm) for paths, steps and other less dominant features.

10. Now trace off all the vertical lines on the plan, holding your set square firmly against the T-square or parallel motion.

11. Use a set square held against the T-square or parallel motion, to trace over all the lines that are at an angle, varying the pen nib size as before.

12. Try to make each area—paving, paths, lawn and so on—look as realistic as possible. Your graphics should communicate your ideas clearly.

13. Indicate areas of soft landscape.

14. Indicate positions of proposed trees and large specimen shrubs, as well as any existing trees to be retained.

15. Write, in clear lettering, what each element or area is. Indicate steps, paths, paving, terrace, pool and so on by writing exactly what it is on the plan. Arrows to indicate steps or ramps should always

point upwards. Use the graph paper to guide your lettering.

16. Draw in the title block, remembering to include the north point and the scale to which your plan is drawn. Extend the vertical lines upwards from the outside edges of the title block to become the space for your notes or information panel. (You may wish to use your computer-generated title block here.)

17. Leave your information panel empty at this point.

18. Release the masking tape and hold the drawing up slightly. Check that you have traced off everything necessary from the plan beneath.

19. Undo the masking tape and take the preliminary garden layout drawing, rolled up in a plastic tube or flat in a portfolio case, to a reprographic office to be printed, either as a dyeline print or photocopy. Ask for two copies so that you can colour up the plan at this stage; colouring may help you check on the proportions of hard to soft material—usually one-third hard landscaping to two-thirds plantings, but two-thirds hard landscaping to one-third plantings can work equally well.

20. Keep both the tracing-paper original preliminary garden layout plan and the copies safe to work with in the next steps.

Above: Views of the French countryside surround this garden. Plants within the garden are clipped or "topiarized" to contrast with natural shapes in the distant landscape.

Above: Unusual modern reinforced glass, timber walls and sliding doors relate this house to its woodland setting. A sturdy pierced timber deck bridges the gap over the lower ground level, allowing snow and rainwater to percolate to the ground below.

Left: Carefully chosen paint and door lighting can transform a property, giving the building an air of individuality. An overhead canopy or porch protects visitors from the elements, and the stone flooring is easily swept.

Above: A garden designer's brief does not always begin with the garden. Here a porch has been added to link the house with the garden. It provides a sheltered place to wait until the door is opened.

Right: In this coastal setting, the vertical plane of the brick and flint house is linked to the horizontal ground plane by the use of a columnar evergreen tree. Brick colours and tones are repeated in the semi-exotic planting.

Above: The columnar cypress acts as an exclamation mark, drawing the eye to the low-built house. The matt or light-absorbent foliage of the cypress contrasts with the grey or glossy foliage of adjacent plants.

Above: This house, its entranceway and its path are of the same stone. The permeable paviours are laid crosswise to emphasize the path width, and the mainly evergreen planting repeats the rough building textures.

Above: The pale green paint used for the door frames and windows of this single-storey house acts as a foil for the dark green foliage that softens the angular lines of the building.

Below: Structural planting emphasizes the entrance to this property. The painted blue doorway is sympathetic to the silver and green foliage tones.

Above: The staggered levels of the timber fence and the covered garden seat set within it help to break what might otherwise have been a harsh line. Multi-stemmed silver birch reduce the impact of the house spire and help to connect house and garden.

Above: Two dominant columns of *Cupressus sempervirens* (Italian cypress) unite the vertical façade of the house and the horizontal plane of this formal garden. A built-in seat attracts attention to the mature *Pinus nigra* (Corsican Pine), which is outside the garden boundary.

Above: The herbs in this garden, which was designed by the late Rosemary Verey, are easily accessible from the kitchen. The curved planted beds soften the angular lines of the house.

Above: Planting at the entrance to this country house emphasizes a sense of arrival. The variegated foliage looks cheerful even during the winter and the clipped box and holly are focal points within the planting.

Above: House and entrance-garden are united by a clipped box parterre. The formality of the planting repeats the formal architectural style of the house.

Above: The vertical impact of this house's dominant façade has been reduced by building on a raised covered terrace or sundeck, providing extra space and allowing viewers to study wildlife in the surrounding woodland.

Above: Hedges and topiary have a strong architectural influence on this space. The lighter foliage of the young mop-head *Robinia* will contrast with the darker green foliage beyond.

Above: Hedges are useful, not only as a windbreak, but also to create a series of garden rooms. Here the bright red flowers of the climbing *Nasturtium tropeolum speciosum* contrast well with the texture of the yew hedge and can be easily pulled free at the end of each growing season.

Above: A long gravel path is broken up by creating a calm, shady clearing accentuated by low-growing box and the pruned columnar "clean" or non-dripping lime, *Tilia ×euchlora*. Although free of aphids, the lime flowers have a narcotic effect on bees.

Above: Planting needed to be scaled up in proportion to this large property. Very large box (*Buxus*) balls, topiarized to varying heights and shapes by an annual clip, break up the space between terrace and lawn.

Above: An example of mass and void, where the lawn flows through the space, held in by the intricate curves of the low box hedge. Planting of foxglove spires, with shrub roses and beech held in by metal tripods, give height to the "mass" of this planting.

Above: During the growing season, this cleverly woven hazel fence merges with the deciduous hawthorn hedge behind. The repetitive detail of the angled finish to the uprights adds to the effect.

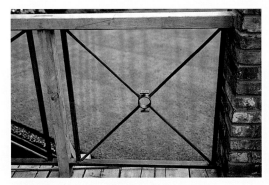

Above: An unusual open combination of copper, wood and brick prevent the danger of falling from this raised walkway. Metal is a material easily worked into intricate patterns.

Above: Recycled birch (*Betula*) logs make an unusual fence. Of slightly differing lengths, the logs are sawn to an angle, seeming to merge with the landscape beyond.

Above: Not strictly a fence, these regular hardwood columns delineate the garden boundary. A similar timber is used for the unusual light fitting.

Above: The robust lines of this bridge parapet are in keeping with the country setting. Detailing includes wooden plugs as opposed to metal screws which could corrode and stain.

Above: A simple post-and-rail fence defines this field while allowing a view of the wildflowers beyond. Only use oak or a timber treated with preservative. Other untreated wood uprights will eventually rot.

USING CIRCLES

Above: The circular grassy landing between the forward and receding stone risers of these steps is fundamental to their design. Treads are generous, and plants are allowed to self-seed in cracks in the risers.

Above: This sunken seating area can double as a fire pit or barbecue. Using a raised metal brazier will protect the decorative tiles. Columnar evergreen conifers emphasize the circular outline.

Above: This raised, wildlife-friendly circular damp or bog garden provides a dramatic change of level. Water spills from the ornate heads into a trough before being pumped and recycled around the perimeter of the planting.

Above: Sustainable and recycled materials create a magical atmosphere in this secluded seating area. The stone and bark chipping flooring is permeable, and green-leaved plants provide contrasting foliage and texture.

Above: A circular theme where bricks delineate the outline of both pool and steps. For ease of mowing, turf has been laid slightly above the level of the pool's brick edge.

Above: A sympathetic planting of *Begonia evansii* and *Helichrysum petiolare* repeat the shades in this terracotta urn.

Above: By placing the larger pot in the foreground, and a much smaller pot behind, the perspective is lengthened.

Above: A colourful planting of the *Tulipa* 'General de Wet' brings out the colour tones of this terracotta urn. Avoid using too many contrasting plants in a pot, especially if the pot is decorative.

Below: These strategically placed display plinths are made of the same monotone material as the paved floor, while white supporting metal uprights echo the silver-barked birch trees.

Above: The mirrored arch helps to break up the length of the wall and brings light into the garden. Flowers and foliage are based on green, yellow, silver and white.

Above: The effect of this border is more dramatic when seen through a dark opening. Shadows and effects of light are often overlooked when considering planting.

Above: In this tiny garden room, the apparent "window" is actually mirrored glass, which brings reflected light into the space. The round, painted, upright posts, planted with the fast-growing golden hop, *Humulus aureus*, support overhead timber shading.

Above: Mirrors may be used to bring light into a garden. Here, a mirror has been fitted into the arch and a gate placed in front of it. The gate helps prevent birds flying into the mirror.

Chapter 3
Finalizing the Garden Layout Plan

Finalizing the Garden Layout Plan

We have looked in some detail at how to develop the elements on the ground plane, or garden "floor", to produce a preliminary garden layout plan. We have also already looked briefly at some of the strategic vertical features. In this chapter we will consider more closely how to give a three-dimensional structure to the garden through the selection of vertical and overhead features. Once the practical and visual roles of each feature have been identified, you will be able to determine the form that these features will take, what they will be made of and how they will be built.

While weighing up the advantages and disadvantages of each design choice, you may want to adapt your preliminary garden layout plan to allow for these new features as you work towards finalizing your garden layout plan. You will also need to be more specific about your choice of materials and the precise design of each area or item as well as considering their impact on the environment. Use locally sourced materials where possible.

After considering materials used for garden surfaces and structures, garden accessories should be taken into account, reviewing the range of items available for use as garden ornaments, furniture, lighting and children's play equipment. Any garden accessories that you choose should blend in with the rest of your design. You will need to indicate their design-style, size, and colour on your garden layout plan.

While this garden layout may also give a general indication of your planting proposals, detailed planting plans are not usually finalized until the final garden layout plan has been accepted. Frequently at this stage the garden designer (or the client) will change his or her mind and decide to alter the original scheme. As any changes would probably have an effect on the proposed borders, the planting plan is usually carried out as a separate drawing (which is covered in the next chapter).

The Role of the Vertical Plane

Vertical features are a crucial element in all gardens. On entering a garden, perhaps from the house or through a garden gate, the eye needs time to focus on the changed scene. It searches momentarily for a strong vertical feature on which to concentrate while adapting to the new location, adjusting rather like an automatic camera. The vertical feature may be a building, a large pot, a sculpture, or even a striking tree. Without something on which to focus, the eye will wander, and the "picture" may be meaningless. This is particularly true of gardens that rely solely on plants, for they rarely provide that strength of outline. Vertical features are vital in holding the different elements of your design together.

The vertical plane is made up of many different materials, varying from hard, architectural elements, such as buildings, walls, fences and pergolas, to tree trunks, hedges and other shrub masses. All these different components can be used to perform specific roles in garden design.

Enclosing Spaces

Vertical features, such as walls, fences or plants, can be used as physical and visual barriers to delineate where one space ends and another begins, whether defining site boundaries or simply separating one internal space from another. The higher the feature, the smaller the enclosed space will feel.

Directing and Screening Views

The height of the vertical plane affects what can be seen from various points in the garden, directing and screening views within the garden and to the surrounding landscape beyond.

Controlling Exposure

The presence of vertical features will affect the exposure (the amount of sun and wind that a garden receives) by modifying extremes of climate. Walls, fences and hedges and other shrub masses can be placed strategically to act as windbreaks or to provide shade.

Directing Circulation

Vertical features, from low walls to planted areas, can be used to determine the route people will take through the space, in the same sort of way that the presence of water can influence movement through a garden.

Unifying the House, Garden and Surroundings

Vertical features can act as an extension of the house, both through continuing the major lines of the force, such as the house walls, and by the repetition of materials. They can also be designed to unite the house with the surrounding landscape—for instance, by echoing the outline of surrounding buildings or hills.

Aesthetic Contribution

Structural features should be built for a purpose, but there is no reason why they should not be objects of beauty in their own right. In selecting vertical elements, choose from the range of textured and coloured materials to complement your design and help to create the desired character of the garden, but always try to maintain a natural effect. Too many textures and colours can look artificial and self-conscious.

Vertical Features

If you are selecting new vertical features, several factors will help guide your choice. You will need to establish the following:

- The height of the feature
- The space available
- The time scale (a yew hedge will require

several years' growing time before it can be an effective barrier, whereas a mixed native species hedge, for instance, will grow more quickly and will provide a better wildlife habitat)
- How the material will integrate with existing features
- Whether it will fit within the budget allocated for the feature
- The sustainability of the feature or material
- Can it be sourced locally?
- Will it benefit wildlife?

Existing House Walls

The walls of the house, or of neighbouring houses adjoining a garden, are often the most dominant vertical features in the site, particularly if there are no trees. If the walls are attractive they can be left exposed, and the same type of material can be used in other parts of the garden (for the vertical pillars of an arbour, for instance), helping to unite house and garden. However, using climbers to clothe the walls can attract many nesting birds and other wildlife.

In some city gardens, particularly small ones, tall house walls can be oppressive. This may be the case where the site is bounded on one or more sides by the walls of neighbouring houses, often consisting of a large expanse of one material, such as brick. One way of "breaking up" or distracting from the expanse is by painting on or adding a "dummy" window or doorway. If you use this trick (or trompe l'oeil) you can enhance the illusion considerably by the careful siting of other garden features, such as a path leading up to the painted doorway. As the wall will probably belong to your neighbour, do ask their permission before beginning any work. To avoid any disputes, all agreements should be put in writing.

Garden Boundaries

Most gardens require some form of vertical boundary to establish the extent of ownership. It may help at

The door and windows are trompe l'oeil features. Slightly larger than life, they reduce the apparent size of the end wall.

Careful planting around a trompe l'oeil can help to add credibility to the illusion.

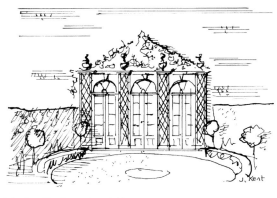

This false "pavilion", on a bare brick wall, is softened by planting.

this point to refer back to your site appraisal. If you have an existing boundary, you will need to integrate it into your proposed design. Look carefully around the perimeter of the garden and consider the following:

- Does the boundary provide privacy where you need it?
- Do you like the materials that have been used, and are they in keeping?
- What parts of the boundary, if any, would you like to expose or conceal, perhaps to frame or to screen particular views?

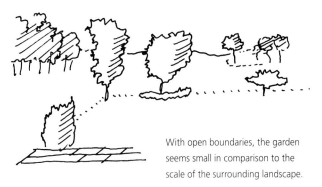

With open boundaries, the garden seems small in comparison to the scale of the surrounding landscape.

Entrances and Gateways

First impressions are important, and the entrance to the garden, or a garden within the garden, should always make a clear statement as to what is to be found within, even if the statement is itself a deception designed to create an unexpected revelation. When low gates are needed to exclude dogs or keep in children, they should make a simple statement of their purpose and be designed to that end. Trying to decorate an obviously utilitarian feature always creates an air of distraction and unnecessary fuss, with results that can often appear quite ludicrous.

The material from which the gates are made is equally important. All too frequently, as soon as an opening is created, the immediate reaction is

Entrances and gateways should be designed to
communicate the intended message.

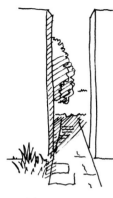

mysterious

domestic, yet mysterious

welcoming

The elaborate ironwork
of the gate cannot be
seen properly against
the background of
the garden—a plain,
understated backdrop is
needed.

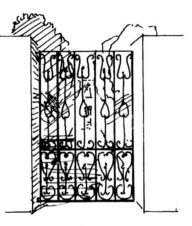

A simple pattern of
vertical bars allows the
house and garden to be
viewed through the gate
without the risk of visual
confusion.

to fill it with a wrought-iron gate, but often this
is not the best solution. Elaborate wrought or cast
iron can only be seen to advantage against a plain
background such as sky, grass or water. Anything
more complex, such as plantings, or even trees and
shadows, immediately sets up confusion between the
two images so that neither can be seen properly. In
such a situation a simple pattern of vertical bars is
the only solution, since it gives an air of proportion
and stability to the background detail.

Often, a better solution is to use well-made wooden
gates, either constructed of plain uprights set more
closely at the bottom than the top (to add visual
weight and exclude rabbits or other pests) or entirely
solid. Unusual gates can be made from recycled
materials, giving character to a garden. Avoid being
too whimsical—there is much to be said for a solid
door that reveals nothing until it is opened, since the
pleasures of the imagination are often greater than
those of reality.

Garden Walls

Walls are the most permanent enclosures used
for gardens, and because of their expense, the
workmanship involved and the protection they
afford, they are often the most treasured. Apart from

To create an element of surprise, use a solid door which reveals nothing until it is opened.

providing a surface for plants to grow up against, they may also provide warmth and shelter for more tender specimens.

Walls are often constructed of brick, although stone or even concrete block walls may be appropriate in certain settings.

Walls may also be used as garden dividers and may be freestanding or retaining. It is most important when deciding on garden walls to match, or in some way echo, the colour, texture and style of any existing walls.

The coping (the top course of masonry on a wall) is made up of either the same material as the rest of the wall or a special coping material. A carefully detailed coping course can make an impressive difference to the finish of a wall.

Garden walls can be divided into two types: freestanding and retaining. Freestanding walls can be used both as boundaries and as internal partitions. They can reduce the effects of noise or wind and can screen views. Retaining walls are used to retain or hold back soil, either where there is a change in level or where raised beds are required. The height of a wall will influence the amount of enclosure provided. Consider the following as a general guide:

The height of a wall determines the amount of enclosure it provides.

High freestanding walls—complete enclosure

Medium height freestanding walls—partial enclosure

Low freestanding walls—minimum/implied enclosure

Retaining walls—used to hold back soil as well as enclose

- Walls higher than eye level, used to form a complete visual and physical barrier, such as boundary walls, should be built to a height of 1.8 m (6 ft.).
- Walls to partially enclose an area, such as a "garden room" or space within the garden, should be 1.2 m (4 ft.) high.
- Low walls acting as a barrier between one space and another, sometimes doubling as extra seating areas or as a base for railings, should be 0.5 m (1.6 ft.) high.
- Retaining walls, used to create changes in level and to hold back soil, may vary in height. A structural engineer should advise on the construction of walls over 0.6 m (2 ft.) in height.

To support the weight of the wall, both freestanding and retaining walls need to be constructed solidly on strong foundations. Retaining walls have an added sideways pressure exerted by the retained soil. The necessity for strong construction is one reason why walls tend to be expensive.

To suit the rest of the garden, walls may be designed in a number of ways—straight or curved, stepped or slanted, rough or smooth, solid or open. A buttressed wall will generate an interesting ground pattern and introduce a sense of rhythm. A smooth-faced boundary used on both sides emphasizes the length and minimizes the width of an enclosure, while one with a rough surface, perhaps allied to slight recesses and projections, will have the reverse effect. A wall of open-work construction, such as a pierced brick screen, allows views to other parts of the garden or its surroundings, whereas a solid wall provides a complete visual barrier.

As well as being used to enclose spaces, walls may be used to support climbers and wall plants or to protect plants from exposure, particularly from wind and sea spray. Brick walls, which retain heat, are often used in temperate climates to protect tender plants and nesting birds.

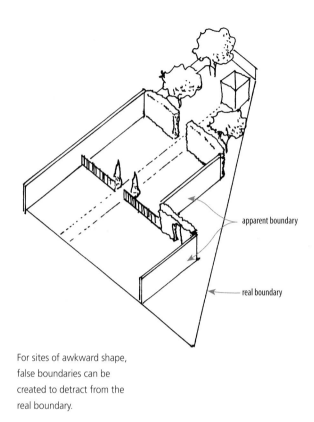

apparent boundary

real boundary

For sites of awkward shape, false boundaries can be created to detract from the real boundary.

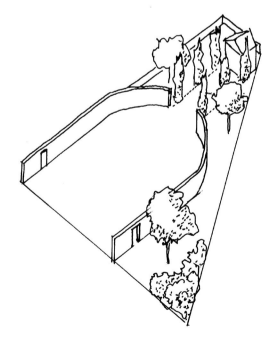

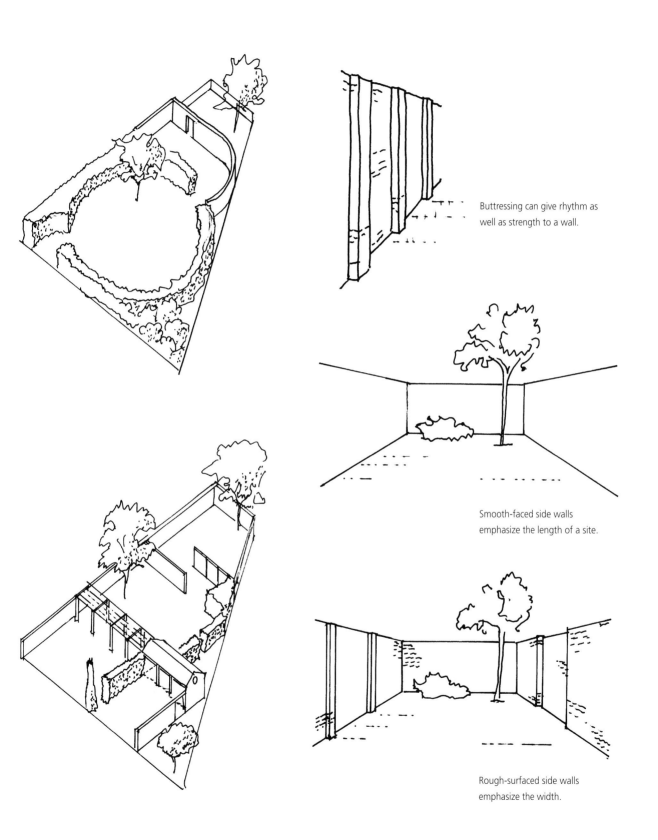

Buttressing can give rhythm as
well as strength to a wall.

Smooth-faced side walls
emphasize the length of a site.

Rough-surfaced side walls
emphasize the width.

Materials

Your choice of materials for important vertical features will have a significant impact on the character of the garden. You may wish to refer to the glossary, which defines many of the materials available.

Walling

Walls can be constructed of many materials, usually stone, brick, concrete or timber. These materials may be used in a variety of designs to complement the design of the garden or, particularly in the case of boundary walls, to blend in with regional styles. When building new walls always try to match their colour and texture to existing structures using, where possible, the best quality of material for the purpose. It is much better, for instance, to have a well-made close-board fence, perhaps mounted on a low brick plinth, than to build an insubstantial wall on inadequate foundations that will blow over in the first gale.

Brick

Brick is a very versatile small-scale material for use in garden design. There are many different types of brick available, but if the whole or part of the house or property is built in a particular type of brick, it is usually best to continue with the same type if it is available. This often necessitates seeking out good-quality, clean, secondhand bricks. If the house is not built of brick, introducing a brick pattern within the rest of the material can break up a monotonous space.

Brick walls can vary in thickness and in the pattern in which they are arranged (referred to as the "bond"). Some regions have traditional bond designs, which are often determined by local conditions.

The colour, texture and strength of the brick itself must also be considered. Facing bricks are often used to finish a wall, the interior being made of less expensive breeze blocks. Engineering bricks, which are darker in colour (from being fired for longer), give greater strength, as they do not absorb as much water. Bricks can have a smooth finish or can be wire cut, with a dragged finish. A coping of weather-resistant bricks, such as engineering bricks, should be used to finish the top of a wall to prevent water from penetrating the walling below.

Brick walls can be finished with a course of bricks on edge, and tiles can be used to create a "lip" or overhang that will help rainwater to drain off without damaging the wall. Compared with stone walls, which can be built to follow the curves of a landscape, brick and concrete block walls are more rigid, although they can be stepped for changes of level.

Stone

Stone will vary according to your region, and your local stone will probably be the most appropriate. If it is limestone or sandstone and can easily be quarried, the stones may be similar enough in size so as to be coursed (with the stones fitting easily together in layers). Other stones, from fields or seashores, will vary in size and can be used in a random fashion. (Since it is illegal to collect stones from some beaches, it is better to buy them from commercial sources.) Traditionally, stone walls were built dry, without mortar to hold them together. If you have a local builder who is skilled in dry-stone walling, this can be very effective, but, as many walls are now constructed from reconstituted stone, mortar jointing is more common. Random stone walls look most authentic when finished with a top course of stones on edge, or stones roughly shaped to an angle (or batter).

Concrete blocks

Concrete block walls, although less beautiful than natural stone or brick walls, are also worth considering because they are considerably cheaper. They may be rendered and brushed, or imprinted in a variety of ways to imitate brick or stone. Alternatively they can be clothed in evergreen climbers. Concrete blocks are usually used to build retaining walls, which can then be faced in natural stone or brick, or rendered.

Steps

Steps that mark changes of level in a garden should be designed with great care so as to be attractive, comfortable and sympathetic in scale and material to the part of the garden in which they are to be sited. Variations in step design are endless, varying from simple straight flights of steps to elegant curving staircases, complete with landings for viewing and highly ornamental balustrades.

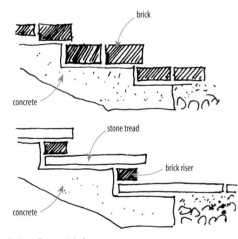

Your choice of materials for steps should be in keeping with the site and meet practical requirements.

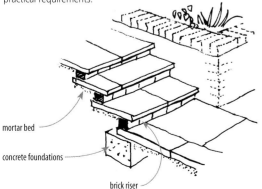

The choice of material to construct steps is diverse. Risers need to be constructed of some solid material, such as stone, brick, concrete or timber, but treads may consist of a loose material, such as gravel or wood chippings. Any loose material will gradually tend to sink and will need topping up every few years. Where growing conditions are right and the stairs will not be subject to heavy wear, grass treads may also be suitable.

Steps may run at right angles or parallel to a change in level. They can change direction as they progress, as in a curving flight of steps, or can change direction partway up the slope, using an intermediate landing. Steps may be recessed, either fully or partially, into a higher level, or project out onto a lower level as a freestanding structure. In the latter case they may need a handrail to provide a safety barrier in the absence of side walls. When designing steps, consider these points:

— To help you get the proportions of steps right, use the following reliable formula: twice the riser height plus the tread depth should equal 680 mm (2.2 ft.).
— Risers should always be the same height, except in very informal situations, such as when using rocks or tree trunks as steps.
— Avoid exceeding fourteen steps in any one flight without the break of a landing.
— A slight projection of the riser material, such as brick or stone, will enhance the visual effect.

Ramps

Usually made out of the same material as steps, ramps are often necessary in a garden, both for easy circulation for the less able and also for ease of movement with a wheelbarrow or mower. If space allows, a ramp can be included within the step area. Crucial in the design of any ramp is the angle of the slope-this should be as gentle as space allows and, for safety, no more than a one-in-twenty slope. For details, see Chapter 2.

Fences

Fences are generally less costly to build than walls, at least in the short term. They create a more instant enclosure than hedges, and for this reason they are often used to provide temporary as well as permanent enclosures. In the long term they can be more expensive; even if treated with preservative, the base of timber fence uprights are liable to rot and need replacing after eight to ten years.

Fences can be designed in a number of ways to suit the location and purpose. They can be designed and built as solid structures, or they can be built more loosely to allow views, light and wind through and to provide a surface for climbing plants to ramble through or over. Whether fences are used for boundaries or for internal divisions, their design should be in keeping with the locality, whether urban or rural. You should take into account both practical and aesthetic considerations:

– What is its function?
– How long will it last?
– How much will it cost?
– What maintenance will it require?
– Is it well proportioned?
– Is it simple and unfussy?
– Does it reflect the local character?
– Is the material sustainable and can it be sourced locally?

There are many kinds of fence, but do avoid larchlap, the most frequently used (probably because it is the cheapest), which is made from thin interwoven slats of wood, generally supported by inadequate posts that are 100 mm (4 in.) square. What is cheap to begin with becomes expensive when it has had to be replaced on several occasions, and it is therefore better to pay more at the outset for something reasonably permanent. A close-board fence of overlapping vertical planks with three, rather than two, arris rails and concrete supports firmly set in the

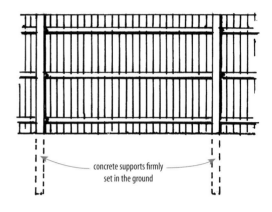

A well-constructed closeboard fence of pressure-treated timber is far superior to fencing consisting of flimsy panels of interwoven slats.

concrete supports firmly set in the ground

ground is a good choice, since only the lowest board, in contact with the soil, will need replacement.

It is quite possible, however, to invent fences of your own that can be made to order by a local carpenter. Many kinds of arrangements, where slats or boards are used alternately on both sides of the supporting cross members, can be useful since light and air can pass through to a greater or lesser degree, depending on the spacing. These are particularly appropriate in exposed situations, as they do not present such a solid barrier to the pressure of the wind. If a neighbour has installed a larchlap fence, staining

Examples of alternating fencing which could be custom-made to order.

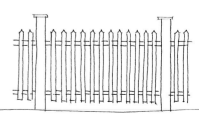

or painting the offending item matt black where it projects into your garden can make it seem to disappear.

Sometimes a chain-link or galvanized mesh fence, hidden by plantings, may be all that is required, but in this case careful thought must be given to its colour. The "green" generally sold for gardens is an impossible colour, far too artificial to be seen in any natural surroundings. Olive, brown or black are better alternatives, being easily camouflaged against the shadow patterns of trees and shrubs. Ivy or other climbers can be grown through the chain link fence, eventually creating a "fedge" that is impenetrable, wildlife-friendly and aesthetically pleasing.

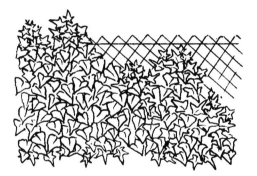

Ivy, especially large-leaved cultivars, can very effectively turn a chain-link fence into a dense, evergreen and narrow "fedge".

Timber fencing

Timber can be used both for urban and rural fencing. It is constructed in a huge range of styles and materials, from rustic wattle hurdle and chestnut paling, to elaborately crafted structures with white pickets and finials. In an urban situation, timber looks good stained or painted to blend in with existing features, while in a country setting, fencing should provide a link with natural surroundings. The positioning of the uprights will depend on what is to be kept in or out, but an imaginatively designed fence can be a great asset in a garden. All woodwork

must be pressure-treated before use. Bamboo fencing can provide an ideal screen for oriental-style gardens, and many recycled materials can also be used effectively.

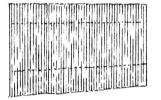

bamboo

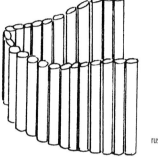

rustic poles

Natural materials like bamboo or rustic poles can be used to creates screens of varying heights and densities.

Metal fencing

Metal fencing is often effective in urban situations, particularly where ironwork has been used locally for railings, street furniture, lighting and so on. Antique wrought-iron railings are sometimes obtainable from an architectural salvage yard, or steel reproductions of old styles can be used. Good-quality ironwork fencing tends to be considerably more expensive than timber fencing, but it is generally more durable. It does, however, require regular painting with bituminous paint to guard against rust.

Log-filled gabions have recently become a popular method of creating a high but impenetrable wall. They carry the advantage of doubling as a home for insects.

Trelliswork

Trellis is a type of fencing consisting of a network of crisscrossing wooden slats, or occasionally steel slats, usually attached to a frame. It is manufactured in units of varying sizes and styles but can also be tailor-made to fit the exact dimensions of a site and complement the rest of the design. When choosing trellis for your garden you should first establish the desired degree of visibility through the trellis panels, particularly the size of the aperture between the slats.

Trellis can be used as a decorative feature in its own right (also known as treillage) or simply to provide an inexpensive support for climbing plants. It can therefore be very useful for screening purposes, whether between different parts of the garden or to extend the height of an existing boundary wall. If you intend to cover a trellis in plants, you will need to select panels of strong construction and provide robust supports, such as thick posts concreted into the ground. For extra durability and to prevent the timber from rotting, posts can be inserted into a

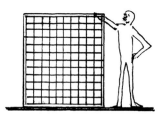
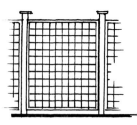

Trellis is usually supplied in panels. To install it, it should be raised slightly off the ground and screwed to supporting posts concreted into the ground.

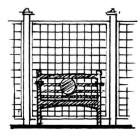

When designing any fencing or trellis work, it is important to consider where the supporting posts should be sited. Try to position posts either side of a foreground feature, such as a bench—rather than having one post bisecting it.

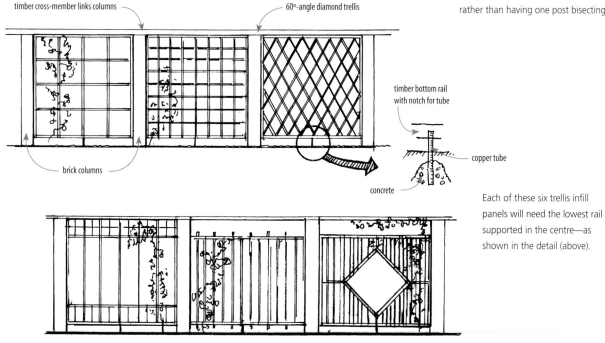

timber cross-member links columns

60°-angle diamond trellis

timber bottom rail with notch for tube

copper tube

brick columns

concrete

Each of these six trellis infill panels will need the lowest rail supported in the centre—as shown in the detail (above).

As an alternative to trellis panels, simple screens can be constructed out of timber or ironwork. In this contemporary garden the screen acts as a division between two areas, but allows light through to the rear of the garden.

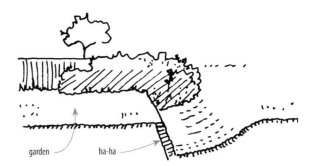

Section through a ha-ha showing the sunken wall and ditch.

The ha-ha prevents livestock from entering the garden.

View from the garden over the invisible, sunken ha-ha.

copper tube that is then bedded into concrete. Ensure that the timber has been treated with preservative. The trellis can also be stained or painted, but this requires more upkeep—and remember that any plants may hamper future maintenance.

Ha-Has

In a large garden, if you want to create a hidden or unobtrusive division, you could consider using a ha-ha, a ditch-type feature that was popular with many garden designers in England in the eighteenth and nineteenth centuries. Originally used as a device to divide the garden from surrounding parkland to prevent the intrusion of deer or farm stock, a ha-ha is a boundary in which a wall—or sometimes a fence—is sunk in a ditch and is therefore invisible from the garden, while still excluding intruders.

Increased production of iron rails and wire netting led to a decline in the popularity of the ha-ha, but the principle can be adapted for use in modern gardens. Although expensive to construct, a ha-ha need not be very long, the ends of the ditch being concealed and the view framed up by hedges or plantings. If you choose this solution, it is important to create a foreground of plain grass, paving or gravel, since any form of ornament will only detract attention from the view.

Structural Planting: Barriers and Enclosures

The more decorative aspects of planting design will be dealt with in Chapter 4, but at this stage you will need to consider the structural role that plants have to play in the design of your garden, defining spaces and directing views in a similar way to walls and fences. The scope for different kinds of "living" boundaries is enormous, varying from strategically placed trees that imply, rather than dictate, a division of space, to dense, impenetrable hedges. Until it is established, it may be necessary to use wire or other netting to protect a young and newly planted hedge from marauding rabbits or deer, which are attracted

Having considered the practical elements, ask yourself what style of planting would complement the house. If the house is tall and imposing, the plants should also be substantial. If it is long and low, a tall fastigiated (conical or tapering) tree could look out of place.

Year-Round Enclosure

Often a green wall, an extension of the building into the garden, is desired. For this, it is necessary to choose a plant with a neat, close habit of growth which will not only accept being clipped into an architectural shape but will also retain that shape

The height of your proposed border planting may greatly influence the degree to which spaces are enclosed.

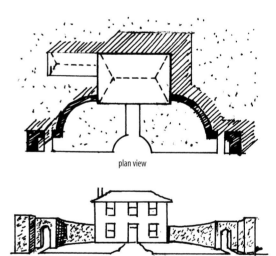

plan view

to any young foliage, even that of poisonous plants such as holly or yew.

Begin to think about the structural planting in terms of its purpose in the design. Ask yourself the following questions:

– What degree of enclosure is needed?
– How high should it be?
– For what portion of the year is the planting needed?
– How much space is available for establishing the structural planting?
– How can it benefit wildlife and bolster the garden's ecosystem?
– What maintenance will be required?

The hedge acts as "wings" and helps link the house to the surrounding landscape.

The hedge is used as a green wall to screen the utility area from the garden.

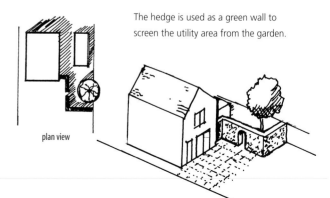

plan view

for a full twelve months (since constant clipping is a time-wasting activity). Some shrubs clip neatly and make a good dense hedge but need frequent cutting to keep them in order, while others, such as box and yew, need only a yearly cut.

Where space allows, you may want to consider hedges that can be left to grow naturally without clipping. They can provide a native habitat for wildlife.

Pleached Trees

Where a tall narrow screen is needed and a hedge would take too long to grow, pleached trees (the branches of which entwine or interlace) are often the answer. In effect, these provide a hedge on stilts. The trees must be pruned every year to keep them

neat, and it is best to use types with an even habit of growth, reasonably flexible wood and no thorns.

If you are growing them next to a fence 2 m (6.6 ft.) in height, you should use trees with clear 1.75 m (5.7 ft.) stems, above which the lateral branches will spread out in even, entwining rows until the desired height is reached.

Tree Screens

If you require a tall screen and you have the space, you can plant a tree screen. Many are far too large in scale and too greedy to be suitable in most gardens, but some fastigiate (or conical) trees, planted perhaps

A screen of deciduous trees can provide an effective barrier in the summer without shading out the garden in the winter.

summer

winter

stretched wires

angle-iron uprights

Before planting the trees, a framework must be constructed. Angle iron uprights, drilled to take heavy gauge wires, are concreted into the ground at intervals of 2–2.5 m. The wires are then threaded through the holes in the uprights and stretched taut by strainers at the end of the wires.

Fastigiate trees are most suitable for tree screens—they can be planted close together and trimmed to shape.

1.5 m (5 ft.) apart and lightly trimmed front and back, will make a tall screen with a lot less effort than pleaching. Like hedges, trees for pleaching or screening must be planted in very well-prepared ground and be fed and watered regularly.

Backgrounds to Decorative Planting

If the hedge or screen is to provide a background to decorative planting, such as a flower border, it must be light absorbent and recessive in character in order to give a foil to the shapes and colours placed in front of it. Yew is ideal for the purpose since it is dark in colour and has a close matt texture when clipped.

Hedges can be used as a backdrop for decorative planting. A well-chosen hedge will provide a neutral foil to accentuate the colour and shape of the plants.

Decorative Divisions

When the hedge is simply making a division of space or concealing some element, such as a vegetable garden, it can be decorative in its own right, perhaps with coloured foliage, flowers or fruit, and of varying degrees of formality. Tapestry hedges, made up of a mixture of different species such as holly, field maple, privet and beech, can be interesting, but as the different species vary in growth rate, clipping can be a problem.

Hedge Cutting

Most hedges will need regular clipping during the growing season, the number of times being dependent on their speed of growth. Privet

(*Ligustrum*) grows quickly and will need clipping every six weeks or so during the growing season, whereas yew (*Taxus*), box (*Buxus*) and native hedges grow more slowly, only requiring clipping two or three times per year. A tapestry hedge will need to be clipped often to contend with the fastest-growing of the species.

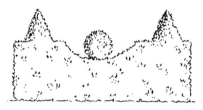

Shaped or topiary hedges lend structure to the garden.

Some plants can be used as a "natural" hedge without the need for regular clipping.

Rosa 'Fru Dagmar Hastrup' provides autumnal hips as well as flowers

Rosmarinus 'Miss Jessopp's Upright' is useful in the kitchen

A tapestry hedge is made up of several types of plants.

Hand-held electric, battery- or petrol-driven hedge trimmers are widely used and give high-quality results; they are much easier and faster to use than traditional hand shears. Check that their weight will suit the user. (Be sure to allow space for a narrow path at the back of the hedge to accommodate ladders and other clipping tools.)

Hand-held rechargeable electric hedge trimmers are useful for lower-growing hedges such as box.

The Role of the Overhead Plane

The overhead plane is created by elements such as pergolas, arbours, tree canopies and umbrellas or awnings. Its main role in the garden is to influence the amount of light entering a space, but it also affects the apparent scale, helps link the garden to the house and gives privacy.

Controlling Light

If your garden is rather gloomy, receiving very little sunlight during the day, you will want to limit any overhead elements as much as possible and place vertical features with great care to avoid shading out what little sunshine the garden receives. If, on the other hand, you have a garden that receives a lot of sunshine, you will need to think carefully where to place the overhead plane so that those using the garden will have some relief from the heat and brightness of the sun at appropriate times of day and year.

Apart from their practical role, overhead features can add greatly to the aesthetics of a garden by creating

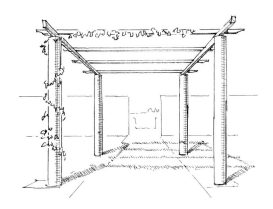

Dramatic shadow lines are created by pergola cross-beams.

interesting shadow patterns on the ground, from the dramatic lines cast by pergola crossbeams to the moving, dappled shade of sparsely foliaged trees.

Controlling Scale and Atmosphere

The presence of overhead features greatly influences how we perceive the size or scale of the garden and is thus largely responsible for its atmosphere. The highest overhead plane is, of course, the sky, which is constantly changing. Even the presence of low cloud or mist lowers it and thereby affects the scale and atmosphere of a place.

Overhead features can give a garden atmosphere. This "awning" has been inexpensively created by training a vine through high wires.

If you want to create an intimate atmosphere—in the entertaining area of a garden, for instance—you could lower the overhead plane, perhaps with an arbour or a large umbrella. Conversely, if a tall tree creates an oppressive feeling, you can open up the canopy by removing some of the overhanging branches or thinning them out. To avoid "bleeding" it is best to do this work in winter when the sap is not rising, but to ensure you achieve the desired finished effect, any branches to be removed should be marked with coloured string or paint before the leaves drop.

Architectural Extension of the House

The overhead plane can be used to link the garden to the house by repeating materials and continuing the line of an indoor ceiling, perhaps in the height of an awning, to provide continuity between the indoor and outdoor space.

The urn at the end of the pergola acts as a focal point to entice one through.

For a contemporary house or one of very plain design, uprights of simple steel tubing set in concrete blocks below ground level can be effective, while Victorian and Regency gardens lend themselves to tunnels of wrought-iron hoops to support climbing roses or clematis. It must be remembered, however, that metal structures have to be repainted at intervals, which can be a problem if they are covered with climbers. In hot countries, metal structures may retain heat and burn the plants that are growing on them.

The line of the indoor ceiling is repeated in this slatted awning, which gives dappled shade on the terrace area.

A pergola constructed of freestanding metal arches may be made away from the site and simply installed in foundation blocks.

Overhead Features

Pergolas

A pergola is a covered walkway designed to provide shade over a frequently used path during the summer months. It must, by definition, lead from one point to another—from a terrace to a tennis court or summerhouse, for instance. When used correctly it should help to integrate the overall space. The view seen through it should entice one to make the journey, and a focal point such as a tree, statue or urn will help to draw the eye and encourage its use.

Proportions are important. Ideally the structure should be wider than it is high, or at the very least should form a perfect square—one that is much higher than it is wide always looks uncomfortable, especially when supporting plant growth on top. Pergolas can be constructed in tunnel form, where the arches are set not more than 1 m (3.3 ft.) apart, but usually the spacing of uprights along the length of the pergola is one-quarter more than the spacing across the walk, which is conducive to easy strolling. If the uprights are particularly large, say 500 mm (1.6 ft.) square, the spacing can be wider, but it must not exceed a reasonable distance for the lengthwise crossbeams. Normally the beams across the path are heavier, making the walk effectively a series of arches, and are linked lengthwise by lighter woodwork over which the plants can scramble. If the pergola or walkway is extensive, it may help to "break" it

occasionally by leaving a gap, allowing the user temporary relief from the tunnel-like effect. Climbers may be used to great effect, but should be chosen carefully so that they do not encroach on the space, attacking people walking through. If climbers tend to hang down from above, wire or sheep netting can be fixed on top of the crossbeams to carry the plants across horizontally. After a few weeks the wire will have weathered and will no longer be noticeable.

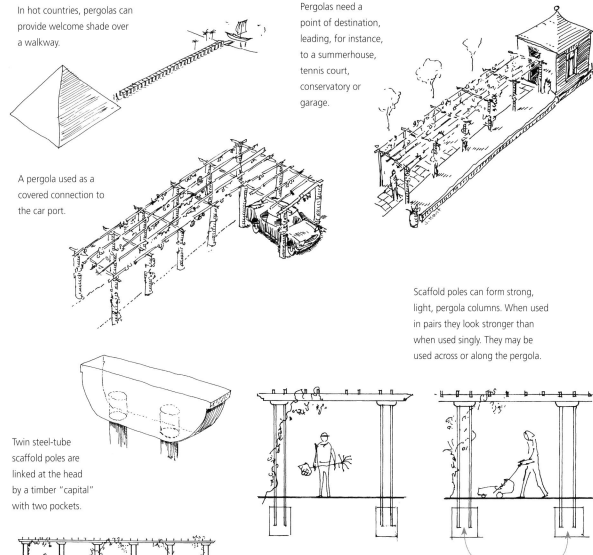

In hot countries, pergolas can provide welcome shade over a walkway.

Pergolas need a point of destination, leading, for instance, to a summerhouse, tennis court, conservatory or garage.

A pergola used as a covered connection to the car port.

Scaffold poles can form strong, light, pergola columns. When used in pairs they look stronger than when used singly. They may be used across or along the pergola.

Twin steel-tube scaffold poles are linked at the head by a timber "capital" with two pockets.

concrete foundations

A hooped or arched pergola, with tension wires, is suitable for training espaliered fruit trees. Space the arches about 1 m apart.

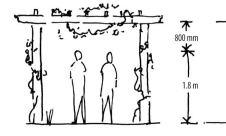

A clear 800 mm below the beams allows for trailing and hanging climbers to grow without interfering with people walking underneath.

When designing a pergola always ensure adequate width and height.

Try to avoid these typical defects in pergola construction.

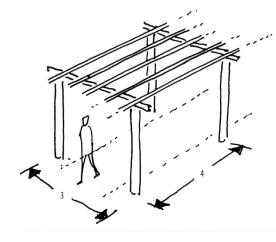

Pergola with robust columns of stone, brick or timber. The spacing of uprights along the length of the pergola is normally one-third more than the spacing across it.

Arbours

An arbour provides shade to a static area, such as a terrace, where one can sit and enjoy some relief from direct sunshine. It should not be confused with a pergola. Again, as it has a strong structural element, the materials used should relate to adjoining buildings and the general style of the garden. For the same reason, the construction must not appear flimsy. The weight and sideways pressure exerted on it by mature climbers can also be considerable.

Arbours may be constructed in a similar way to pergolas, perhaps with back and sides infilled with trellis, or vertical slats, possibly arranged in alternately slatted fashion to give greater protection while still allowing light and air to enter. The roof crossbeams may also be closer together, since shade for sitting needs to be denser than that over a walkway.

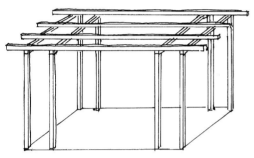

The basic framework for an arbour can be quite straightforward. However, with additional trelliswork and infill panels, it may be modified to suit the owners' needs and their surroundings.

This timber arbour makes use of an existing old wall for some of its support.

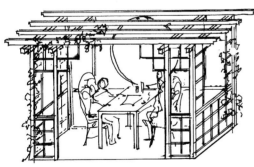

This arbour is created by wires stretched between two buildings. Tensioning turnbuckle wire strainers hold the cable taut. They are available from yacht chandlers and specialist suppliers. The wire can span long distances and support vines.

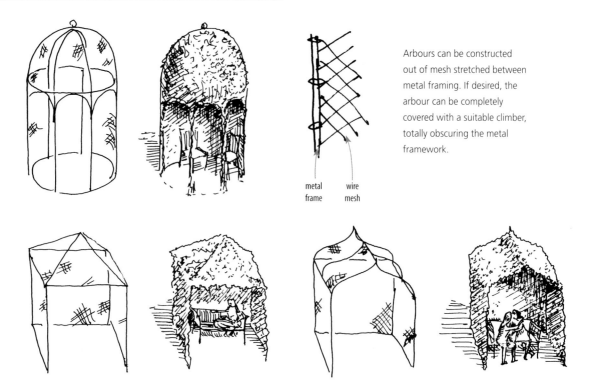

Arbours can be constructed out of mesh stretched between metal framing. If desired, the arbour can be completely covered with a suitable climber, totally obscuring the metal framework.

metal frame   wire mesh

Garden Buildings

A more solid garden building may be required for use on cold bright days and for protection from wind. There are many types available commercially, but before making any decisions, examine the garden itself. Are there any unused outbuildings which, with alteration (such as glazed doors or new and larger windows) might be adapted to suit your purpose? Such a solution may well be cheaper and more satisfactory than building or buying something new.

Look into any building proposals carefully, and try to discover any hidden problems, either of construction or maintenance, since the superficially attractive may prove to be badly made, poorly proportioned or impractical to use. As with all other elements that make up a total design, the appearance must suit the style of the garden and its surroundings.

Disused outbuildings may be able to be adapted as garden rooms.

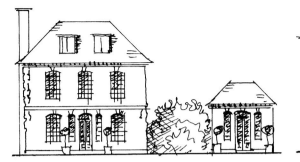

New garden buildings are more successful when they look as though they were built at the same time as the main house.

It may be wiser to adapt an outbuilding than to dispose of it altogether.

Choose the styling of your garden buildings with care. This Chinese-style kiosk looks most odd in this European country garden.

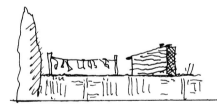

An unwanted garage …

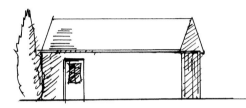

… exposed a neighbouring eyesore when removed.

Trees

The siting of trees in a design is as important as any other element. Trees capture space and, by doing so, shelter a garden and provide it with a sense of security. They should be chosen and positioned with great care.

Before deciding on a particular species you should think carefully about the effects you want to create with different forms, foliage, colours and so on. Consider how a rounded or domed tree, such as a hawthorn (*Crataegus prunifolia*) or maidenhair tree (*Ginkgo biloba*), might look in the space, then try a tall slim vertical shape, such as a columnar Irish yew (*Taxus baccata* 'Fastigiata'). Each of these will create a different effect, and the outline shape, seen perhaps when leafless in winter, should always be the first consideration. Avoid reaching for your

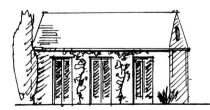

However, it could have been kept and easily adapted for another use.

fastigiate   columnar   rounded   spreading

weeping   picturesque   pyramidal   umbrella-shaped

The outline shape of a tree is the first thing you should consider when making your selection. Do not forget to anticipate how the ultimate size of a tree will affect the space that it occupies.

catalogue until this has been decided, or you will be overwhelmed by choice.

The character of a tree varies enormously, depending on whether it is evergreen or deciduous. The colour, size and texture of leaves, trunk and bark; the ultimate height, breadth and growth rate; the density of the canopy and how well the light penetrates through—all of this needs to be taken into account.

Garden Accessories

Once the surfacing and structural elements of a garden have been established, there are many supplementary items, used to furnish the garden and enhance its layout, which need to be finalized. These may be vitally important for making a particular design statement or allowing an area to function in a certain way, or they may simply provide the finishing touches to a design.

Ornaments

If you leave the choosing of ornaments to the end of a project, you may find that there is little left in the budget to do justice to these elements. This is a mistake, because ornaments, if used, should be an integral part of the total scheme; they should be carefully chosen at the same time decisions are made about the hard landscaping so that they complement other features.

What you choose need not be new, elaborate or expensive. Indeed, ornaments and objets d'art that may have been collected over the years will give a garden individual character—similar, perhaps, to the house interior. A simple approach is often best. It is not what you use but how you use it that is important. There may even be old statues or urns already in the garden, which could be restored to create an important focal or talking point.

Large objects, particularly when placed high in relation to normal eye level, give a feeling of drama and aspiration very suited to an extrovert garden, while those that are small or placed below eye level are more appropriate to creating a feeling of introversion in a scheme.

Simply because a garden is small, it does not follow that everything in it must be small; carried to an extreme, this could suggest a garden for dolls rather than humans! A bold feature, well chosen and placed, can give an air of grandeur to even the most modest space, providing that its general character is suitable to the position.

Architectural Salvage

Searching for a particular object can be fun, and over the past few years a number of specialist salvage companies have sprung up, carrying out a thriving trade in old chimney pots, doors, pedestals and so on, recycling the unwanted objects of others. Local auctions, house sales or junk shops can be worth investigating. Garage sales, car boot sales and flea markets often provide interesting items at reasonable prices.

Chimney pots, with their bold shapes and slender outlines, can look very good either alone or in groups, as can large drainpipes set at varying levels, particularly in a modern garden. Old sinks, complemented with rocks or stones, are now much sought after as planters for a selection of alpine plants.

Old sections of sculptured ornaments from demolished buildings, broken columns and lengths of cornice may find a place in the more romantic garden, perhaps set low among the natural sculpture of dramatic foliage.

Reproduction Ornaments

Often easier to obtain are the many reproductions—some excellent, others much less so—of antique ornaments that are widely available. Provided they are cast from fine original pieces, as many of them are, both lead and reconstituted stone items are very satisfactory and, when weathered, almost indistinguishable from the originals. They are, indeed, better in some respects since they have not had to endure a century or two of exposure to the climate, and if they should be stolen they are easily and relatively cheaply replaced.

The new appearance of reconstituted stone items can be tempered by brushing them over with yoghurt (which encourages moss) mixed with soot if a darker colour is desired. Manure water will have much the same effect but is less than pleasant to apply.

Reproductions that are cast or moulded in plastic are often finished with crude detailing and so are best avoided.

Natural Objects

Natural objects such as interesting bits of driftwood and sections of tree trunk can look effective if placed in an appropriately wild or naturalistic setting. Ideally, every garden should contain a small pile of rotting-down wood as a home for all manner of creatures, helping the natural ecological balance to combat pests and disease. "Wild" stones and boulders can be bought from garden centres, which is a better option than removing them from environmentally sensitive areas.

Rocks and boulders can look effective in a naturalistic setting.

An untidy pile of logs provides hiding places for many garden creatures.

A–Z of Ornamental Ideas

In addition to the more usual types of garden ornament already mentioned, many other items can add a personal touch to your garden. For easy reference, these are listed here in alphabetic order.

Balls and finials are basically ornaments for gateposts, the ends of walls or the corners of buildings. The simplest, and often the best, are variations on the theme of the stone ball, but pineapples and closed urns with lids to keep out the weather can also look attractive. Eagles and heraldic beasts can look pretentious and are best avoided. A finial on a well-designed column can make a striking object and terminate a vista or form the centrepiece of a large circular feature.

The uniform shape of stone balls is an effective contrast to the informal shapes of plants.

Balustrades are used to create a safety barrier at the edges of retaining walls, terraces and steps. Reconstructed stone rails or copings of classical design are easy to purchase, as are cast iron ones. A lighter effect can be achieved by creating your own designs and having them made up in wrought iron by the local blacksmith.

Birdbaths and feeders, provided they are kept clean and constantly supplied with food and water, can bring a lot of life and interest to the garden. Placed in an open position, well away from trees or hedges where cats can lurk, they can be very decorative in

themselves, although the design and the material used must accord with the character of the garden. The level should be above the spring of a cat, and there should be a strong overhang to discourage marauding squirrels. Providing water for birds also reduces the risk of their attacking foliage in search of moisture.

This simple bridge of two planks has a balustrade for safety.

Bridges are practical necessities for crossing stretches of water or streams and must be designed primarily for safety. However, their design should also suit the character of the garden, both in style and in scale. Although they can be highly ornamental, especially when reflected in water, bridges tend to look ridiculous unless they serve some functional purpose, such as linking one part of a garden to another.

Cisterns made in lead, or occasionally cast iron, were originally used to collect rainwater, for which purpose they are still admirable, and are far more attractive than a plastic water butt. Filled with soil, they are also good for planting, since they allow ample room for the roots of permanent plants. Fibreglass imitations of lead cisterns are available, but these do not weather down to the matt texture of natural lead.

Old lead cisterns make ideal planters.

Clair-voyées are essentially grilled openings made in the garden boundary, whether wall or hedge, to give a view out onto the countryside beyond. Unless the view is of sky, or a very distant landscape, it is best to have a plain grill in upright wood or metal bars, since any elaborate pattern will tend to clash with whatever detail lies beyond. A squared trellis can be equally effective, and concrete screen-blocks of simple design can look good in a modern garden setting. Sheets of plate glass can been used, but birds may injure themselves trying to fly through these.

Clair-voyées, traditional and contemporary, provide views out to the surrounding landscape.

Dovecotes are an interesting addition to a large garden, particularly if stocked with some of the more unusual varieties of doves or pigeons. Since they tend to breed rapidly, it is best not to provide too much accommodation, so that the surplus stock is encouraged to move elsewhere. Like other animals, birds need proper feeding and attention, and they can create problems with their droppings and occasional forays into the kitchen garden.

Flower pots of the ordinary terracotta variety, in various sizes, can be grouped on steps, at the corners of terraces and beside seats to very good effect. Some may contain permanent plants (brought out from the greenhouse or conservatory in the summer), while others can hold bedding plants or lilies that may be exchanged for something else when they have finished blooming. If possible you should try to have a small space where things that are finished, or not yet ready, can wait. Generally speaking, the simplest and most traditional designs are best, but if the pots are to stay year-round, they must be made from frost-proof clay. However practical, plastic pots do not look attractive on display, although they can be placed behind clay pots in large displays, allowing only the plants to be seen.

Mirrors, used with care, can magically extend the apparent size of a small garden, but they should always be set at a slight angle to the viewer-it is disconcerting to suddenly meet oneself face to face! They must also be protected from the weather and be placed so that soil cannot be splashed up onto them. Birds often injure themselves trying to fly through the mirror. To avoid this, a mirror fixed in an arch or doorway can be placed behind a metal gate or frame, making it less attractive to birds and more realistic to the viewer.

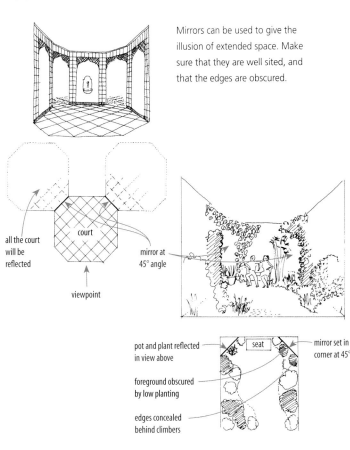

Mirrors can be used to give the illusion of extended space. Make sure that they are well sited, and that the edges are obscured.

all the court will be reflected

court

viewpoint

mirror at 45° angle

pot and plant reflected in view above

foreground obscured by low planting

edges concealed behind climbers

seat

mirror set in corner at 45°

FINALIZING THE GARDEN LAYOUT PLAN

Sundials, although hardly useful, are both decorative and popular, forming an excellent centrepiece for a formal garden. They range from grand and complex armillary spheres to simple columns topped with a plate and gnomon (the rod or pin that indicates the time by the position of its shadow).

Topiary is essentially living sculpture. Generally made from box or yew, both of which are long lasting but need only a once- or twice-yearly clip, topiary specimens can represent almost anything, the limiting factors being the time they take to grow and the ability of the gardener. They are often supplied grown through a light frame of bamboo and wire to get the main proportions right; you can then gradually add finishing touches as fancy dictates. It must be remembered that however architectural in form, they are still plants and require feeding, watering and cultivation.

Topiary specimens can represent almost anything.

Treillage (trelliswork) is generally used as a decorative feature to give character and interest to a large blank wall. Since the treillage itself is a feature, any planting against it should be restrained—vigorous climbing plants can quickly obscure the design and destroy the effect (and often the treillage itself, since it tends to be rather fragile). Ready-made treillage is now available in metal and can be fixed to a wall to give a variety of effects.

Treillage can be used to create a false perspective as on the side wall of this terrace.

Trompe l'oeil, the painted scenes meant to trick the eye, have been used to create the illusion of space for many hundreds of years (there are some famously fine examples at Pompeii). A trompe l'oeil scene must be undertaken by a good artist, since a bad painting can completely ruin a garden. Although a wide wall painted with an extensive landscape view can look fine, even a blank archway in the wall of a small garden, painted to show a path to another garden

A trompe l'oeil can add an extra dimension to a small garden.

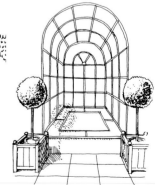

A false perspective is enhanced by the positioning of the topiary balls.

enclosure, can add an extra dimension. The painting should be sited in a place that affords protection from the rain.

Urns and vases are generally important objects in their own right, the plant material used to fill them being mostly secondary decoration. They may be of stone (or, more frequently, of reconstituted stone), marble, lead, bronze or cast iron, generally standing on plinths to give them greater importance. Flanking steps or doorways, at the end of a walk or along the edge of a terrace, they are invaluable, but the design and material must always match the position. If they are of a material that must be painted, it is best to choose a neutral colour, such as grey, grey-blue or dark bronze-green. Decorative urns are often best left unplanted to avoid a conflict of interest.

Garden Furniture

For many people, one of the great pleasures of having a garden is that it provides a place to sit outdoors, whether to lounge and relax or to dine. To do this in comfort, garden furniture is essential, and the more inviting the furniture and the view of the garden from it, the more a garden will tend to be used.

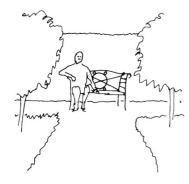

A bench positioned at the end of a path acts as a focal point and provides a pleasant viewpoint of the garden.

As always, you need to think of function first, deciding what is actually needed and where you should position your furniture. Consider the following points:

– From where can the best views of the garden and its surroundings be seen?
– Would these areas provide an appealing place to sit?
– Who is likely to use this seating, and how many people might use it at the same time?
– What are the dimensions of the terrace? For dining, what type of table will you need, and how many chairs will be required on a regular basis?
– Would an occasional seat, carefully placed at the end of a path (and also acting as a focal point in the design), allow you to enjoy your garden from a specially selected viewpoint?
– Will the furniture need to be stored inside during the winter?

Permanent or temporary furniture

From a practical point of view, there are basically two types of garden furniture: permanent, which may remain out all year, and temporary, which comes out only when required. Temporary furniture is most useful where space is limited, provided there is somewhere convenient to store it when it is not in use.

Permanent furniture, which needs to be weather-resistant, is usually constructed of materials such as stone, wrought iron, cast iron, timber or plastic. Temporary furniture can be of any material (usually cane, canvas or plastic), as long as it is light enough to be easily transported and stored.

If you intend to move furniture around, choose items that are not too heavy.

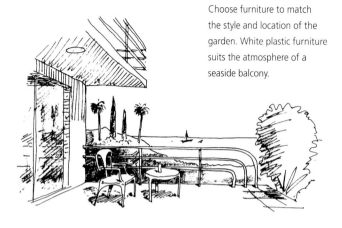

Choose furniture to match the style and location of the garden. White plastic furniture suits the atmosphere of a seaside balcony.

The same furniture in a cottage garden would be out of keeping with the place.

Choosing a design

Once you have established what type of furniture is needed in the garden and where it is going to be placed, you can start to consider the design of each item. There is now a vast range of garden furniture available to suit most styles and budgets. As a general rule, opt for simple, well-made products that blend into the garden as you will be less likely to tire of them in the long run. There are many furniture makers who copy classic designs such as the Lutyens bench, and others who supply a comfortable and often lightweight contemporary range. Whatever design you choose, make sure that it complements the style of your garden and its surroundings. White plastic patio-style tables and chairs may not look out of place on a yacht or on the balcony of an

apartment in Spain or Florida, but they would ruin the carefully planned effect of a cottage garden in a romantic, natural setting.

Comfort is another important factor. Many seats, particularly those made of wrought or cast iron, will benefit from the addition of cushions. These should be made out of tough, washable fabric and brought indoors or under cover when not in use.

Some garden seating can be very uncomfortable.

If you already have some old garden furniture that is suitable for your needs, you may consider having it repaired, cleaned up and repainted. This is often preferable to buying newer furniture of inferior craftsmanship. Remember also that you can design your own seating. You do not have to be a master carpenter or stone mason to create simple sawn log seats, suitable for a woodland garden, or to place

An octagonal tree seat provides a shady place to sit.

a slab of stone on two sections of an old column to create a simple bench, ideal perhaps for a small country garden. Painted garden furniture, especially seating, will need an occasional scrub or wash to keep it clean.

For permanent seating, you may also consider furniture that is built in to the hard landscaping of the garden, such as a seat wall or a bench incorporated into a decked area. Built-in seating can be particularly effective where space is limited.

Natural or painted finishes

Hardwood seats generally look best if they are allowed to weather naturally, but if stained or painted, choose a dark, neutral colour such as grey, dark brown, very dark green, or even a deep blue to blend in with the rest of the garden. Ironwork usually looks best painted black. For more striking effects, brighter colours such as orange, yellow or red can look effective, particularly in a contemporary setting. Beware of using white as a colour. Far from being safe and neutral, white is a glaring colour that always demands attention.

The same rules apply to choosing colours for temporary furniture (often of cane or plastic). When selecting canvas chairs or fabric-covered cushions, note that natural canvas will tend to blend in gently with other features, while patterns and stripes are less easily absorbed. If colour is desired, it is usually best kept plain and carefully related to the colours already used in that part of the garden.

Umbrellas

Sometimes, if the garden is in full sun, a large garden umbrella may be needed. The designs modelled on those found in outdoor cafés in Italy are large enough to shade four or six people, giving a feeling of privacy in overlooked town gardens. Contemporary designs are now available from some yachting sail manufacturers seeking a new outlet for their product.

Umbrellas can provide privacy as well as shade in gardens that are overlooked.

Barbecues and fire pits

Barbecues can be built into a terraced area or may be freestanding. If you would prefer a permanent structure, be very careful about where you site the barbecue. The prevailing wind (and any other freak winds!) can play havoc with the smoke produced, sometimes rendering the terrace unusable while cooking is in process. Freestanding models can be moved out of the wind and are often more practical.

A fire pit is usually a low, freestanding metal brazier or bowl made to hold and burn logs outside, giving warmth to people seated around it. Sometimes a fire pit is a fixed item, built of stone or brick, perhaps with a low wall to be used as seating surrounding the pit area. It can be built to specification by a local metal worker, and in some cases a metal fire pit can double as a barbecue. If a glass top is used as a cover it can also function as a low table. Unless fire pits can be covered, they should be cleaned out and stored inside during the winter.

glass cover

fine wire cover

A typical metal fire pit has either a fine wire cover or a glass cover that can serve as a table.

Children's Play Equipment

Children love to play outside, and it is often possible to allocate a particular area of the garden, perhaps visible from the kitchen window, as a play area, always remembering that children soon grow up and that this particular area may need to be reintegrated into the main garden layout in five or ten years' time. A sandpit, for instance, might convert to a pond or water feature when the children are older.

With small, simple items it is better to try to design your own and integrate them into your garden layout plan. An existing tree, provided the branches are sound, might make an exciting climbing frame, or an old garden building could be adapted as a playhouse.

A children's playhouse is later transformed into a summerhouse.

Sandpits

These can give many happy hours of play and are fairly easy to construct out of timber or brick. A sunken square or circular area is often best, and a low surrounding wall of three or four brick courses can double as a seating area. A light, removable or folding wooden cover will help keep the sand clean and prevent it being soiled by cats and other animals. Sand is readily available from most builders' merchants and may need replacing annually.

Playhouses

An unused garden building, perhaps once a coal shed, may well convert into a playhouse, complete with a scaled-down door, door knocker or bell, curtains at the windows, and possibly the children's names or an imaginary house name clearly written outside. Children love to indulge in games of fantasy and will be able to do so in the safety and privacy of their own space.

A sandpit can later be converted to a pool.

A mature tree might be adapted as a tree house.

Tree houses, swings and ropes

You may be fortunate in having a mature tree that can be adapted as a tree house or as a fixture for a swing or climbing rope, but check that all the branches are sound before proceeding. Sometimes, instead of being removed, a fallen tree can be put to use for climbing games.

Climbing frames

Climbing frames, complete with swing and slide, can give hours of fun. There are several manufacturers who produce natural timber frames that merge well into a garden layout, but these tend to be expensive. You may, with a little ingenuity, be able to adapt some existing feature to serve the same purpose. Children usually love these custom-made facilities, and they are more fun and easier to live with than the brightly coloured objects usually offered commercially.

Lighting

Most gardens will benefit from some form of lighting, whether for security, to discourage intruders, for access, to define steps and pathways or for aesthetic effect. Lighting can dramatically enhance a garden at night, highlighting special features, such as a statue, a tree or the texture of ground cover, while allowing other features to recede.

Lighting techniques

The choice of fittings will depend on the effect required but may vary from a single fixture—illuminating a terrace, for instance—to a complex scheme employing many different types of fittings, including uplighters, path lights, underwater lights, spotlights and so on. Similar to interior light fittings, garden lights can be a decorative feature in themselves, or they can be discreet and designed to be concealed. When developing a lighting scheme, it is vital to establish early on in the design process how you want your lighting to function. Often, cables will need to be laid and buried during the

Low-level downlighters cast pools of light, accentuating surface texture.

An uplighter emphasizes the form and foliage of a shrub.

construction of the garden and certain fittings, such as recessed step lights, installed as part of the building process.

There are several lighting techniques that can be used alone or in combination to create the desired effects. With all types of lighting, use a qualified electrician to install watertight sockets, cables and fixtures, according to the safety regulations in your area.

Uplighting is created by placing a light source directly underneath features and is particularly effective when used with shrubs and trees with an interesting internal structure, such as intertwining branches. The effect created is dramatic, especially when used in winter through bare stems and branches.

Spotlighting is used extensively in gardens to highlight the detail of a particular feature, such as an intricately carved urn. For maximum shadow and detail, position the light source to one side of the feature rather than directly in front of it. This form of lighting is most effective when the light source is hidden. When choosing spotlights, note that the spread of the beam is variable as is the intensity of the light source. Often a pinpoint beam works best because, when correctly positioned, the area lit can be limited to the feature.

Silhouette lighting is a dramatic yet subtle form of lighting used to define the outline shape of features with strong form, such as well-defined plants. The object is lit from behind, usually from below, and the light source is hidden.

Path lighting and step lighting are usually achieved by using downlighters. These cast pools of light onto the ground, accentuating the surface texture. Path lighting is primarily functional, but it should be carefully designed so that it does not detract too much from other features. When used for entrances and drives, it should be soft and welcoming. Path lighting may be concealed so that it is not apparent during the day, or you can use decorative lights of different design and finishes—often of mushroom or globe shape—that are a feature in their own right. For step lighting, the light source may be attached or built into the supporting wall, the underside of the step or the step itself. For all step lighting a diffuser should be used to direct light downwards onto the tread of each step.

Step lighting built into the supporting wall can be a useful safety feature.

Underwater lighting can bring a pool to life at night. In a still pool, backed by a wall, the flickering shadows cast by the movement of fish can animate the garden in a way that would be impossible during the day. Underwater lighting is also effective for highlighting fountains and waterfalls, especially when used in conjunction with spotlights.

Moonlighting provides an effect that simulates the soft glow of the moon and stars. It is achieved by using several fittings fixed high above the ground, usually in trees, to cast diffuse, dappled light onto the ground below. It is particularly effective in rural gardens where excessive lighting can detract from the enjoyment of the moon and stars.

Security or access lighting

In most countries, elaborate security lighting systems are available, many with built-in sensors activated by body warmth and movement. The sensor does not distinguish between animals and humans, and it can be alarming to find the garden illuminated in the early hours of the morning, even if the intruder is only an innocent cat or fox. These sensored systems are easily installed and can be very useful to light up a path from garage to front door or around the house to a rear entrance. The systems can now be purchased from some hardware stores, but an experienced electrician is often needed to fit them to the best advantage. Care must be taken to position the light bulb away from any timbers or other inflammable material.

One drawback of security lights is that they cannot distinguish between humans and animals.

Security lights should be chosen to complement the style of the house and should be positioned with care.

Gardens can be dramatically enhanced by lighting schemes, but equally, if badly used or overused, artificial lighting can be crude and garish. Moveable spotlights are highly versatile fittings that can be placed anywhere in the garden, provided their cables are long enough. The most useful versions are either mounted on spikes for easy insertion into soil, or incorporate a simple clip for fixing to items above the ground, such as trees and fences. These discreet spotlights, which are normally finished in black, are easily concealed. They can be used for all kinds of lighting effects, from uplighting to silhouette lighting. The advantage of moveable spotlights is that they are easily relocated to take advantage of seasonal changes and plant growth.

A simple fixture beside a doorway is often sufficient for both security and ease of access. Try to choose a fitting with clean simple lines in a style that is suitable for the architecture and locality, rather than opting for a utilitarian model. It may take time to find an appropriate fitting, but it is worth making the effort as the wrong lighting can often spoil an otherwise carefully planned scheme.

Think carefully about the positioning of the fitting. It should be neither too high nor too low and should not shine directly into the eyes of anyone approaching. Unless you need a great deal of light, a fairly low wattage or energy-saving bulb may be all that is necessary.

Night lighting of garden features and plants can have some interesting effects, depending upon where the light is coming from.

Lighting for aesthetic effect

Avoid spotlighing objects from across the garden.

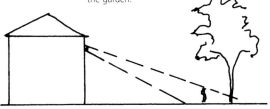

While for security and access lighting it may be essential to have artificial light permanently in place, for aesthetic effects you can create a magical atmosphere by using natural flame from candles, flares or torches. For most outdoor settings, candles will need to be encased in lanterns, which may be of any material—glass, paper, metal and so on—to blend in with the rest of the garden design.

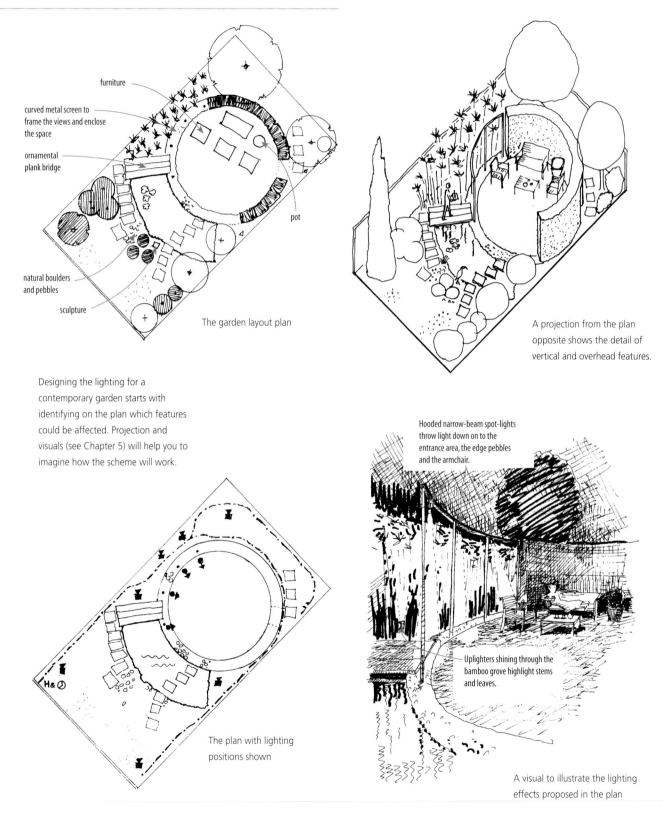

furniture

curved metal screen to
frame the views and enclose
the space

ornamental
plank bridge

pot

natural boulders
and pebbles

sculpture

The garden layout plan

A projection from the plan
opposite shows the detail of
vertical and overhead features.

Designing the lighting for a
contemporary garden starts with
identifying on the plan which features
could be affected. Projection and
visuals (see Chapter 5) will help you to
imagine how the scheme will work.

Hooded narrow-beam spot-lights
throw light down on to the
entrance area, the edge pebbles
and the armchair.

The plan with lighting
positions shown

Uplighters shining through the
bamboo grove highlight stems
and leaves.

A visual to illustrate the lighting
effects proposed in the plan

Practical Considerations

There are a number of important practical considerations that may influence costs and your choice of materials and accessories. Before making final decisions about the garden layout plan (whether on the horizontal or vertical plane), you need to consider how you will access and prepare the land, whether the soil is in the right condition and how services (such as water and electricity) will be brought onto the site.

Site Access and Clearance

An obvious point, but one frequently overlooked, is how you or the contractor will get into the garden in order to carry out the work. Can the garden only be reached by going through the house? For large items, such as classical columns or mature trees with wide root balls, access simply may not be feasible through the house or a narrow side alley. In towns the only realistic access for large items may be by hired crane over the roof. There may be restrictions on parking, making unloading difficult. It is worth considering access problems early on, as this may have a direct bearing on feasibility and cost.

Normally, before any work can begin, some site clearance is necessary. This will depend on the state of the site and the work proposed. It may mean simply removing a tree or a shrub and applying weed killer, or erecting a temporary protective fence around trees and shrubs that you want to preserve, or it may mean bringing in earth-moving equipment. An area may need to be set aside for a bonfire. This should be in the open to avoid scorching any existing trees, and the local regulations on burning rubbish will need to be investigated.

Soil Preparation

If topsoil is to be removed, this should be done first and the topsoil stacked separately from the subsoil beneath it. If excavating for pools or ponds, ground shaping may be necessary. This will all be done in subsoil, the topsoil only being returned after grading work is finished. The depth of topsoil required depends largely on what is to be grown. Grass or lawn requires a minimum depth of 50 mm (2 in.), while shrubs need a minimum of 250 mm (10 in.).

Care must be taken to prepare the soil for the planting areas. It should be thoroughly dug over and all pernicious weeds removed or sprayed off. If the soil is impoverished, humus should be incorporated to improve the texture; nutrients may also be needed. The rate of plant growth will be greatly affected by the soil structure, so extra care taken at this stage will pay dividends later.

Drainage and Water

Water is one of our most precious resources, and many gardeners are beginning to take responsibility for using it economically and wisely. The extraction of freshwater from rivers has serious effects on the creatures and plants that rely on freshwater ecosystems, but by adopting a responsible approach at the outset of planning the garden, the extent to which we waste this resource can be greatly reduced.

If there is a drainage problem in the garden, there is no point in replanning the garden without first taking

If heavy machinery is required for site clearance, ensure that access to the site is sufficient.

Build bonfires in open areas to avoid scorching trees.

some positive action. If the site is waterlogged, a drainage system may need to be installed. When the house was being built or during subsequent levelling and grading, the soil may have been compacted by heavy machinery. It may simply be a question of aerating the soil, or there may be a more serious inherited problem of subsoil dumped over free-draining soil, disguised with only a thin layer of topsoil. The compacted soil may need to be spiked with a fork and have fine grit incorporated to help break it up.

Your builder should be able to advise you on which system to use, and it should be installed early on when the ground work is being prepared, while machinery and access are available.

Soakaways, French drains and tile drainage systems

A soakaway is a hole that can be dug under a damp spot to drain the water off the surface and down into the ground below. The hole should be approximately 1 m (3.3 ft.) square and 1 m deep and filled first with coarse rubble, then with a layer of ash, and finally backfilled with topsoil before replacing the turf.

French drains are steep-sided trenches filled with coarse stone or gravel. They act as water-conducting channels, or temporary drains, which eventually become blocked by a gradual accumulation of silt and soil. French drains are used in preference to open ditches on the sides of paths or driveways to control any seepage.

Tile drainage is a more extensive drainage system, in which clay tile drains are laid underground with the outlet going to a ditch or watercourse. They can be laid in a single line or, for more thorough drainage, in a herringbone pattern. Gradients of the laterals should not be greater than

Underground tile drainage systems

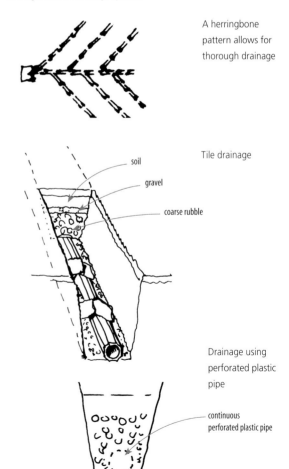

A herringbone pattern allows for thorough drainage

Tile drainage

soil

gravel

coarse rubble

Drainage using perforated plastic pipe

continuous perforated plastic pipe

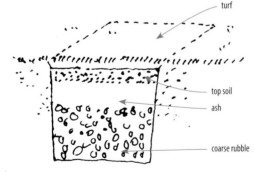

turf

top soil

ash

coarse rubble

A soakaway

ash

coarse rubble

A French drain

1:250, with the main drain similarly graded to the outfall. The depth and spacing at which these tile drains should be laid will depend on the type of soil, closer spacing being required for thinner sandy soils.

Septic tanks

If your house requires a septic tank for sewage (or an oil tank for fuel), you will need to consider its position with regard to access for vehicles and the route of any pipes leading to and from the tank before you finalize your garden layout design.

Water points and irrigation

Most plants require regular feeding and watering to help their roots become established and to encourage them to grow quickly. Imagine a prolonged period of hot dry weather during which your plants may need to be watered once or twice daily. Have you included sufficient garden taps, irrigation points or trickle irrigation to give thirsty plants a thorough watering? Using a watering can is time-consuming, and too often results in the foliage being given a light overhead sprinkling rather than a thorough watering that reaches down to the roots.

Water points should be sited at suitable positions around the garden, perhaps with one near the house and another at the opposite end. The pipes for these will need to be tapped into the main supply and will also need to be laid beneath the soil surface. Install more points than necessary, as it is easier to do this at the outset than to disturb the garden by digging up the ground and laying pipes at a later stage.

Water points should be sited at convenient locations around the garden.

You may also wish to include some form of irrigation, such as a surface drip system to moisten soil around plants, or a pop-up underground system that will spray lawns. In areas such as roof terraces or basements where much of the planting may be in containers, "spaghetti" or drip line irrigation can be moved around easily.

Rainwater contains more air and nutrients than piped water, and using it in the garden helps to conserve

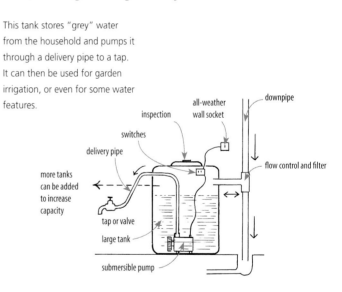

This tank stores "grey" water from the household and pumps it through a delivery pipe to a tap. It can then be used for garden irrigation, or even for some water features.

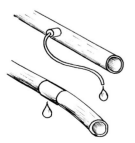

"Spaghetti" lines (top) and drip lines (bottom) help to conserve resources by delivering small amounts of water to individual plants.

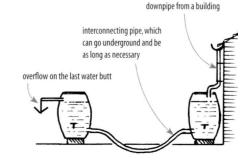

Water butts can be connected to provide water to different parts of the garden. If they are to fill up reasonably equally, they need to be fairly level with one another.

resources. A system of water butts and rain traps, linking and overflow kits can be strategically placed to serve many irrigation requirements.

To avoid unnecessary transpiration the most effective times for watering plants, including areas of grass and lawns, are early in the morning and in the evening.

To reduce the reliance on watering systems, every garden owner should consider using plants whose water requirements are compatible with the conditions in the natural climate. For areas of minimal moisture or where drought commonly occurs, a more sustainable system such as xeriscaping (using drought-tolerant plants, such as cacti) should be considered.

In areas where monthly rainfall is inconsistent and where you cannot assume that your plants will naturally receive the required water, a sprinkler system should be considered. By throwing an arc or jet of water, a large area can be covered in one application. Sprinklers can be very wasteful, and should only be used on plants that really need the water, which may mean planning the garden layout to locate needy beds and lawns where water access can be most efficient. Sprinklers can use as much water in an hour as a family of four would use in one week.

If gaining access to water is a problem, you may consider sinking a borehole (see page 107).

Choosing a watering system

The method of irrigation will depend on location, budget and the needs of your particular garden. Usually there are irrigation specialists who will be happy to advise and quote on a suitable system, but if your garden is small you may simply need to enquire at a good garden centre to see what is most suitable. There are several main systems to consider.

The first option is water taps, from which you can conveniently fill a watering can or run a hose with a sprinkler attachment. These should be carefully sited so that they are accessible from each part of the garden, not just from the terrace or back door. By using a watering can, you can direct the water solely to the needy plant, so there is little waste. However, the cans can be heavy and time-consuming to carry, especially for the elderly or disabled.

A sprinkler system usually involves tapping into the main line. The system can be broken down into zones where you can have a variety of different watering options, perhaps one zone for potted plantings near a terrace, a second zone for the lawn and a third for the perennial border. These zones are broken up into areas that need the same frequency of watering as well as a similar delivery method (for example, pop-up sprinkler heads, soaker hoses, bubblers or sprays). A central timer can be installed and set to manage all of the various zones through the use of programmed rotating watering.

Another option is a trickle irrigation system, consisting mainly of a perforated hose that can emit a small amount of water over a prolonged period. Connected to the water taps and coupled with an automatic timer, this will allow you to have watering control even during long absences from your garden. The hose is often black (sometimes made of recycled tyres) and can either be dug in below ground or laid on the soil surface and moved occasionally to give greater coverage.

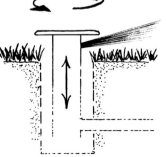

Pop-up sprinklers are mainly used on grassy areas. Although they distribute large volumes of water, they can be programmed to treat specific segments within a 360° circle.

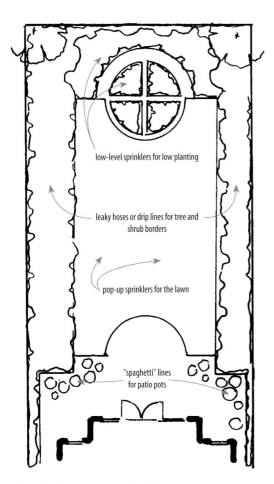

low-level sprinklers for low planting

leaky hoses or drip lines for tree and shrub borders

pop-up sprinklers for the lawn

"spaghetti" lines for patio pots

To avoid using too much water, divide the garden into different irrigation zones depending on the plants' needs.

Automatic pop-up irrigation systems are usually used in gardens with large areas of plants and lawn, often in hot, dry countries where water is at a premium. They tend to be wasteful, but may be programmed to use less water.

A further option is a system connected to a well or borehole within your property. This system is sometimes expensive to install, but the running costs are cheaper. You should seek professional advice locally if you are considering this option.

Recycling "grey" water from domestic use—with the exception of water from washing machines, dishwashers or any water that has been used to wash pets or nappies (diapers) or that may contain bleach,

disinfectants or household cleaners—allows the reuse of small quantities of water through out the year, saving it from disappearing into the sewer or septic tank system. As it may contain bacteria, grey water is not recommended for food crops. To collect the water, you can connect a diverter and water butt to the waste pipe in an upstairs bathroom, or fit a more complex system to siphon it off. Make sure the system adopted will comply with the rules set by your local water authority.

Electricity

Electricity may also be needed in the garden, either for lighting, for operating water pumps or for running barbecues. The cables to the power points should be protected in armoured casing and marked and buried below the level of the topsoil where they cannot be easily damaged by spades or other tools. Always ask a qualified electrician for advice.

Finalizing a Scheme for the Final Garden Layout Plan

The suggestions in this chapter are not meant to be comprehensive, and there is always room for the innovative use of different materials in a garden setting. Once you have decided on the precise design of your garden and taken into consideration any practical factors, you are ready to finalize and draw up your garden layout plan. This plan completes the hard landscaping proposals (both horizontal and vertical) for your garden.

The plan must be accurately drawn so that you will be able to use it in a practical way, both to set out the design on the land and to estimate the materials required for the hard-landscaping elements of the construction. To calculate quantities of materials, measure the area and depth (or volume) of the material, then multiply these figures to find the amount. Alternatively, take the area and depth dimensions to your local builder's merchant and ask them to calculate the required quantity for you.

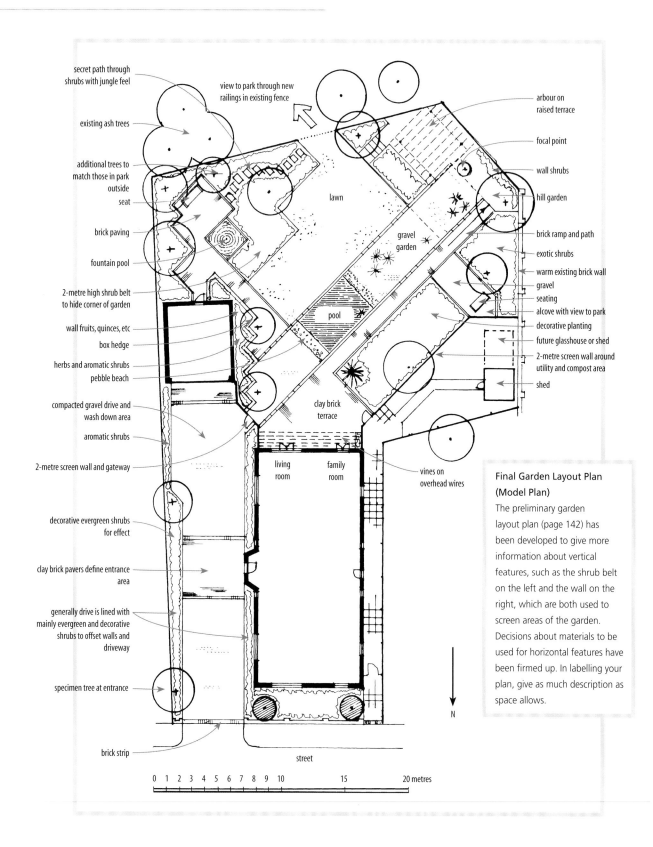

secret path through
shrubs with jungle feel

view to park through new
railings in existing fence

arbour on
raised terrace

existing ash trees

focal point

additional trees to
match those in park
outside

wall shrubs

seat

hill garden

brick paving

lawn

fountain pool

gravel
garden

brick ramp and path

exotic shrubs

2-metre high shrub belt
to hide corner of garden

warm existing brick wall

gravel

wall fruits, quinces, etc

seating

box hedge

alcove with view to park

herbs and aromatic shrubs

pool

decorative planting

pebble beach

future glasshouse or shed

2-metre screen wall around
utility and compost area

compacted gravel drive and
wash down area

shed

aromatic shrubs

clay brick
terrace

2-metre screen wall and gateway

living
room

family
room

vines on
overhead wires

decorative evergreen shrubs
for effect

clay brick pavers define entrance
area

generally drive is lined with
mainly evergreen and decorative
shrubs to offset walls and
driveway

specimen tree at entrance

**Final Garden Layout Plan
(Model Plan)**

The preliminary garden
layout plan (page 142) has
been developed to give more
information about vertical
features, such as the shrub
belt on the left and the wall on
the right, which are both used to
screen areas of the garden.
Decisions about materials to be
used for horizontal features have
been firmed up. In labelling your
plan, give as much description as
space allows.

N

brick strip

street

0 1 2 3 4 5 6 7 8 9 10   15   20 metres

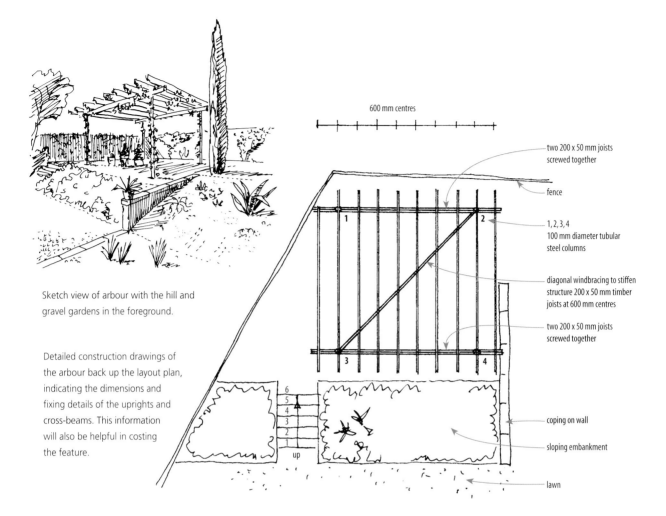

600 mm centres

two 200 x 50 mm joists screwed together

fence

1, 2, 3, 4
100 mm diameter tubular steel columns

diagonal windbracing to stiffen structure 200 x 50 mm timber joists at 600 mm centres

two 200 x 50 mm joists screwed together

coping on wall

sloping embankment

lawn

up

Sketch view of arbour with the hill and gravel gardens in the foreground.

Detailed construction drawings of the arbour back up the layout plan, indicating the dimensions and fixing details of the uprights and cross-beams. This information will also be helpful in costing the feature.

Drawing up the Final Garden Layout Plan

The garden layout plan may be drawn in pencil or ink. Technical drawing pens or disposable fine-line pens will give a more professional finish, particularly if you vary the line width by using different nib sizes. Draw the more important or dominant features such as the house or the garden boundary with a wider line, then a thinner line for less dominant items. If you use a pencil, keep it well sharpened.

1. Fix the preliminary garden layout plan to the drawing board, and attach a second sheet of tracing paper over it (on which you will work up the final garden layout plan). Take care with the layout, arranging the plan slightly to the left of the sheet, leaving enough space above, below and at the sides to allow for any notes or labelling. You will require an information panel on the right-hand side with a title block at the bottom of this, together with a north point and scale.

2. Look at the ground plane elements on the preliminary plan, starting at the terrace or another critical point that links house and garden. Decide on your exact choice of materials and how you will use them (a brick path in a laid basket-weave pattern, for instance). Are you happy with them, or do they need adjusting?

3. Continue doing the same with paths, steps and any other ground plane elements. If you are content with what you have drawn on your preliminary garden layout plan, you will simply need to trace over the previous drawing. Remember that the idea is to communicate the design or pattern of your ground plan elements, not necessarily to produce a work of art.

4. Now draw up any new ground plane elements individually to scale. Imagine you are looking down on them from overhead, and show the outline shape of the feature as well as the design in which the material is arranged (if appropriate). Indicate the latter by detailing to scale only a small area. If bricks or other materials are too small to be drawn to scale on the plan, you can supplement it with separate detail sheets. Alternatively, you could try to indicate your intentions graphically, possibly by magnifying them in a diagram drawn alongside the plan. If you use this technique, make sure that you number or label your details to key them to the plan so that their positions are instantly identifiable.

5. Next draw in all vertical and overhead elements, beginning with the outer or boundary walls, gradually moving inwards to include any trellis, pergolas, arches and so on. Remember that you are viewing the objects from above. Label all vertical features (for example, "Brick wall: 1.8 m in height", "Hardwood trellis, stained dark blue: 1.2 m in height").

6. Draw in the canopies of any existing or proposed trees, and indicate with a cross where they are to be planted. Refer back to page 76 for symbols for these.

7. Provide a short descriptive label for each area of border or planting to indicate your broad intentions (for instance, "Scented mixed border for summer interest").

8. Are there are any elements that need to be shown in more detail, such as a pond or pergola construction? You may not be able to show sufficient detail on your plan drawing, and these should be drawn on a separate sheet. (Make a note of these. Drawing sections and other visuals will be dealt with in Chapter 5.)

9. Once you have completed it, remove the final garden layout plan from the drawing board. The plan will have taken you time to draw and is therefore an important document. Take at least two copies (either dyelines, blueprints or photocopies), and keep the original flat and safely stored as you may need to make amendments to it later if you change your ideas. You may want to colour one of the copies (see page 249) when you have decided on the planting for the garden, which is the next stage in the design process.

10. You should now have an accurate garden layout plan, which can be used either by you for constructing the garden or by the builder to give you a price for the work. The next stage is to decide on the plantings for your new garden.

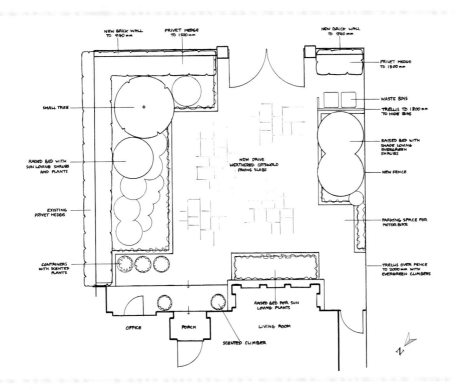

NEW BRICK WALL TO 990 mm
PRIVET HEDGE TO 1500 mm
NEW BRICK WALL TO 990 mm
PRIVET HEDGE TO 1500 mm
SMALL TREE
WASTE BINS
TRELLIS TO 1800 mm TO HIDE BINS
RAISED BED WITH SHADE LOVING EVERGREEN SHRUBS
RAISED BED WITH SUN LOVING SHRUBS AND PLANTS
NEW DRIVE WEATHERED COTSWOLD PAVING SLABS
NEW FENCE
EXISTING PRIVET HEDGE
PARKING SPACE FOR MOTOR BIKE
CONTAINERS WITH SCENTED PLANTS
TRELLIS OVER FENCE TO 2000 mm WITH EVERGREEN CLIMBERS
RAISED BED FOR SUN LOVING PLANTS
OFFICE
PORCH
LIVING ROOM
SCENTED CLIMBER
N

This simple layout for a front garden is drawn in black and white. A detailed planting plan will be produced once the layout has been approved by the client.

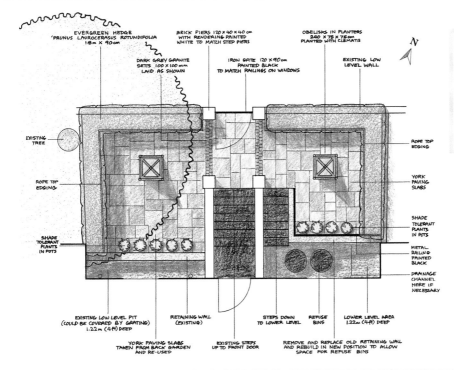

EVERGREEN HEDGE 'PRUNUS LAUROCERASUS ROTUNDIFOLIA' 1.8 m x 90 cm
BRICK PIERS 120 x 40 x 40 cm WITH RENDERING PAINTED WHITE TO MATCH STEP PIERS
OBELISKS IN PLANTERS 240 x 75 x 75 cm PLANTED WITH CLEMATIS
N
DARK GREY GRANITE SETTS 100 x 100 mm LAID AS SHOWN
IRON GATE 120 x 90 cm PAINTED BLACK TO MATCH RAILINGS ON WINDOWS
EXISTING LOW LEVEL WALL
EXISTING TREE
ROPE TOP EDGING
ROPE TOP EDGING
YORK PAVING SLABS
SHADE TOLERANT PLANTS IN POTS
SHADE TOLERANT PLANTS IN POTS
METAL RAILING PAINTED BLACK
DRAINAGE CHANNEL HERE IF NECESSARY
EXISTING LOW LEVEL PIT (COULD BE COVERED BY GRATING) 1.22 m (4 ft) DEEP
RETAINING WALL (EXISTING)
STEPS DOWN TO LOWER LEVEL
REFUSE BINS
LOWER LEVEL AREA 1.22 m (4 ft) DEEP
YORK PAVING SLABS TAKEN FROM BACK GARDEN AND RE-USED
EXISTING STEPS UP TO FRONT DOOR
REMOVE AND REPLACE OLD RETAINING WALL AND REBUILD IN NEW POSITION TO ALLOW SPACE FOR REFUSE BINS

A detailed layout plan for a front garden gives information on all hard landscaping. Colour applied to the printed plan brings it to life.

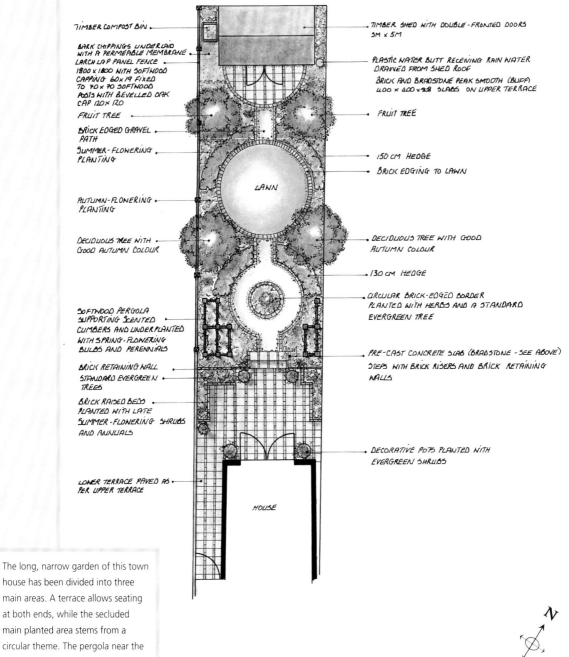

TIMBER COMPOST BIN

BARK CHIPPINGS UNDERLAID
WITH A PERMEABLE MEMBRANE
LARCH LAP PANEL FENCE
1800 × 1800 WITH SOFTWOOD
CAPPING 60 × 19 FIXED
TO 70 × 70 SOFTWOOD
POSTS WITH BEVELLED OAK
CAP 120 × 120

FRUIT TREE

BRICK EDGED GRAVEL
PATH

SUMMER-FLOWERING
PLANTING

AUTUMN-FLOWERING
PLANTING

DECIDUOUS TREE WITH
GOOD AUTUMN COLOUR

SOFTWOOD PERGOLA
SUPPORTING SCENTED
CLIMBERS AND UNDERPLANTED
WITH SPRING-FLOWERING
BULBS AND PERENNIALS

BRICK RETAINING WALL
STANDARD EVERGREEN
TREES

BRICK RAISED BEDS
PLANTED WITH LATE
SUMMER-FLOWERING SHRUBS
AND ANNUALS

LOWER TERRACE PAVED AS
PER UPPER TERRACE

TIMBER SHED WITH DOUBLE-FRONTED DOORS
3M × 3M

PLASTIC WATER BUTT RECEIVING RAIN WATER
DRAINED FROM SHED ROOF
BRICK AND BRADSTONE PEAK SMOOTH (BUFF)
400 × 400 × 38 SLABS ON UPPER TERRACE

FRUIT TREE

150 CM HEDGE

BRICK EDGING TO LAWN

DECIDUOUS TREE WITH GOOD
AUTUMN COLOUR

130 CM HEDGE

CIRCULAR BRICK-EDGED BORDER
PLANTED WITH HERBS AND A STANDARD
EVERGREEN TREE

PRE-CAST CONCRETE SLAB (BRADSTONE – SEE ABOVE)
STEPS WITH BRICK RISERS AND BRICK RETAINING
WALLS

DECORATIVE POTS PLANTED WITH
EVERGREEN SHRUBS

LAWN

HOUSE

The long, narrow garden of this town
house has been divided into three
main areas. A terrace allows seating
at both ends, while the secluded
main planted area stems from a
circular theme. The pergola near the
terrace unites the vertical façade of
the house with the horizontal plane
of the garden.

N

0 1 2 3 4

SCALE 1:100

Above: Making the most of a small sunken space, steps serve as easy seating at various levels, and an unusual backdrop of sustainable timber cubes provides privacy.

Above: An octagon works well in this change of level. Railway sleepers back-filled with gravel help to unite these steps with the surrounding countryside.

Above: Wide steps cope with a steep change of level, while the back-filled, soil retaining wall is built at a slight angle to allow water runoff, providing good drainage for plants.

Above: Subtle changes of level, combined with a selection of carefully placed recyled pots and artifacts as well as contrasting foliage, distinguish this coastal garden

Left: Steps can be used to change the direction of a path. The combination of gravel, stone overhang and smaller stone off-cuts blend with the local landscape.

Above: In this small shallow pool and bubble fountain, the water level falls just below the stone edging, and the pool base is covered in shingle.

Above: This shallow rill is "musical"; as each break in the flow of water occurs, different stones vary the sound of moving water, providing a cooling yet intriguing effect.

Above: Shallow bog planting by the stone edge of a larger pool allows water creatures easy access, although invasive bog plants will need regular thinning-out if amphibians are to thrive.

Above: Water trickles gently down these stepped stone risers into a natural pond where a small central island encourages ducks to nest without fear of marauders.

Above: In a densely planted garden, an area of quiet simplicity comes as a relief. Tactile swaying grasses surround a timber deck and "dip" pool, giving privacy for sunbathing on the warm sustainable timbers.

Left: A decorative, recycling water feature where wall-mounted stone "shells" trickle water by means of a pump into a shallow pool. Deliberately slightly overgrown and mysterious-looking, it attracts wildlife; wall climbers make a protective habitat for nesting birds.

Below: Guttering and a downpipe deliver water into this recycled water barrel. Water drains through a tap, to which a hose could be attached for irrigation.

Above: This old tin bath serves to trap and reuse water. In a hot, dry climate the wooden lid prevents evaporation.

Left: A dry "stream" made from stone pieces evokes the effect of water. Narrow enough to step over, its curve is repeated in the outline of the hedging and lawn.

Left: The rounded shapes of plants in this garden are a contrast to the unusual vertical sundial. The different shades of green include both matt and light-reflective foliage.

Below: Use of the overhead plane by means of tree canopy, parasol or pergola, makes a garden feel more secluded.

Above: Brick inserts break up this expanse of stone paving. Setting the height of the paving level just below the level of the lawn allows the mower to skim over without damage to the cutting blades.

Above: Contemporary and classic materials combine to indicate a strong directional flow. Slate panels (pre-cut to a template), blend with the edging of stone chippings.

Above: In this seating area, a roughened surface prevents slipping, while the plants between pavers create interest and allow for water runoff.

Above: Permeable timber decking and narrow brick pavers indicate the directional flow of this garden floor, while dark-coloured furniture contrasts with carefully arranged planting.

Above: Sustainable seating hewn out of old tree trunks is in character with this garden's woodland setting, and can be left out in all weathers.

Above: A white rendered wall brings light into a small space. Permeable perforated metal is used for steps and to edge the raised timber deck. The seemingly natural close planting is sourced from local markets and allows no space for weeds.

Above: The locally sourced, recycled table, chairs and metal container outside this green-roofed garden shed make an interesting seating area.

Above: Here the backdrop and retaining walls are formed from thin rough-hewn slate, contrasting with the carefully balanced and eye-catching seating arrangement.

Above: Three easily accessible compost bins allow for the gradual rotting-down of vegetation. Covering the bins with old carpet speeds up the process and deters airborne weeds.

Above: Recycled car tyres delineate the path between salad vegetables and medicinal plants in this eco-friendly garden where water conservation and composting are prioritized.

Above: A green roof planted with drought-tolerant sedums offers insulation, waterproofing and a means of drainage; permeable filter layers underlie the soil or growing medium.

Above: This turf and wildflower roof keeps the building well insulated. Turf can be supplied ready-grown, or a combination of seed mix and plug plants may be used.

Left: Concrete sewage-carrying pipes have been stacked to make unusual containers, giving height and a purpose to the curved stone steps.

Right: This simple mossy container, lined with black polythene and planted with drought-tolerant sedums, requires minimal watering.

Chapter 4
Creating a Planting Plan

Creating a Planting Plan

For many people who are planning a garden, the most exciting and challenging part of the process is choosing the plants. It is not simply a question of going to the local garden centre or nursery and filling up a trolley or shopping cart. Each plant has its own characteristics, situation and soil preferences, and you need to consider how the plants that you want to use will relate to your garden. As every site is different, there is no standard solution.

To design with plants, you need to know them—not just from photographs in a reference book or catalogue or by keeping a plant notebook (see page 277), but most importantly from frequent observation and, if possible, from growing them yourself. However, a collection of plants does not necessarily make a good garden. This chapter gives you guidelines for choosing plants that will create memorable, lasting groupings. Consideration is given to the importance of outline shape and also the texture and patterns of foliage.

Colour can be provided in both foliage and flowers, but flowers are fleeting and subject to seasonal change. Enduring far longer than flowers, foliage is often secondary in consideration to flower colour. A memorable planting scheme usually relies on outline plant shape, texture of leaves, colour of both leaves and flowers, and the relationship between each individual plant and neighbouring plants.

Much effort, time and money may be spent on the garden layout. Now the planting should be planned to harmonize with it and set it off, softening and contrasting with the harsher lines of man-made materials. It is usually the planting that most people remember.

The Role of Planting

You probably associate planting with bringing colour into your garden, which is a perfectly acceptable expectation. However, as plants play many more functional roles, such as providing a garden with structure, colour should not be the first consideration. Examining the different roles planting can play will help you identify your own planting objectives.

Structure and Enclosure

While developing the garden layout plan, you considered certain aspects of the planting, such as using plants to create the garden structure. For instance, you should have decided already which trees to include, and the location and type of any hedges. In shaping the various spaces, these decisions need to be taken early on in the design process because structural planting is as important as hard landscaping.

Plants chosen for structure are usually trees or shrubs which will provide height and bulk throughout the year, but remember that there are also many large herbaceous perennials that can dramatically affect the structure of the garden. Some taller perennials can reach the staggering height of 2 m (6.6 ft.) during the growing season, before dying right back to the ground in winter. Try to think through the effect of seasonal change in relation to the structure and height in your garden. The bare winter appearance will be very different from high summer when the flower-filled borders are at their peak.

There should be sufficient structural planting to enclose and shape each individual space, creating a series of garden "rooms" which can be enjoyed during the different seasons.

Enhancing Hard-Landscape Features

For a garden to read as a unified whole, the plants should work in harmony with the hard-landscaping features. Plants may be used as focal points, such as an ornamental tree at the end of a vista, or a topiary feature drawing attention to an alcove. Plants can also be used to direct movement through a garden, either by forming impenetrable masses or by marking a change in direction.

When choosing plants to function closely with hard structures, they should be of appropriate size, shape and growth potential. Avoid using vigorous plants for quick effect, which may result in narrowed paths, obscured views, and much thinning out later.

Relating the Garden to Its Surroundings

Whether in an urban or rural setting, you can use plants to unite the garden with the landscape beyond. In a country situation a garden can appear to merge with the local landscape by repeating native plants, or their ornamental forms, within the garden. In city gardens the shape of neighbouring buildings can be echoed or contrasted through the selection and arrangement of the plants.

In Chapter 1 the importance of considering a garden's setting to determine its style was emphasized. There are many different styles of planting, or ways of combining plants for different effects. Often, the climate, soil and aspect will rule out inappropriate styles. To take an extreme example, a woodland garden would not be appropriate, or even survive, on an urban rooftop. There are certain styles of planting that, although possible, would be out of character with the house and its surroundings. In a country setting particularly, the view for others may be spoilt if your planting detracts from the surrounding landscape. Think about the prevailing conditions of your site, and try to ensure that the chosen plants share the ability to thrive in them. Drought-resistant species that are able to cope with dry, hot seasons and desiccating winds will not live happily beside woodlanders that need shade from overhanging tree canopies and moisture in the soil.

Changing Scenes

Plants alter as they mature and adapt to the changing seasons. Just as a bare winter garden may look very different in summer when it is in full flower, a newly planted garden will look very different twenty years later.

One of the greatest challenges of designing with plants is to arrange combinations that create successional interest throughout the year. Seasonal changes can be dramatic, but try to take advantage of this by capturing the energy and rhythm of the seasons in your choice of plants.

Nonvisual Qualities of Plants

Probably the greatest role that plants play in a garden is their visual appeal, particularly when well grouped to provide an appealing arrangement of forms, textures and colours, but they also have other important qualities that should not be overlooked when choosing plants.

Scent

For most gardeners, scent is an important attribute. Some people have a strong sense of smell, and for them, too many contrasting scents in a small space can be disturbing. To the uninitiated it may be assumed that all roses have a scent, but the strength of the scent will vary from plant to plant, and this may affect your selection.

Not all scents are welcome in the garden. While flower blossom often has a sweet or perfumed scent, leaves and bark may be aromatic, some plants have a strong odour to attract flies, and others have an unpleasant pungent scent. *Salvia sclarea* is nicknamed "hot house maids" or "smelly socks" for a reason.

Sounds

Plants may produce sounds through their movement, such as the rustle of bamboo leaves in a breeze, and through the wildlife that inhabit them, such as the song of birds attracted to the garden. The bird population can increase rapidly as a garden matures, especially if the garden can be planned as a wildlife habitat.

Tactile appeal

For children in particular, the enjoyment of touching plants can give great pleasure. Feathery plumes of grasses, silken catkins and rough-textured bark are just a few examples. Other plants, such as the yucca with its spiky leaves, are an obvious deterrent.

Food for the table

Fruit, vegetables, herbs and nuts can make a garden useful as well as pleasurable. Distinguishing between edible and poisonous plants is crucial in designing gardens for young families. Organic produce is relatively expensive to buy and it is far more pleasurable to grow your own, even in a small space.

Principles of Planting Design

Plant material can also be used to fulfil particular requirements. Rather than focusing on different kinds of plants, concentrate on their general qualities of scale, form, colour and texture. Try also to sustain plant interest throughout the year, and match plants to your own site conditions while still giving them enough space to develop.

Scale and Proportion

The scale, or outline shape, height and spread of plants that you choose for a particular site can have an enormous influence on the mood of the garden. It is vital to get this right, because if plants are too large, a space may be claustrophobic, and if they are too small, the space may be exposed and unprotected. The scale of the planting should relate to adjoining buildings, to the size of the garden and to the scale of the human figure.

To achieve a sense of harmony in a garden, different groups of plants should relate to, or be in proportion

with, one another, both in scale and number. Try to achieve a balanced rhythm of different sizes and effects. If, for instance, you decided to place a large shrub on one side of the garden, you would need to balance this on the other side. An obvious thing to do would be to place another of the same on the other side, but if you wanted to use a smaller type

In this typical suburban plot, the neighbouring houses are very intrusive.

The same plot with some planting added. The tree helps to enclose the garden and give some privacy, but the other plants are too small, allowing the fences to dominate the scene.

Here, where the scale of the planting has been increased, the atmosphere of the garden is vastly improved. The trees relate well in scale to the size of the house and the shrubs are human-scaled. A good balance of enclosure and openness has been achieved.

If plants are too large in scale for the house, surroundings and size of plot, the garden may feel rather airless and cramped.

To achieve a sense of balance in the planting, one plant, or group of plants, must equal the mass of another.

The natural growth habit of the climber softens the brick wall.

Informal shrub planting contrasts with the straight lines of the border.

Low topiary masses reinforce the geometry of the house.

Here, a large shrub is counterbalanced by a group of smaller shrubs.

A tall slender tree, with low ground cover beneath, is balanced by a mass of shrub planting, which is intermediate in height.

Within the border, tall upright forms contrast with more rounded forms of different sizes, providing accents and rhythm to the composition.

of shrub, one would not be enough to balance the visual weight of the large shrub, so you would have to use several, perhaps three or five. Odd numbers create a natural effect, while even numbers can be more formal.

Shape and Form

Once you have established the scale of your planting, you should consider the shapes and forms for your plant groupings. At this stage, think about the plant outline rather than the shape of a particular leaf or flower. Drawing elevations (projecting your planting plans onto a vertical plane) is a useful way of trying out different ideas (see page 228). What you are aiming for is a group of contrasting forms

that combine to form a balanced whole, just as if you were composing a still life grouping for a painting. For inspiration, observe the garden's surroundings. Are there any obvious shapes, such as distant hills or rounded clumps of trees that you may like to echo or contrast? If the surrounding area is flat and dry, it might be better to use fairly low clumps of planting, occasionally interrupted with a taller architectural shrub or eye-catching cactus.

Grouping plants

Plan the planting with groups of plants rather than individual plants. A single iris, for instance, could not balance a large rounded shrub, but a large group of irises could do so effectively as the volume, or mass, would be similar.

Repeating plant groups

When planning the outline form of your planting, be sure to repeat effects across the garden to relate one area to another. Repeating plants is one way of restricting the variety of plants used in a plan, usually resulting in strong, bold effects as opposed to the "dot" approach (one of this here, one of that there) which always looks restless.

Layers of planting

Try to plan the planting in layers, whether horizontally or vertically. Make beds that are large enough to accommodate more than one plant's width, so that plants can be placed in front of, or behind, other plants. This layering effect, where some plants are partly obscured by others, will give your planting depth.

Where space is at a premium and beds are narrow, plants can be layered vertically, similar to the way they sometimes coexist in nature. In woodland, for example, the plants arrange themselves in several "storeys", with the foliage of large trees at the top, smaller trees and shrubs directly beneath them, and herbaceous plants and bulbs at the bottom. Planting that is planned in this way can occupy the same area of ground for several effects, since both spring and autumn flowering bulbs may be planted between herbaceous plants. Above these, the shrubs and overhanging trees may each have two seasons of interest, enhancing the overall composition.

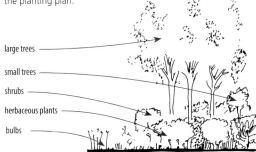

Imitating the layering of natural plant groups works effectively to create depth in the planting plan.

large trees
small trees
shrubs
herbaceous plants
bulbs

Texture

Texture follows on from deciding on the shape and form of the planting, and is mainly defined by the leaves of a plant. Like fabric, plant leaves have varying qualities of roughness and smoothness, from very coarse to extremely fine, and as many different finishes. Their surfaces may resemble such materials as fur, velvet, suede, sandpaper, leather and plastic. To show off the textural qualities of a plant to greatest effect, contrast it with another of very different texture. In some plants, the underside of the leaf contrasts markedly with the top side.

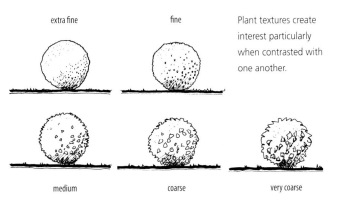

extra fine

fine

Plant textures create interest particularly when contrasted with one another.

medium

coarse

very coarse

Light quality

Texture affects the quality of light reflected or absorbed by a plant. The leaves of some plants are shiny and light-reflective, while others are matt and light-absorbent. A mass of bright glossy leaves can bring life to a dark corner, while a plant with matt leaves may provide a perfect foil for more colourful or decorative subjects.

Experiment with using different textures in your garden, varying the proportion of rough textures with smooth, metallic with furry and so on. It is usually best to allow one texture to predominate, repeating it across the garden to relate one area to another.

Colour

The concept of colour in a garden always seems to be associated with planting, although all hard-landscaping features, such as walls or paving, will also give colour to the overall composition. Although you may prefer a certain colour palette in planting, it may not suit the existing hard-landscape colour. Often it is wiser to consider the backdrop first and then choose your colours to complement or contrast with this.

Using plant colour to influence perspective

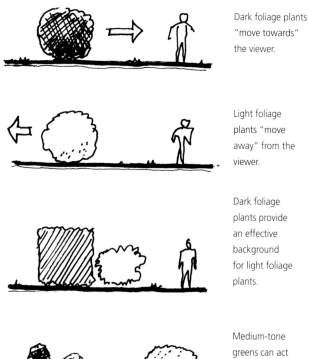

Dark foliage plants "move towards" the viewer.

Light foliage plants "move away" from the viewer.

Dark foliage plants provide an effective background for light foliage plants.

Medium-tone greens can act as a transition between dark and light greens.

Spatial tricks

The overall design can be accentuated by using plant colour. For instance, it can be used very effectively to influence perspective. Cool colours, such as pale blues, pale browns, whites and greys, introduced

at a distance, will have the effect of lengthening a view, while hot colours, such as strong reds and vivid oranges, clamour for attention and tend to advance towards the viewer. For this reason you should avoid using strong colours in the path of an important view, as the colours will compete with the view and distract attention from it. However, if something needs to be hidden, strong colours will arrest the eye, distracting it from the scene beyond.

Colour from foliage, bark and stems

Although flower colour seems to be most people's primary concern, when you are designing with plants, you should concentrate on more permanent colour, particularly in leaves, bark and stems.

Leaves have a wide range of colours. Within the green range alone there are yellow-greens, grey-greens and glaucous or blue-greens, not to mention purple, crimson and yellow foliage. Leaves may also be variegated or have margins that are a different colour from the main leaf. In some plants the emergent leaves are a fresh pale green, yellow or even pink, but as they mature they dull down. Consider seasonal colour variations as an unexpected asset. Particularly with plants partial to acid soils, autumn leaf colour can vary from bright oranges through vibrant reds to rich purples, and can transform the appearance of the garden towards the end of the growing season when rich, vibrant tones show up the autumn sunlight.

Some plants, particularly certain deciduous trees and shrubs, can have the additional attraction of coloured bark and stems to provide interest in the winter months.

Light

Our perception of colour is affected by light, which is why painters traditionally opt for studios facing north, where the light variation is minimized. As light intensity increases, all colours tend to fade, but stronger hues, such as vivid reds and oranges, retain more brilliance than muted colours, which may be completely "bleached out" by the fierce sunlight typical of tropical countries. In the bluish light of temperate climates, colours are perceived differently—muted colours tend to glow, while stronger colours can look garish. As evening approaches and the sun begins to redden, bright colours tend to be enriched and then deepen to violet and black. Paler colours, particularly white, will continue to glow long after the brighter colours have faded. This effect can be applied to planting in shade. Whites and pale yellows will tend to gleam, while warm reds, greens and blues will become darker. Use paler shades if the garden is mainly to be used in the evening; stronger colours, such as reds and purple, tend to disappear as daylight fades.

Adjacent colours

As well as being modified by light, the hue of a colour is affected by its neighbours. When you place one colour next to another, both colours will be affected by each other's presence, and the difference between them will become more exaggerated. This applies not only when colours are seen simultaneously but also when one colour is observed immediately before another. This is why white gardens, filled predominantly with white flowers and grey foliage, appear more intense if approached through an area of hot colour.

Altering mood

Colour affects people in different ways, but in general, reds are associated with warmth and stimulation and blues and greens with coolness and tranquility. You can use these associations creatively to change the perception of a space. For instance, a hot courtyard, on which the sun blazes down, can seem cooler if planted with silvers, cool blues and harsh whites, while a cold, north-facing area can be enlivened by flame, orange, apricot and yellow. In deep shade, however, these strong colours will darken and disappear. You can make a rather sunless area appear brighter with yellow flowers or foliage, much of which will thrive better in shade than in direct sunlight.

Colour themes

The easiest, but nonetheless very effective, way of using colour in planting is one that frequently occurs in nature—to have a mass of one type of plant providing the colour statement at a given time. Far from being boring, the eye often appreciates a rest from being besieged with colour.

Single-colour schemes are particularly effective if used with foliage of a contrasting or complementary colour. Good examples of this technique include yellow flowers or leaves combined with grey foliage, and red flowers with bronze or purple foliage.

An extension of the single colour theme is to use a combination of plants with the same basic colour but subtle variations of hue and intensity. This can be very striking, and there is a tremendous amount of plant material available. For success, try to achieve a balance of deep, medium and pale shades.

Broadly, all flower and foliage colour is based on either blue or yellow. In the blue range are the hard whites, all the bluish pinks, magentas, crimson-reds and purples, as well as the true blues. In the yellow range are warm whites, yellow, orange, orange-pinks (apricot, salmon and the sunset shades) and all the scarlet-reds. If either range is used alone, there will never be a clash, since all the colours derive from a single base. Sometimes a good clash is needed to enliven a space or to stimulate our colour appreciation, preventing a bland effect. Lead up to a clash with an arrangement of less demanding tones, allowing a good stretch of neutral colouring before introducing another clash.

In the fashion trade, colour preferences come and go, and there are similar fashions in planting. To make an occasional very bold statement in your planting, contrast form, texture and colour at the same time. Be careful not to overdo it, however, or the statement will lose impact and become irritating.

Seasonal Changes in Plant Compositions

To achieve well-balanced seasonal effects you need to consider your proposed planting throughout the year. To do this you should observe plants in every season. The effect of spring foliage is just as important as flower colour, berries and autumn leaf colour, while the colour and texture of winter stems and twigs may be a greater asset than the heavy foliage produced by these plants in high summer. To observe plants in intimate detail, there is no substitute for growing them yourself. Even failing to grow them satisfactorily will teach you something about their needs! But if this is impossible, you should at least regularly observe the same plants over the seasons in your local park or botanical garden.

You may find it a challenge to introduce and arrange plants to provide interest throughout the seasons. In some gardens, or in parts of gardens that are only used at certain times of the year, this may not be wanted, but most people will want at least one part of the garden to have some interest in the winter. Avoid scattering little bits of interest throughout the garden; although this may provide something in bloom every month of the year, the overall visual result is rarely effective. Far better to designate a particular season of interest to different areas, so that each area in turn holds the attention, while the remainder of the garden forms a quiet green background, awaiting its moment to perform.

The level of seasonal change differs throughout the world. Some are very extreme, some almost constant. In temperate areas, there are four clearly defined seasons that present four distinctively different pictures (unless the planting is entirely evergreen).

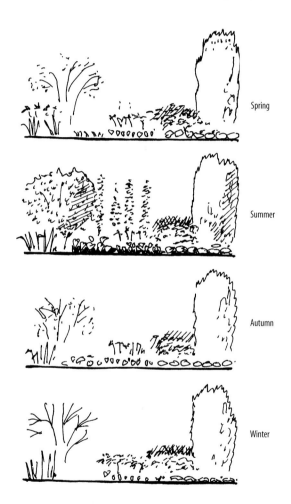

Spring

Summer

Autumn

Winter

Small elevation sketches will help you to consider the effect of the seasons on a planting plan.

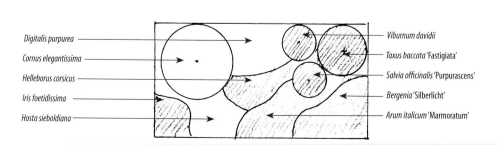

Digitalis purpurea

Cornus elegantissima

Helleborus corsicus

Iris foetidissima

Hosta sieboldiana

Viburnum davidii

Taxus baccata 'Fastigiata'

Salvia officinalis 'Purpurascens'

Bergenia 'Silberlicht'

Arum italicum 'Marmoratum'

Spring effects

In spring, trees and shrubs will be covered in developing foliage, with the branch and twig structure still clearly visible, while herbaceous plants of varying height begin to appear through the ground. In both cases, leaves may predominate and be at their most attractive when young and fresh.

Summer and autumn effects

Summer shows solid outlines of texture, with herbaceous plants gradually becoming taller as the summer progresses. In many gardens, the flowering season is at its peak in late spring to midsummer. Individual plants tend to merge into groups, and it is hard to reconcile the overall abundance with the bare winter scene. From midsummer to late summer, this abundance becomes less interesting, many plants having "gone over" and no longer flowering but still providing greenery in the foliage. By early autumn, interest is rekindled as late-flowering plants come into bloom, often set off against a background of richly coloured autumnal foliage.

Winter effects

Although gardens are mainly dormant in winter, they can still look beautiful. Often this is because the bones of the design, which give a garden its strength, are only revealed as the foliage recedes. Most herbaceous plants and many ground covers will have gone below ground. Trees and certain shrubs will have a skeletal outline, while other more twiggy shrubs will still appear very solid. Evergreen plants will retain their bulk and outline. Plants that appear quite recessive during the other seasons (a light-absorbent conifer, for instance) may now become the dominant feature. An appealing winter garden relies heavily on structural plants that are selected for their outline shapes, helping to maintain interest year-round.

Practical Considerations

Although there are numerous plants to choose from when you are designing a garden, the physical conditions of a site—the soil, aspect, exposure and climate, for instance—will restrict what can be grown in a particular place. Unless your plant knowledge is good, you will need to do some research to check on individual plant preferences.

To understand these individual preferences, try to find out where plants originate, be it Japan, Switzerland, South Africa or the Mediterranean. By planting them in conditions that are as similar to their natural habitat as possible, they should have an

What is hardy in one area may not be elsewhere.

In a seaside location salt winds can desiccate plants.

Plants must be chosen for their tolerance of given conditions. Many plants can tolerate the fumes and pollution of a traffic-side location.

increased chance of thriving. If you cannot offer such conditions, do not try to grow the plant. Lavender, for instance, found in dry, sandy soils in the Mediterranean would never do well in shady, damp conditions. In addition to plants that originate in foreign countries, there are many native wildflowers and shrubs that are garden-worthy and may be easier to grow than introduced species. They too need the appropriate type of soil and growing conditions. Although we all want to place our plants where they will look attractive, it is even more important to plant them where they will thrive. Choosing plants that will only succeed by undertaking artificial fertilizing, watering and other unnatural conditions is always a mistake, as they will look out of place even if they do survive, and will use up a great deal of resources in the process.

Using Existing Plants

You may wish to retain certain existing plants, which can either be moved or kept where they are. Mature small trees or shrubs may need to be root pruned six months prior to the move, and the overall height and spread reduced by a third. Root pruning is achieved by digging around the plant while it is in its existing position, to reduce the spread of the roots. This process encourages the plant to send up new, smaller rootlets that will adapt more readily to the subsequent new position. Reduction of the overall height and spread reduces the amount of energy a plant must use to support its overall size, and as it is smaller, this reduces the likelihood of root damage caused by wind rock.

An existing plant will often look out of proportion in association with newer plants, but with careful pruning to reduce the overall bulk, the plant can be more easily integrated. Existing clumps of herbaceous plants may be split up into several smaller clumps and reused elsewhere in a planting scheme. If you are replanning a mature garden, the kitchen garden could perhaps be used as a temporary holding area, allowing you to dig up the existing

plants, line them up in close knit rows and then replant them in new borders later.

Existing clumps of herbaceous perennials may be suitable for dividing.

Plant Spacing

When drawing up a plan of your planting on paper, you will allocate spaces to be occupied by mature plants (a standard approach is to show them at their approximate height and spread after five years). On your planting plan, you will only need to show the spread, but you may also wish to draw an elevation, which will show both height and spread.

A mature shrub may eventually reach 600 mm (2 ft.) in height and 900 mm (3 ft.) in spread, but when first planted it may take up as little space as 150 × 150 mm (6 × 6 in.). Do not be tempted to overplant the remaining space by placing shrubs too close together. This can quickly lead to overcrowding as the plants grow, resulting in poorly shaped trees and shrubs. Far better to use filler plants that can later be removed as the main plant matures.

Ideal filler candidates include annuals and bulbs, as well as fibrous-rooted shrubs that not only grow quickly but also have a short lifespan. In five years or so, these plants tend to become rather straggly and can easily be removed. In the meantime, the slower-growing, longer-lasting shrubs will gradually fill in the lessened gaps. It is unwise to apply the same system to trees, since quick-growing "filler" trees take too much moisture and nutrients out of the soil. Vigorous ground covers should also be avoided, at least in the first two or three years, as they tend to compete with young shrubs for soil nutrients. Ground cover can always be added later, possibly when the infill shrubs are removed.

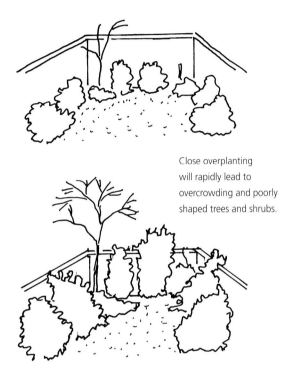

Close overplanting will rapidly lead to overcrowding and poorly shaped trees and shrubs.

Planting Styles

Before you begin drawing up the planting plan, you should reconsider your original ideas for the garden. Now that the hard-landscaping decisions have been made, think how you will complement these with the plantings. Try to imagine that you are walking through the garden—beginning, for instance, at the terrace adjacent to the house—and ask yourself two important questions: What style of planting would be appropriate for each area? What season or seasons would you expect a particular bed to peak or perform at its best?

A clear idea of the style of planting needed to complement the garden layout plan may have

evolved while you were working your way through the planning stage. Now you need to translate this style into its essential parts. This stage is rather like painting a picture. It is very difficult to paint something if you do not have a clear idea of what you are trying to paint.

We have already considered how the architectural and interior style should be repeated in the garden design, and you should adopt a similar approach when choosing your plants. House, garden and plants should work together as a unified whole, each enhancing the qualities of the others. In this way it is often the house or the location that will determine the planting style.

First decide whether the style should be formal or informal. Which is most appropriate to the house and its setting? Formal designs are based on straight lines, often with a strict pattern of clipped box or yew outlining geometric shapes of squares, rectangles or circles. An informal design may be based on the more natural lines of gentle curves and meandering paths with plants spilling over the edges. Consider also how your design will affect the surroundings and environment, using locally produced and sourced materials where possible. Think through the impact of the workload you are imposing on the site; maintenance, or the lack of it, may be a wise point to consider at the outset.

Formal

Many people feel more comfortable creating a formal garden, reassured by the simplicity of the style. It is still possible, within the strict geometric shapes, to have luxuriant groups of flowing plants set off or framed by the formal scheme to create a romantic effect. The simplicity of a formal design is not only confined to historical associations but also blends well with modern minimalist buildings. Repetition of plants and a limited number of genera is often the hallmark of a formal garden.

Informal

Informal gardens may imitate the bends and curves of nature, but in nature there is usually a reason for the bend or curve, such as to avoid a tree, large rock or pool. Curves should be generous, allowing you to move around them slowly, and should be emphasized at the widest point by a tree or group of shrubs. Any curves may be created by cutting the border outline around a garden hose laid out on turf. Unless you make your curves generous, not only will they look unnatural and self-conscious but the wiggles will also be emphasized when viewed in perspective from the house. Informal planting allows the use of many relatively modern plants such as grasses and herbaceous perennials, or hostas, ferns and other woodland plants.

Romantic

The romantic style is perhaps personified by the cottage garden, often appearing to have a simple and tender charm where roses, honeysuckle and lavender mingle with fruit and vegetables. Our current popular perception of a cottage garden is an idealized version of a style that evolved from the need to survive on what could be grown on a small holding. Then and now the planting is insubstantial and only performs for a limited season. Romantic gardens tend to have curves, hidden seating, framed vistas and plants whose scent is seductive or nostalgic. Planting in romantic gardens relies on old favourites such as roses, honeysuckle (*Lonicera*), catmint (*Nepeta*), phlox and other scented plants.

Natural

Natural gardens, now enjoying a resurgence of popularity, were originally the concept of the Victorian gardener William Robinson. Through the developed world, our current positive movement towards conservation has resulted in a style of wildflower gardening that mimics natural habitats, working with nature and with plants that would occur organically in these conditions. Poppies,

cornflowers and the semi-parasitic yellow rattle (*Rhinanthus minor*) all combine for the natural effect.

Japanese

Japanese gardens fall into two distinct categories: the "borrowed" garden, a landscape garden that incorporates distant scenery as part of its design, and the "small courtyard" or "tea" garden, an enclosed space where carefully placed stones, gravel, trees and shrubs combine with lanterns and water basins. Space, illusion and the careful control of natural elements are part of the Japanese culture. They can be very effective in a small space and work well with modern or minimalist buildings. Many of our favourite plants originated in Asia, and include a wide range of shrubs such as bamboo, camellia, hydrangea and viburnum.

Modern

Modern-style gardens can be very functional and are an antidote to the traditional English image. These are usually gardens in which Perspex, steel tubing or other modern material is used instead of traditional brick or timber. They might incorporate walls painted in strong contemporary colours that combine with plants in complementary or contrasting colours. The cone flower (*Echinacea*), eryngiums, sedums and other herbaceous perennials and grasses are appropriate in a modern setting.

Sustainable

In areas where drought or times of water shortage makes growing plants difficult, it makes sense to grow plants that will survive with less water, using those that are not only drought tolerant but that also look attractive. A 6-in. (150-mm) minimum layer of gravel or a similar mixture of eighty percent grit and twenty percent loam allows for drainage during wet periods, and this can be topped by a 2-in. (50-mm) mulch of crushed stone, glass chippings, sea shells or other sustainable locally sourced (carbon-neutral) material.

Planting is usually best done just after the autumn downpours, when the soil may stay reasonably moist until the spring, allowing the plants to establish their roots without being dependent on watering. Use plants that provide food sources and habitats for animals, and that take minimal management. Drought-tolerant shrubs include *Skimmia*, the castor oil plant (*Fatsia japonica*), holly (*Ilex*) and *Euonymus fortunei*. Perennials may include spurge (*Euphorbia*), hardy geraniums, ice plants (*Sedum*), sea holly (*Eryngium*) and many bulbs.

Productive

Few types of gardening are as rewarding as growing your own vegetables, herbs and fruit. A productive garden is a simple step towards a more sustainable lifestyle, and it can be surprisingly easy and satisfying.

Even a small space can be productive, either by interplanting ornamental vegetables such as carrots and parsley between the flowering plants, planting thyme (*Thymus*) between cracks in paving, growing tomatoes and other crops in growbags or containers, using decorative wooden or metal tripods to support climbing runner beans, cucumbers or gourds, devoting an area of the garden to kitchen crops or taking on an allotment where possible. The cabbage family do best under netting, the smaller butterfly netting preventing birds and the cabbage white butterfly from laying eggs (which eventually turn into hungry caterpillars) on the leaves. Slower-growing crops such as cabbage can be interplanted with faster-growing ones such as lettuce or radish to ensure you make the most of the space. Three- or four-year successional crop rotation will be necessary to prevent exhausting the soil and to avoid disease such as club root on cabbages.

Soft fruit such as raspberries and currants are best grown under netting to deter birds. Fruit trees can be very decorative and one or two will produce enough fruit for the average family. A decorative potager, perhaps edged with box (*Buxus*), wild strawberries or parsley, looks very attractive and need not take up much space.

Arid

Arid environments must rank as the most challenging to the existence of plants. Typically arid areas are baked by the sun during the day, often freezing cold at night, buffeted by wind and parched by lack of rain. Plants that do well here have cleverly adapted themselves to cope with these conditions by leaf and root modification. Tiny leaves, such as those of thyme (*Thymus*), help to cut transpiration due to their small surface area; slim or incurved foliage like that of *Pennisetum orientale* and many other grasses serves a similar purpose. The thick, fleshy leaves of *Sedum* and *Agave* store food and moisture as a thick, sticky sap. Silver foliage, like that of lavender (*Lavandula*) reflects the sun, and hairy leaves trap any moisture in the air, even if the plant is growing straight out of rock as in the case of *Saponaria*.

Lower-growing plants are less likely to be uprooted by wind, especially during their formative years. Many plants survive by putting down a tap root, searching deep for water and nutrients, storing the food and moisture and locking the plant into the soil at the same time.

Coastal

Coastal gardens are usually buffeted by salt-laden wind, with tree branches and other taller vegetation being swept in the leeward direction. Often frost free, this climate allows a wide range of plants to thrive. Trees and shrubs are most likely to succeed if planted firmly when small, allowing their roots to grip the soil before they become tall enough to be affected by the wind. Silver plants, such as *Buddleja* and *Crambe* and evergreens like *Arbutus* and *Choisya* should do well, as will *Hydrangea*, *Hebe* and *Fuchsia*.

Native

A burgeoning popular interest in biodiversity and encouraging wildlife has been leading many gardeners to seek out more natural-looking plants whose pollen- and nectar-rich properties are attractive to indigenous wildlife. Many of these are wild plants not necessarily native to Britain, continental Europe or the United States; often they have been selected and propagated or bred from the wild for their garden-worthiness. They may not be able to take the place of native flora in providing food sources for many invertebrates, such as butterflies, which depend on specific food plants such as lady's smock and hedge mustard. However, in providing some native species among the ornamentals, even a clump of stinging nettles, you will encourage a wider range of wildlife. Make sure that any native plants bought have been legally sourced, and try to obtain locally propagated stock; otherwise the plants may not have the same genetic characteristics.

Naturalistic

In the naturalistic style of gardening, plants are selected for their similar cultural requirements so that they can grow together with minimal human intervention. The principle of "right plant, right place" is central to this movement; rather than placing dry sun-lovers right next to plants that prefer a nutrient-rich soil and plenty of water, plants are placed in the garden spots where they are most likely to thrive naturally. Many of the plants commonly used in this style have either occurred in the wild or been bred to retain their toughness while enhancing their foliage or flowering qualities. As naturalistic planting requires less watering and maintenance, it uses fewer natural resources and is a sustainable alternative to more traditional planting styles.

The large-scale plantings of Piet Oudolf and James van Sweden using grasses and herbaceous perennials have been hugely influential in promoting a naturalistic approach, but the scale can easily be broken down to fill a much smaller space. For instance, billowing perennials such as *Echinacea*, *Persicaria* and *Helianthus* might be combined with grasses such as *Miscanthus*, *Panicum* and *Stipa*. With the plants growing together, there is no need to stake individual plants. This "prairie" style attracts wildlife and provides pollen and seedheads; best from summer until early frosts, the seedheads themselves provide winter interest. Naturalistic planting and design may look haphazard, but to get it right demands skill and attention to detail.

Water and Aquatic Habitats

Of all the elements deployed to increase sustainability and biodiversity in gardens, water is of the greatest benefit, attracting a wide range of creatures from those that live in or on the water to occasional visiting animals that may use it to drink or bathe. Unless their numbers are strictly controlled, ornamental fish have a tendency to consume other smaller water inhabitants, disrupting the natural balance. A wide range of pond plants will increase the presence of wildlife and create a natural appearance. These plants can be divided into three groups: submerged, bog and marginal plants. Submerged plants and oxygenating species include the water hawthorn (*Aponogeton distachyos*) and water lilies (*Nymphaea*), which create shade and help prevent algae from growing; bog plants such as the yellow skunk cabbage (*Lysichiton americanus*) and the umbrella plant (*Darmera peltata*), which provide cover for amphibians to get in and out of the water, as well as providing a leafy edge to the pond; and marginal plants, such as the marsh marigold (*Caltha palustris*) and the yellow flag iris (*Iris pseudacorus*), which bridge the transition between the water's edge and the bog plants. Always ensure that the pond's edge includes a small semi-submerged level area to allow wildlife to get in and out of the water.

Following the Theme

Once you have decided on a style, you can begin to select plants to carry the theme through. Always do this with conviction, keeping in mind the effect that you want to create, rather than allowing yourself to be seduced by some pretty but inappropriate plant that you have just discovered in a catalogue.

Base your decisions on how the garden is going to be used. If it is unlikely that you (or the garden owner) will stroll down to the far end of the garden in winter, think of placing plants for winter interest near the house, where they can be enjoyed from an indoor window on a winter day. Similarly, scented plants should be placed where they will be most appreciated, such as surrounding a paved terrace or on top of a low retaining wall, where the scent will be nearer to your nose as you pass.

Creating a Planting Plan

You may intend to plant the garden yourself, or you may ask a contractor or nurseryman to plant it for you, but in either case a detailed planting plan will be necessary. A planting plan is a working drawing—it will be taken onto the site, and each plant will be set out on the soil in the position indicated on the plan. Often this work takes place in the wind or rain, so the planting plan must be clear, legible and easy to understand. Plant names should all be written at the same angle, with spacing and numbers clearly indicated. If the garden is large, several smaller planting plans for small areas are more easily handled than one large sheet.

What to Include

The planting plan is drawn up on a simplified form of the garden layout plan. It shows, using symbols, the planting position and spread of every plant (after about five years' growth) that you intend to include in the garden, labelled with its precise Latin name (genus, species and cultivar or variety), correctly spelt, and the exact number of plants in any grouping. The plan will also include any existing plants, in their original positions or sited elsewhere.

In the accompanying plant list, all the plants will be grouped according to category—tree, shrub, climber and so on—and then arranged alphabetically, with the precise number of plants required in each case. Since the objective of compiling a plant list is to enable you to place an order for the plants, it will be appreciated by the supplier or nursery if your list follows the same format as the catalogue pages. Most nursery catalogues categorize plants as follows:

— Trees
— Shrubs
— Climbers
— Roses
— Herbaceous perennials
— Ferns
— Bamboos and grasses
— Bulbs
— Annuals and half-hardies

The plan must be drawn up so that the positions, names and numbers of the plants are clear, legible and easily understood by whoever may be carrying out the planting. With so much information to communicate, it is always quite a challenge to produce a plan that is well labelled. In many text books this problem is circumvented using a key or number system in which, to identify a particular plant or plant grouping, the reader must consult a separate list. This approach is both tedious for whoever is studying the plan and difficult to follow when planting. It is far better to label each plant as near to its symbol as possible, ensuring that label lines do not cross.

The Stages Involved

Begin a rough draft of your planting plan, and try out ideas on a simplified version of your garden layout plan, perhaps also experimenting by drawing elevations to see the effect of contrasting heights. After you have finalized the selection and placement of all the plants you intend to use on a rough sheet, draw up the plan properly on a separate sheet. When

Small garden
A simplified garden layout. The horizontal plane (the garden) and the vertical plane (the house) will be linked once the structural planting is added.

Far right: structural plants (trees and shrubs) are the first to be put in place. The trees and topiary give important vertical emphasis to the space.

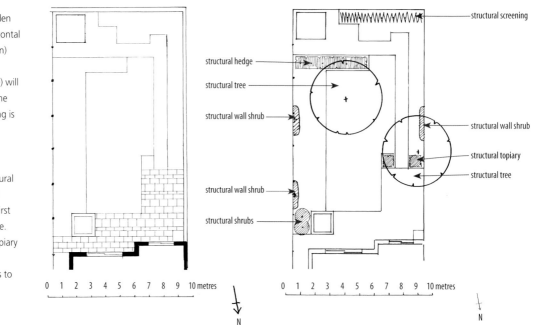

structural screening

structural hedge

structural tree

structural wall shrub

structural wall shrub

structural topiary

structural tree

structural wall shrub

structural shrubs

0 1 2 3 4 5 6 7 8 9 10 metres

N

0 1 2 3 4 5 6 7 8 9 10 metres

N

all the graphic symbols are in place, carry out your labelling.

The easiest way of working up a planting plan is to start with the largest items (including the trees from the final garden layout plan), then the structural and key planting, working down gradually towards the smallest plants. The stages of planning the planting for a small garden shown in this chapter demonstrate the way the different elements can be built up. These stages are structural planting (including trees), key planting, decorative planting and herbaceous planting.

Structural Planting

Start with the structural plants (mainly trees and shrubs), and try to think through their seasonal effects. Consider the following questions:

— Are there any additional areas where you would like to see some permanent form?
— For these areas, would you like the plant or group of plants to be evergreen, or would you prefer a deciduous plant with a twiggy winter outline?

— Think about climbers and wall shrubs. Are there any parts of the garden that require these to emphasize the framework?
— Imagine the garden in winter. Will there be enough structural form to hold interest when many herbaceous plants have disappeared below ground?

While developing the structural planting, remember to repeat plants across the garden diagonally. This repetition will help link one area to another, acting as a foil for the more transitory seasonal or colour groupings. It will also provide continuity and prevent a restless effect.

Try shading in the evergreen plants on the plan. This will remind you to look for a good balance of evergreen and deciduous plants, such as one-third of one type to two-thirds of the other. It will also help you in the next stage to position the more decorative shrubs, whose delicate foliage or pretty flowers may be enhanced against an evergreen backdrop.

Trees, when viewed from a distance, are arresting perpendiculars that link sky, house and garden.

Choosing a tree or trees for a garden is always an exciting task; most of us will not plant many trees or see them mature during our lives, so the long-term effect and consequences (of shade, for instance) must be considered. Planting trees can also offset carbon emissions, and provide shelter or a wildlife habitat.

Trees and shrubs

The difference between a tree and a large shrub is often unclear, but for the most part a tree is a woody plant, evergreen or deciduous, that has had the lower branches removed at an early stage, resulting in a single clear main stem or trunk. A shrub has either several stems, or a main stem with branches along most of its length. The exceptions to this are multistemmed trees, which have two or even three main stems deliberately left for aesthetic effect. These can be very effective on a corner or to give a natural effect, the disadvantage being that as they mature, the leaf canopy becomes heavier and occasionally one of the stems or trunks breaks off, spoiling the effect and outline shape. Occasionally a large shrub, having outgrown its allotted space, may become too dense, casting heavy shade onto the space beneath the branches. Consider the effect of removing several of the lower branches—this way, the large overgrown shrub may be turned into a multistemmed tree or a specimen with a single main stem or trunk.

Using existing trees

There may be existing trees in the garden, perhaps serving the purpose of screening or giving shade. The majority of trees mature slowly, and it may be wiser to improve the outline shape by tree surgery or by judicious thinning or pruning rather than removal

or replacement. If the canopy of a mature tree is reduced by carefully removing up to thirty percent of its branches, more light will be admitted, often showing off the tree silhouette better and giving dappled, as opposed to dense, shade. Decisions on which limbs or branches to remove are best made when the tree is in active growth or full leaf, but the actual cutting or tree surgery should be left until growth subsides in late autumn or early winter. The offending branches can be clearly marked with paint and removed later. Dead branches should always be removed to prevent disease, decay or injury.

Evergreen versus deciduous trees

Deciding between evergreen and deciduous trees may depend on whether something needs to be hidden or screened. Deciduous trees (those that shed their leaves in winter) will only be fully effective while leaves are in full growth. However, even a leafless tree in winter can interrupt and therefore dilute the full impact of what is hidden in summer. The eye will rest on what is in the foreground and often will not stray beyond. A line of deciduous trees can blur the vision of what lies beyond, as well as making it more difficult for neighbours to see into your property. There is usually a wider choice of deciduous trees, but if an evergreen variety is needed, the decision must be based not only on what tree is wanted but also the size of the foliage and whether the leaves are glossy and light-reflective or matt and light-absorbent.

Conifers

Used judiciously to avoid an overpowering effect, conifers provide a year-round statement, and are

With careful pruning, a shrub can be trained to resemble a small tree.

effective in removing harmful particle pollution from the air. However, dense coniferous planting can appear alien to the surroundings and many conifers will grow to a great height unless kept under control; their thirsty roots tend to dry out the surrounding area, making it difficult to grow other plants nearby.

Choosing trees

Most trees live fifty to two hundred years or more, so it is vital that your decision takes into account both short-term and long-term effects. Consider the following points:

— Outline shape or form (for example, rounded, dome, pencil and weeping)
— Classification as deciduous or evergreen (this will depend on the desired effect and whether screening is needed)
— Leaf texture, shape and colour (including texture or colour on the underside of foliage and whether the tree is early or late into leaf)
— Flower shape, colour and scent, and the time of flowering
— Berry or hip shape, colour and attractiveness to birds
— Trunk or stem bark type and colour

rounded

The size of a tree and its outline shape are significant factors in choosing a tree.

upright or fastigiate

horizontal

weeping

decorative

— Winter silhouette (if the tree is deciduous, this varies enormously)
— Size at maturity (among the most important aspects to consider)
— Whether they blend in or contrast with the local landscape or other planting

Tree size

Large forest-type trees, such as beech, ash or oak, should only be considered if there is plenty of space and if you are prepared to wait for the trees to mature. If the garden backs onto a beech wood, for instance, a copper beech or a red oak might stand out against the native varieties beyond. Many of these trees will eventually have a spread of 30 m (100 ft.) or more, their intrinsic beauty being in their outline shape. If planted too close to a building or to each other, the effect will be lost, and the roots may cause damage. Choose a smaller tree, or group of trees, in preference to lopping off oversized branches and spoiling the outline shape. Large mature trees can be found but are heavy to lift and plant, need support by staking and are expensive.

Medium-sized trees are usually preferable for most gardens and tend to grow more rapidly. With a wide variety to choose from it is particularly important to consider all aspects when making your choice. In a small garden a medium-sized tree must have all the attributes to earn its keep. Try to see mature specimens in a park or botanical garden so that the different features can be compared. Research the origin of the tree to ensure that local conditions are suitable, and bear in mind that trees also have preferences for acid and alkaline conditions. When bulk is needed, perhaps at the end of a drive or to give height at the end of a garden, a group of three, five or more of the same variety will look more natural than a mixed group.

Small ornamental trees are useful when used singly as focal points in smaller gardens and can also be grouped together to give a formal or informal effect.

Buying and ordering trees

It is always wise to inspect a tree before you order or buy. Many trees are raised close together in rows, sometimes under a polytunnel (hoop house), resulting in a deformed canopy which can take several years, if ever, to regain its classic outline shape. The tree, like many shrubs, may also be pot-bound or suckering from the base of the stem, or from where it has been grafted onto the parent stock. In their formative years all trees need staking to prevent wind rock until the roots spread and grip the soil. It is usually easier to order tree stakes and tree ties to be delivered at the same time. Less visually demanding native genera such as beech (*Fagus*) and oak (*Quercus*) may suit an informal design and are often more easily sourced.

Shrubs as structural plants

Shrubs must be solid or structural enough in character to form part of the framework of the garden. Flimsy leaves and spasmodic flowers will not give a feeling of permanence and security. Ultimate size must be considered, but a solid effect can be achieved with tall columns of Irish yew, low-clipped balls of box, or other structural plants such as *Mahonia* or *Choisya ternata*. To be effective, structural plants often need to be repeated, either formally as "exclamation marks" through a border or as informal singles or groups. Structural plants usually need to be evergreen to retain their effect.

Use structural plants to emphasize the pattern or shape of your garden layout. A group of five, nine or more low shrubs, all of the same type, can frame the corner of a border or can lead the eye around a circle or curve, acting as a perpetual contrast to the other more ephemeral planting.

Key Planting

Key plants are those that will provide important focal points in your garden, and these need to be identified next. These plants have strongly defined outlines and can be used occasionally or repeatedly for accent. They will act as strong key elements on which the eye will

Small garden
Key planting is added to the structural plants. The strongly defined shapes of these key plants will allow the eye to rest before taking in the other plantings.

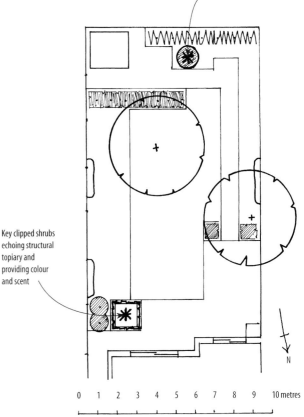

Key shrubs providing strongly defined shape, contrasting with hedges

Key clipped shrubs echoing structural topiary and providing colour and scent

0 1 2 3 4 5 6 7 8 9 10 metres

N

rest before continuing to take in other plantings. Key plants should stand out from the rest of the plants with some distinctive quality, such as a strongly defined or contrasting shape, texture or colour. Key plants are often also structural, forming a link to the surrounding landscape, or they may act as pivots, emphasizing a change of direction in the hard landscaping.

Key plants should be used sparingly in a garden or border. Use too many and they all vie for attention. Consider them like actors or actresses playing a starring role, not to be confused with the rest of the cast or chorus line.

CREATING A PLANTING PLAN

Elevation of a mixed border

Drawing Elevations: It is helpful to test out planting proposals by using sketch elevations of details of the planting plan. A sketch elevation can be drawn by translating the approximate measurements of the mature plants into an imaginary view of them on the vertical plane. Fully developed elevation or section drawings can be made from the plan (see page 258), and used to supplement the information.

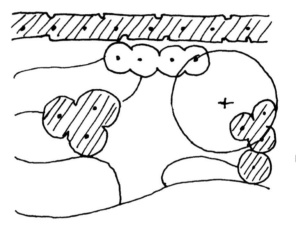

Planting plan

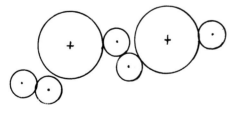

Planting proposal 1: When drawn in elevation, the scheme looked "spotty" and disjointed.

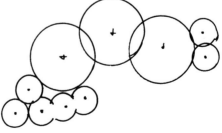

Planting proposal 2: An elevation of a scheme that uses the same plants, but in different numbers and positions, reveals that massing the plants achieves a much better balance.

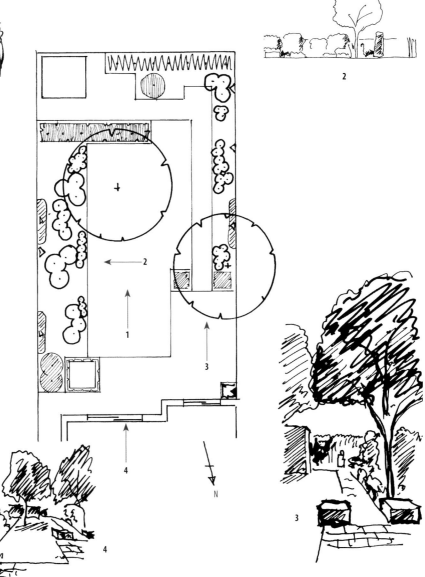

Small garden

Decorative shrubs and climbers are added. These soften the stronger outlines, the criteria for choice being form, shape, texture and colour. Thumbnail sketches and elevations drawn from the plan help to visualize the effect of the planting.

Decorative Planting

Once the structural and key plantings are in place, more decorative elements can be identified. These are composed of shrubs and climbers chosen for a pretty outline or attractive flowers, foliage or berries. Use elevations to help you to visualize your ideas, bearing in mind the importance of contrasting shape and form, texture and colour.

Decorative plantings give balance and contrast to structural or key plantings and usually only demand attention for a short period of time. In working up your decorative plantings, it is helpful to consider four main points: leaf size, leaf shape, flower colour and time of flowering.

Roses

For many people, roses epitomize the English gardening style. Since the 1950s there has been a surge of interest in the older roses, mainly brought about by the influence of the English rose-grower Graham Thomas. Through his books and the rose gardens he has created, old roses and their hybrids have replaced many of the hybrid teas and floribundas previously grown. Catalogues list myriad different varieties, seducing you with their names, photographs and descriptions but rarely pointing out their disadvantages.

A distinction should be made between climber and rambler roses. Ramblers are much more vigorous and, as they often reach 9 m (29.5 ft.) or more, are not recommended for house walls, because they would need hard pruning and tying into a framework of wire. They should be grown through trees or to cover an unsightly building; in the wrong place, their long summer growth could be a nuisance.

Climbers have much stiffer stems, larger flowers and smaller trusses than ramblers. Pruning and maintenance is much reduced, as flowers are borne on the framework of mature wood which is more or less permanent. When choosing a climber for a wall, consider the flower colour and how it will look against the stone, brick or other backdrop.

Try to build up a repertoire of reliable and high-performance plants that you are confident about using in your plans. The main points to look for are as follows:

- **Constitution**. For a rose to be worth its keep in any garden it should be healthy, and some are more prone than others to black spot, mildew and other disfiguring ailments.
- **Period of flowering**. Generally roses either flower once, perhaps with a spasmodic later "flush" or occasional flower. In Britain once-flowering roses generally flower in late spring, usually in May or early June, or in summer from mid-June to the end of July. Other roses are recurrent or repeat-flowering, and some flower almost continuously throughout the summer. In the United States the time and period of flowering depend on the area. Several British rose growers have suppliers in the United States.
- **Hips**. Some roses have attractive hips, making them useful in the autumn border or as features in the wild garden where they attract birds.
- **Foliage**. Ranging from glossy green through to glaucous and reddish tones, foliage can be effective even when the flowers have faded.
- **Other uses**. Other useful types of rose are ground cover or procumbent roses, useful near terraces or at the front of a border, and hedging roses, such as *Rosa* 'Fru Dagmar Hastrup', whose flowers turn to colourful hips in autumn provided they are not deadheaded.

Shrub roses can produce an attractive informal hedge.

Herbaceous Planting

Herbaceous plants are generally, but not always, smaller in scale than the decorative shrub plantings. In a mixed border they look most effective planted in drifts, weaving in and out of structural and decorative shrubs to hold the composition together and provide some movement. Herbaceous plants vary enormously in shape, texture and colour; they can be strikingly architectural or rounded and soft in texture.

Avoid using too many different types of plants, which can result in borders that look restless and unbalanced. To give continuity, repeat certain important groupings. To help you decide which to select from the huge range available, herbaceous plants can be divided into those that give broad-brush effects (long-lasting shrubs and perennials) and those that create fleeting effects (short-season perennials and bulbs which will give flashes of seasonal delight).

Broad-brush effects

Broad-brush plants provide not only large drifts of long-lasting colour but also attractive foliage. Some

Small garden: Herbaceous drifts and infill plants have been added. These hold the structural composition together and provide movement.

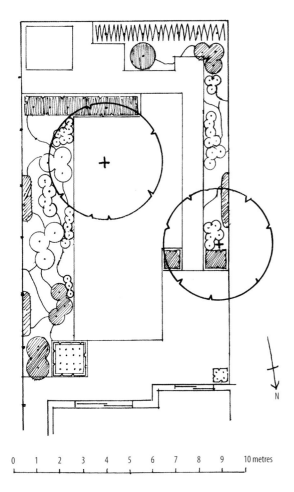

0   1   2   3   4   5   6   7   8   9   10 metres

are chosen for their foliage, with any flowers being an incidental extra. The diversity of their outline, colour and texture allows you to counterbalance plants, contrasting spears of iris or crocosmia with the silver filigree of artemisia, for instance, or placing arching blades of grass against the glossy foliage of aconitum or the soft velvet of *Stachys byzantina*. Try to use plants that contrast both in the way they look and their texture. Herbaceous plants should be chosen for their varied outline shapes. Incorporate verticals, such as foxgloves or hollyhocks; horizontals, such as sedums and achilleas; spikes, such as iris or hemerocallis; and mounds, such as agapanthus or *Alchemilla mollis*.

Fleeting effects

Fleeting effects create occasional interest or highlights that interrupt the longer-lasting broad-brush plants, providing finishing touches that enliven a border or group. They give a flash of seasonal interest and prevent plantings from being monotonous. Bulbs, annuals, half-hardies and short-lived perennials fall into this category and can be divided up seasonally. For example:

- Spring: snowdrops, tulips
- Early summer: lupins, poppies
- Late summer: cannas, tobacco plants (*Nicotiana*), lilies, gladioli
- Autumn: colchicum, cyclamen

Balancing the broad-brush effect with incidents of colour results in an ever-changing seasonal canvas that rarely fails to delight. Even in a small garden, broad-brush plants should be arranged in bold groups of uneven numbers, say five, nine, eleven or fifteen of one plant, giving a more natural and restful effect. Fleeting plants can be used in smaller groups of, say, three or five. Repeat the groups diagonally across the garden, weaving them through structural and key plants until the planting plan fits tightly together rather like a jigsaw, leaving no space, when mature, for uninvited guests such as weeds.

Bulb underplanting

Allium giganteum/10 - with *Perovskia*

Tulipa 'Queen of the Night'/10 - with *Achillea*

Fritillaria persica/10 - with *Foeniculum*

Muscari botryoides/100 - with *Iris/Acanthus/Geranium*

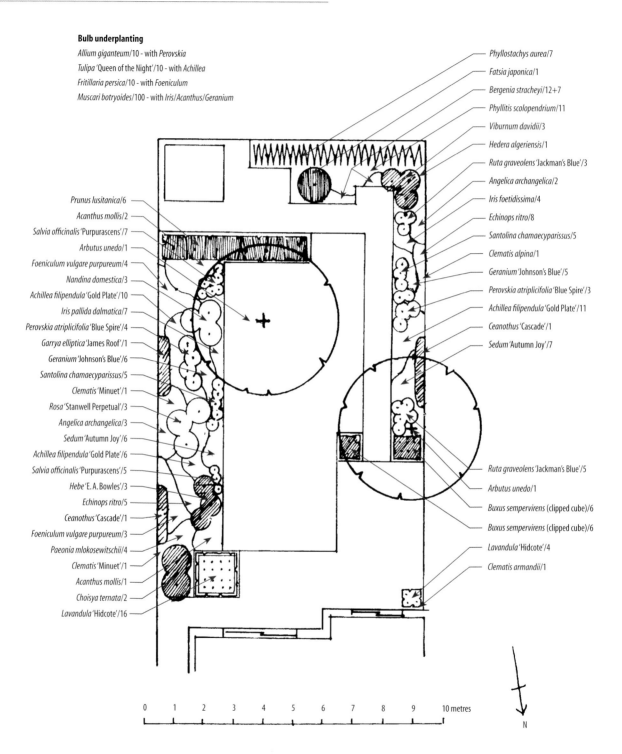

Phyllostachys aurea/7

Fatsia japonica/1

Bergenia stracheyi/12+7

Phyllitis scolopendrium/11

Viburnum davidii/3

Hedera algeriensis/1

Ruta graveolens 'Jackman's Blue'/3

Angelica archangelica/2

Iris foetidissima/4

Echinops ritro/8

Santolina chamaecyparissus/5

Clematis alpina/1

Geranium 'Johnson's Blue'/5

Perovskia atriplicifolia 'Blue Spire'/3

Achillea filipendula 'Gold Plate'/11

Ceanothus 'Cascade'/1

Sedum 'Autumn Joy'/7

Prunus lusitanica/6

Acanthus mollis/2

Salvia officinalis 'Purpurascens'/7

Arbutus unedo/1

Foeniculum vulgare purpureum/4

Nandina domestica/3

Achillea filipendula 'Gold Plate'/10

Iris pallida dalmatica/7

Perovskia atriplicifolia 'Blue Spire'/4

Garrya elliptica 'James Roof'/1

Geranium 'Johnson's Blue'/6

Santolina chamaecyparissus/5

Clematis 'Minuet'/1

Rosa 'Stanwell Perpetual'/3

Angelica archangelica/3

Sedum 'Autumn Joy'/6

Achillea filipendula 'Gold Plate'/6

Salvia officinalis 'Purpurascens'/5

Hebe 'E. A. Bowles'/3

Echinops ritro/5

Ceanothus 'Cascade'/1

Foeniculum vulgare purpureum/3

Paeonia mlokosewitschii/4

Clematis 'Minuet'/1

Acanthus mollis/1

Choisya ternata/2

Lavandula 'Hidcote'/16

Ruta graveolens 'Jackman's Blue'/5

Arbutus unedo/1

Buxus sempervirens (clipped cube)/6

Buxus sempervirens (clipped cube)/6

Lavandula 'Hidcote'/4

Clematis armandii/1

0 1 2 3 4 5 6 7 8 9 10 metres

N

Small garden: The planting plan, complete with plant names, planting positions (for trees, shrubs and climbers) and numbers of plants that are required. The numbers of each plant, or how many are in each group, are critical as the same plant may be used in several different positions.

Drawing up the Planting Plan

1. Tape down the final garden layout plan over a graph-paper backing sheet on the drawing board. Tape a fresh sheet of tracing paper over the layout plan, then trace over the house and garden boundaries and any areas that will contain plantings (including containers such as window boxes or pots). Use a sharp pencil or pen (the latter will be easier to read through subsequent sheets of tracing paper). This should be a simplified version of the layout plan; avoid putting in all the detail so that you leave room for the plant details.

2. Remove the garden layout plan from the drawing board, and make sure the newly traced sheet (which will become the planting plan) is firmly stuck down. You will work up the planting plan on this sheet in draft form and transfer it later onto a final sheet of tracing paper.

3. Refer to the site appraisal (see page 62) to remind yourself of existing conditions, such as soil type, aspect and so on, and to help you define the function of different planted areas.

4. Begin the draft plan working in pencil, drawing shapes freehand. Start by drawing in any existing plants that you intend to retain, referring back to the symbols on pages 76–77. Label existing shrubs or groups of herbaceous plants (for example, "Existing *Iris foetidissima*: 4").

5. Now draw in the main structural plants that you require for the plan (some of which will already have been identified on your garden layout plan), stating how many plants you require in each case. When planning a hedge, check a reference book for the recommended spacing between each plant, indicating with a dot the exact planting position of each. Do not forget to include any structural climbers or wall shrubs.

6. Decide on the key plants, then draw them in and label them.

7. Using a blunt pencil, shade in the evergreen plants.

8. Start to develop elevations (see page 228) for each planting area. First contrast shape and form, then texture and colour. You can experiment with different ideas as you develop the plan further. These elevations can be drawn either on the same sheet of tracing paper, if you have room, or in a notebook. Although they are intended to be experimental, it is important that they are drawn to scale, if only approximately.

9. Use the elevation sketches to help you decide on the decorative plants. Draw these in on the draft plan and label them.

10. Developing the elevations still further, decide on the herbaceous plants, broad-brush or fleeting, that you want for each area, designing these in drifts to flow around and between the structural and decorative planting.

11. When your draft plan is completed, check that you have a good balance of evergreen and deciduous plants, that there is a succession of interest in the garden, that you have repeated groups of plants diagonally across the garden and that the chosen plants are suitable for the site conditions.

12. When content with the draft plan, place it underneath a further sheet

of tracing paper and stick it down. You are now ready to draw up the final planting plan on this new sheet. Remember to leave space for your information panel and title block. Your plant list will occupy the information panel. Trace over the draft plan and draw (in pencil or ink) all the plants, using the appropriate symbols. On this same sheet, label each plant (as shown in the examples on pages 232, 236 & 237). Give the full botanical name and, in each case, the number of plants in each group, even if there is only one plant. You may wish to use labels cut from a printout generated by your computer. These look very professional but are also time-consuming to cut out and stick onto the plan.

13. If you have space, your final planting plan could show an elevation. This will need to be titled, showing the view from where it will be seen but there is no need to label the plants themselves, as this information is on the planting plan.

14. At the top of the information panel, before the plant list, it is sometimes helpful to include a note on the reasoning behind your choice of plants, such as the style or colour combination that you are trying to achieve. List the plants according to category (trees, shrubs, climbers and so on), and arrange them in alphabetical order within each category. Give the full botanical name of each plant and the number of plants in each group, even if there is only one plant. When there are several groups of the same plant, they should be subtotalled, as shown on the opposite page and on the planting list of the model plan on page 236. This information should be put onto the information panel, either handwritten or as a printout from your computer in the same style as the rest of the plan.

15. Fill in the title block information, remembering to include the north point and the scale to which you have drawn the plan.

16. After double-checking that you have included all the necessary information, remove the planting plan from the drawing board.

17. Keep the tracing-paper original plan safe. The planting plan will be invaluable both for ordering your plants and for placing them in their allocated positions on the soil. You may need to refer to it at a later stage if any alterations need to be made to the final planting plan. Make at least two copies of it, either dyeline prints or photocopies. You can add colour to one of these.

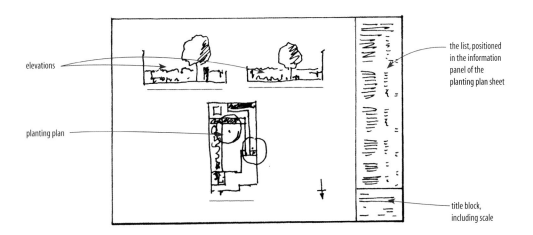

elevations

the list, positioned in the information panel of the planting plan sheet

planting plan

title block, including scale

The completed sheet shows the planting plan, elevations and plant list.

Small garden: The completed plan sheet for this garden includes the planting plan and two elevations. The planting list is positioned in the information panel of the plan sheet, giving the details needed to allow the garden to be planted according to the plan. If space on a plan is limited, use a separate sheet of paper for the plant list.

The plant list

		QUANTITY	SUBTOTAL
TREES	ᴍᴍᴍᴍ	2	2
	ᴍᴍᴍᴍ	1 + 2	3
	ᴍᴍᴍᴍ	1	1
		TOTAL	6
SHRUBS			
	ᴍᴍᴍᴍ	2 + 4	6
	ᴍᴍᴍ ᴍ	2	2
	ᴍᴍᴍᴍ ᴍ	2 + 3	5
	ᴍᴍᴍ ᴍ	1	1
		TOTAL	14
CLIMBERS			
	ᴍᴍᴍᴍ	2	2
	ᴍᴍᴍᴍ	3	3
		TOTAL	5
HERBACEOUS			
	ᴍᴍᴍᴍ —	1	1
	ᴍᴍᴍᴍ —	4 + 5	9
	ᴍᴍᴍ ᴍᴍ	2	2
	ᴍᴍᴍᴍ	5	5
		TOTAL	17
BULBS			
	ᴍᴍᴍ	25	25
	ᴍᴍᴍ	20 + 10 + 10	50
	ᴍᴍ .	10	10
	ᴍᴍᴍᴍ	10	10
		TOTAL	95

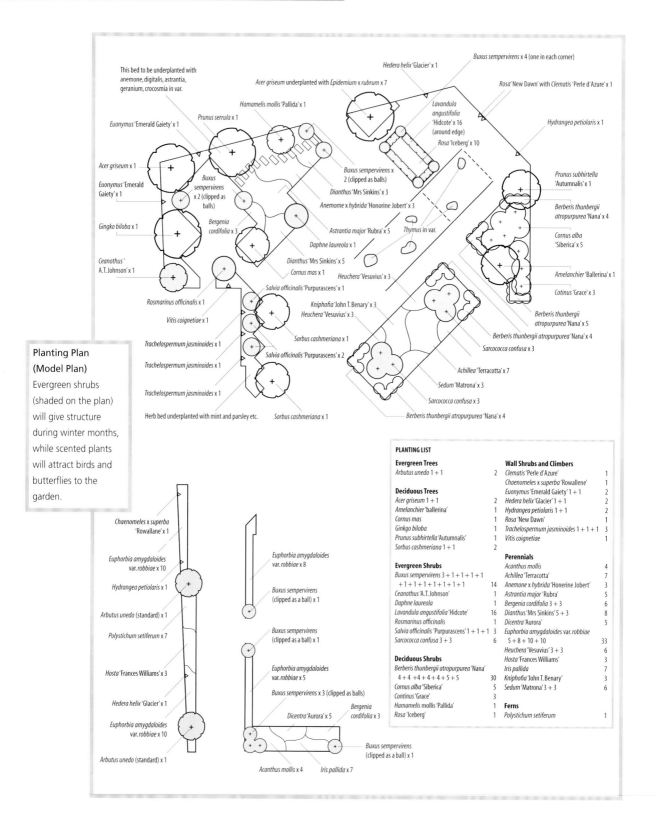

This bed to be underplanted with
anemone, digitalis, astrantia,
geranium, crocosmia in var.

Hedera helix 'Glacier' x 1

Buxus sempervirens x 4 (one in each corner)

Acer griseum underplanted with Epidemium x rubrum x 7

Rosa 'New Dawn' with Clematis 'Perle d'Azure' x 1

Hamamelis mollis 'Pallida' x 1

Lavandula
angustifolia
'Hidcote' x 16
(around edge)

Hydrangea petiolaris x 1

Prunus serrula x 1

Euonymus 'Emerald Gaiety' x 1

Rosa 'Iceberg' x 10

Acer griseum x 1

Buxus
sempervirens
x 2 (clipped as
balls)

Buxus sempervirens x
2 (clipped as balls)

Prunus subhirtella
'Autumnalis' x 1

Euonymus 'Emerald
Gaiety' x 1

Dianthus 'Mrs Sinkins' x 3

Berberis thunbergii
atropurpurea 'Nana' x 4

Anemone x hybrida 'Honorine Jobert' x 3

Gingko biloba x 1

Bergenia
cordifolia x 3

Cornus alba
'Siberica' x 5

Astrantia major 'Rubra' x 5

Daphne laureola x 1

Thymus in var.

Amelanchier 'Ballerina' x 1

Ceanothus '
A.T. Johnson' x 1

Dianthus 'Mrs Sinkins' x 5

Cotinus 'Grace' x 3

Cornus mas x 1

Heuchera 'Vesuvius' x 3

Rosmarinus officinalis x 1

Salvia officinalis 'Purpurascens' x 1

Berberis thunbergii
atropurpurea 'Nana' x 5

Kniphofia 'John T. Benary' x 3

Vitis coignetiae x 1

Heuchera 'Vesuvius' x 3

Berberis thunbergii atropurpurea 'Nana' x 4

Sorbus cashmeriana x 1

Sarcococca confusa x 3

Trachelospermum jasminoides x 1

Salvia officinalis 'Purpurascens' x 2

Trachelospermum jasminoides x 1

Achillea 'Terracotta' x 7

Sedum 'Matrona' x 3

Trachelospermum jasminoides x 1

Sarcococca confusa x 3

Herb bed underplanted with mint and parsley etc.

Sorbus cashmeriana x 1

Berberis thunbergii atropurpurea 'Nana' x 4

**Planting Plan
(Model Plan)**

Evergreen shrubs
(shaded on the plan)
will give structure
during winter months,
while scented plants
will attract birds and
butterflies to the
garden.

Chaenomeles x superba
'Rowallane' x 1

Euphorbia amygdaloides
var. robbiae x 8

Euphorbia amygdaloides
var. robbiae x 10

Buxus sempervirens
(clipped as a ball) x 1

Hydrangea petiolaris x 1

Arbutus unedo (standard) x 1

Buxus sempervirens
(clipped as a ball) x 1

Polystichum setiferum x 7

Euphorbia amygdaloides
var. robbiae x 5

Hosta 'Frances Williams' x 3

Buxus sempervirens x 3 (clipped as balls)

Hedera helix 'Glacier' x 1

Bergenia
cordifolia x 3

Dicentra 'Aurora' x 5

Euphorbia amygdaloides
var. robbiae x 10

Buxus sempervirens
(clipped as a ball) x 1

Arbutus unedo (standard) x 1

Acanthus mollis x 4   Iris pallida x 7

PLANTING LIST

Evergreen Trees	
Arbutus unedo 1 + 1	2
Deciduous Trees	
Acer griseum 1 + 1	2
Amelanchier 'ballerina'	1
Cornus mas	1
Ginkgo biloba	1
Prunus subhirtella 'Autumnalis'	1
Sorbus cashmeriana 1 + 1	2
Evergreen Shrubs	
Buxus sempervirens 3 + 1 + 1 + 1 + 1	
+ 1 + 1 + 1 + 1 + 1 + 1 + 1 + 1	14
Ceanothus 'A.T. Johnson'	1
Daphne laureola	1
Lavandula angustifolia 'Hidcote'	16
Rosmarinus officinalis	1
Salvia officinalis 'Purpurascens' 1 + 1 + 1	3
Sarcococca confusa 3 + 3	6
Deciduous Shrubs	
Berberis thunbergii atropurpurea 'Nana'	
4 + 4 + 4 + 4 + 4 + 5 + 5	30
Cornus alba 'Siberica'	5
Continus 'Grace'	3
Hamamelis mollis 'Pallida'	1
Rosa 'Iceberg'	1

Wall Shrubs and Climbers	
Clematis 'Perle d'Azure'	1
Chaenomeles x superba 'Rowallene'	1
Euonymus 'Emerald Gaiety' 1 + 1	2
Hedera helix 'Glacier' 1 + 1	2
Hydrangea petiolaris 1 + 1	2
Rosa 'New Dawn'	1
Trachelospermum jasminoides 1 + 1 + 1	3
Vitis coignetiae	1
Perennials	
Acanthus mollis	4
Achillea 'Terracotta'	7
Anemone x hybrida 'Honerine Jobert'	3
Astrantia major 'Rubra'	5
Bergenia cordifolia 3 + 3	6
Dianthus 'Mrs Sinkins' 5 + 3	8
Dicentra 'Aurora'	5
Euphorbia amygdaloides var. robbiae	
5 + 8 + 10 + 10	33
Heuchera 'Vesuvius' 3 + 3	6
Hosta 'Frances Williams'	3
Iris pallida	7
Kniphofia 'John T. Benary'	3
Sedum 'Matrona' 3 + 3	6
Ferns	
Polystichum setiferum	1

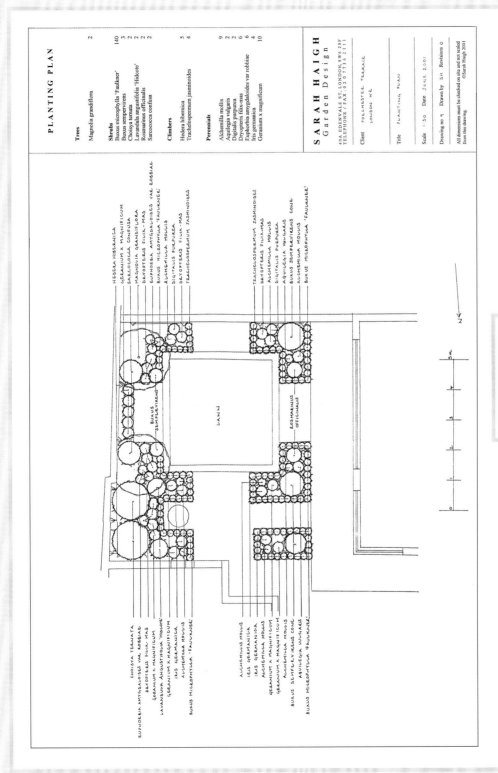

Sculptural evergreens provide a strong framework against which a succession of flowering perennials provide a long season of summer interest.

Above: In this green- and white-themed area, structural clipped box plants are clipped to the same height and width as the stone cube.

Above: Instead of being removed, an old tree may be clipped to form a focal point. Without the tree as a vertical feature, this garden would be less interesting.

Above: Box and clipped Irish yew frame the planting in this traditional rose garden. The fountain provides a central feature as well as a cooling influence.

Above: A double border where shrub roses are interplanted with clipped fast-growing variegated buckthorn (*Rhamnus alaternus* 'Argenteovariegata'). Trained into columns, they provide evergreen interest against the backdrop of a yew hedge.

Above: In this damp and shady border, the strong foliage contrasts of a large-leaved hosta and rodgersia are highlighted by slim blades of the variegated grass *Phalaris arundinacea* 'Picta'. Flower colour is of secondary importance here.

Right: Ferns and hostas are congenial companions, enjoying similar soil and aspect. The intriguingly twisted, white variegated foliage of *Hosta undulata* var. *undulata* draws attention to the change in level.

Above: In a natural setting, a tree house and swing invite children to play creatively. Steep steps add to the excitement, and binocular use is encouraged to record birds and other wildlife.

Above: A woodland edge planting where plants have been chosen for their leaf texture, contrasting foliage and ability to survive dry shade. The unplanted pot collects rainwater.

Above: Made entirely from reclaimed materials, this front garden provides vegetables and herbs for the whole family. The non-slip path is made of old, hard-wearing stable paviours.

Above: In this vegetable garden, raised beds with added compost allow soil manipulation where needed. Beans and cucumbers can be trained up stakes, while straw mulch prevents soil damage to strawberries.

Above: A naturalistic garden need not look messy. Colours are random, but varying heights, foliage shapes and scented plants planted in groups create a sense of order. Bulbs and late-flowering perennials will extend the seasonal display.

Above: Rammed earth walls surround this dry garden which is planted mainly with agaves and sedums. Spaces between the permeable stone paving slabs accommodate low-growing plants.

WET GARDENS

Above: This waterside planting relies on contrasting shape and texture of foliage as opposed to flower colour.

Above: Water lilies should be selected according to the depth of water, and planted in metal baskets inlaid with upturned turves.

Above: This garden stream has been designed and planted for a natural effect. The water flows over a series of shallow steps and the small structure above the waterfall acts as a focal point.

Right: Natural water is a bonus to be exploited in any garden. The huge leaves and flowering spikes of *Gunnera manicata* depend on a damp environment to perform well.

Left: This early summer colour scheme in restful blue-purple and white has been carefully coordinated, with pots and raised planters coloured a darker blue. The small, horizontally branched dogwood *Cornus florida* 'Welchii' (syn. 'Tricolor') shields the view from the house.

Above: The symbolic and studied placement of rocks and trees and absence of colour evoke calm in this Japanese garden.

Above: A "hot colour" border is set off by the red backdrop. Use of these vibrant colours can bring a dark area to life.

Above: The aromatic foliage of purple-leaved sage (*Salvia officinalis* 'Purpurascens') is enhanced by the varied pink tones of these shrub roses. Both plants enjoy sunny, well-drained conditions.

COLOURFUL COMBINATIONS

Above: An informal planting of tall shrub roses highlights this meandering grass path, while the lower herbaceous plantings interplanted with bulbs give gentle relief to the colourful scene.

Above: Our perception of flower colour and tone is affected by the quality of light. Yellow foliage and flowers can bring life to a dull or dark area.

Above: A decorative stone urn is framed by blue catmint and the dark red foliage of the *Rosmarinus* 'Rosemary Rose'). The blue tones of *Hosta* 'Halcyon' frame the planting and play up the colour scheme.

Right: The hot colours of red-hot pokers, half-hardy dahlias and cannas are cooled by the surrounding green foliage.

Left: Although the climbing rose that covers this arch has a slightly bluish tone, it is not strong enough to clash with the hot colour planting beyond. Nasturtiums and other annuals mix through the perennial planting.

Above: This two-colour border concentrates on blue and apricot. The spikes of the kniphofia complement the rounded forms of the other plants.

Above: Herbaceous clump-forming perennials such as *Paeonia lactiflora* 'Pillow Talk' are a useful addition to an early summer border. In spring, the deep reddish emergent

Left: The sharp spikes of the variegated New Zealand flax (*Phormium tenax*) contrast with the bulbous purple flowering garlic (*Allium cristophii*). Both cope with drought conditions and are easy to maintain.

Above: In this courtyard garden, yellow- and white-flowering plants are set off by a clipped box hedge. Topiary in pots adds interest around the pool area.

Above: The large glaucous foliage of *Macleaya* x *kewensis* and the deep red leaves of *Cotinus coggygria* 'Royal Purple' are a foil for the tall spikes of *Eremurus* 'Shelford Hybrids'.

Above: The lower petals of *Monarda* 'Croftway Pink' match the dark purple foliage of *Cotinus coggygria* 'Royal Purple'. These purple tones will contrast later with the sealing wax orange hips of *Rosa moyesii* 'Geranium'.

Above: Spikes of *Eremurus bungei* (*E. stenophyllus*) or fox-tail lily draw the eye to the variety for plants in this border. The rampant deep blue herbaceous *Clematis heracleifolia* needs supporting at an early stage, although it is not a climber.

Right: Although the pale flowers are set off by the dark foliage, the planting is too busy to be effective. The large-leafed hosta in the background will be more evident when some of the taller flowering spikes are removed.

Left: Old-fashioned roses and alliums are a useful partnership. After the flowers have faded, allium heads still look decorative.

Left: The strap-like leaves of the phormium are an effective contrast to the rounded leaves of *Hosta sieboldiana*. Dark foliage and flowers help show up the scented flowers of *Rhododendron luteum*.

Above: A very tactile plant, beloved of children, this grass, *Pennisetum villosum*, stands out against other plants until late autumn.

Above: Flowering grasses bring life and movement to a border in summer and early autumn. These flowerheads create a fountain-like effect but be careful as some grasses are invasive.

Above: Flowering from midsummer to early autumn, the long-lasting, upright, spiky thistle (*Eryngium ×oliverianum*) is an essential architectural element in dry, well-drained areas.

Above: Easily grown in sunny areas and tolerant of poor but well-drained soil conditions, the architectural *Euphorbia wulfenii* (spurge) is long lasting. When cutting, avoid coming into contact with the latex-like sap—it is a notorious skin irritant.

Left: The delicate, dissected foliage of *Acer palmatum* is outstanding in autumn.

Below: Bulbs bring the garden to life during long winter days. The orange-red tones of the strong upright-stemmed *Tulipa* 'Ballerina' are accentuated by the grass (*Anemanthele lessoniana*) in the background.

Above: Foliage that develops good autumn colour should be included in any garden. Here, the leaves of *Vitis coignetiae* reflect the rust tones of the brick wall.

Left: As shrub roses develop, their flowers often become paler. Some roses only have one period of flowering during the growing season, while others, such as the china rose (*Rosa* 'Perle d'Or') offer recurrent or continuous bloom.

Chapter 5

Visualizing and Constructing the Design

Visualizing and Constructing the Design

At the end of the process of creating the garden design and planting plan, you should have a very clear idea of how the garden will look once it is built. However, it may be helpful for both you and others involved to see a further visual or an artist's impression of how the finished work will look. Although flat, two-dimensional plans have their limitations, they can be enhanced with colour or tone to represent light and shadow. Further drawings will explain your intentions and are helpful when read alongside the plan.

Axonometric, or measured, drawings are constructed from the garden layout and planting plan. While working up these drawings, anything you have overlooked (such as the number and width of treads and risers in a flight of steps) will soon become apparent. This is a useful method for double-checking any inaccuracies and will give you an opportunity to fill in any missing details on the garden layout plan.

Drawing sections of a garden will give you a view of the plan that can be investigated at any stage of the work and might be particularly useful when you are developing the preliminary garden plan. Sections and elevations are useful because they help to clarify the vertical elements, but they do not show how all the different planes (the garden floor, walls and any overhead features) work together as a unified whole. For this you need to create three-dimensional drawings, such as an axonometric drawing or photographic overlay.

Photographic overlays are particularly effective because they instantly relate any new proposals to the existing site. In this way they can help to give the new design a credibility that is rarely matched by other visuals, such as artistic impressions, which can have an unreal quality about them.

Once your plans have been agreed on, the site can be prepared, building work can begin, the plants can be brought in and planted, and thoughts can turn to maintenance and future development.

Enhancing the Plan

Some excellent effects can be achieved by applying tone, and it is fun to experiment until you find a method that suits your particular drawings. Colour is enormously helpful in bringing a plan or visuals to life. What you use may well depend on the available media and your time.

Using Colour

When choosing your colours in whatever medium, try to select earthy or natural tones that include a wide range of browns, greens and greys. Much of your hard landscaping will be in shades of brown or grey, and a variety of greens will help you depict variety in your plant selection. A greyish purple can be very useful for shadow effects.

You may already have a range of crayons, felt-tips or watercolours, and perhaps you only need to buy one or two more shades to extend your colour range. It is worth considering several options to see which suits your style.

Colour applied directly onto tracing paper does not usually reprint, so you will need to apply it to a copy of your drawing. It is wise to have two or three copies made so that you can experiment. You may have your work reproduced as a dyeline print or photocopy, choosing a slightly heavier paper, perhaps with a finish or texture that will look effective when coloured. Shiny surfaces can be used, but they do not absorb crayon, felt-tips or watercolours readily. If using watercolours, specialist watercolour paper is recommended, but often the reproduced print lines will not adhere properly to heavier papers. Experiment before making up your mind.

Coloured Crayons or Pencils

These can be anything from a child's set of primary colours to an extensive artist's range. Some manufacturers supply a good selection in packs of about eight or twelve earthy colours. Alternatively, by selecting your crayons individually you can build up your own range, concentrating mainly on browns, greys and greens, and including yellow, red and blue to enliven the more muted shades.

When applying colour, always try to work in one direction, not pressing too heavily. To obtain an area of regular well-blended lines, a good effect can be achieved by supporting your crayon or pencil against the set square, parallel motion or T-square and moving this gradually down your sheet as you draw a series of lines in one direction. Aim to build up colour intensity gradually rather than applying it heavily when you begin.

Mixing two colours can create a realistic effect. Brown could be used in conjunction with red or yellow to illustrate brick, a light grey and dark grey could be combined to show paving, and a light bluish green and darker green could indicate plants or areas of grass.

Try testing out these mixtures of colour beforehand on a separate sheet of paper. When you like a particular combination, note down the crayon reference numbers so that you will remember them.

Felt-Tip or Marker Pens

These are also available in a wide colour range. Marker pens, with their wider tips, are useful for covering a larger area in a single stroke. They too should be used in a single direction, pushed against the ruler, parallel motion or set square. If the colours are water-soluble they may bleed into each other. Practice is required to apply the colour evenly, and at the end of each stroke it is best to lift the felt-tip to avoid a heavier intensity at one end. If you persevere with this medium you should be able to achieve some good effects.

Watercolours

These can produce delightful effects, but the amount of water used tends to make normal paper buckle, so heavier paper (or watercolour paper) is recommended. Again, take time choosing and mixing your colours, and use a variety of good-quality brushes—perhaps a thick one for covering areas of lawn or paving, a fine one for detailed areas and a short, firm brush for effects such as flowers or shadow. When mixing colours try not to use too much water to avoid making the paper buckle.

Applying Tone and Rendering Texture

A quick and effective way of giving textural interest to a drawing is by producing a rubbing. You simply lay the dyeline print or photocopy of the plan over an embossed surface (sandpaper, an old book cover, a briefcase) and, using a soft pencil, rub over the area of your plan or drawing that you want to give texture.

It is also possible to render onto tracing paper if you are using a thick or good-quality sheet combined with a soft, dark lead pencil, such as 5B. For a drawing on tracing paper, always apply the lead finish to the reverse side so that it does not smudge on the surface. The lead can then be spread, if required, by rubbing it lightly with your finger or a paper tissue. This treatment is particularly effective for shadow effects. If you vary the pressure you can indicate the light direction.

Shadow can be added to a plan to give it a three-dimensional quality and to bring it to life. To achieve this, choose a realistic position for the sun, and determine the length of the shadow by the angle of the sun (as shown on page 252). Lightly mark the areas in pencil that would be cast in shadow, and hatch them with lines.

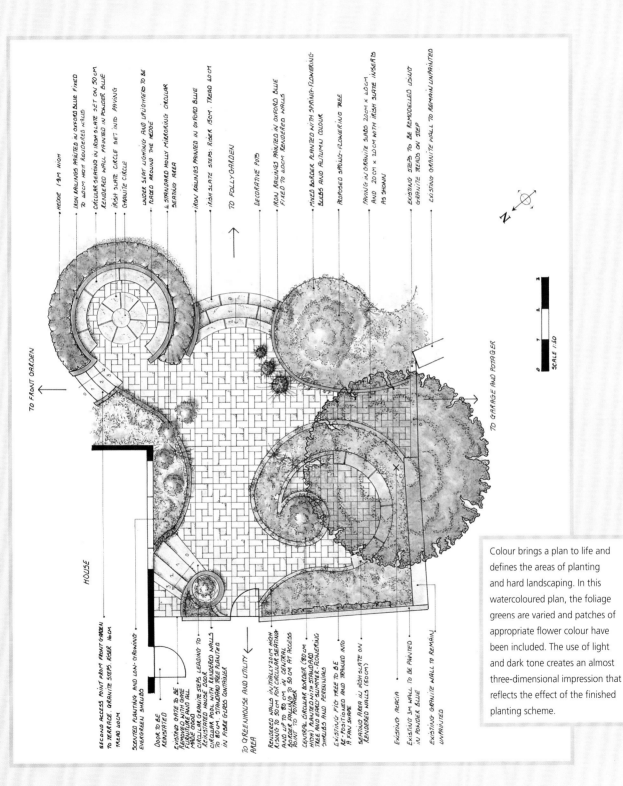

HEDGE 1.3M HIGH

IRON RAILINGS PAINTED IN OXFORD BLUE FIXED TO 40CM HIGH RENDERED WALLS

CIRCULAR SEATING IN IRISH SLATE SET ON 50CM RENDERED WALL PAINTED IN POWDER BLUE

IRISH SLATE CIRCLE SET INTO PAVING

GRANITE CIRCLE

UNDER SEAT LIGHTING AND UPLIGHTERS TO BE PLACED AROUND THE HEDGE

4 STANDARD HOLLY MIRRORING CIRCULAR SEATING AREA

IRON RAILINGS PAINTED IN OXFORD BLUE

IRISH SLATE STEPS. RISER 15CM. TREAD 40CM

TO FOLLY GARDEN

DECORATIVE POTS

IRON RAILINGS PAINTED IN OXFORD BLUE FIXED TO 40CM RENDERED WALLS

MIXED BORDER PLANTED WITH SPRING-FLOWERING BULBS AND AUTUMN COLOUR

PROPOSED SPRING-FLOWERING TREE

PAVING IN GRANITE SLABS 20CM x 40CM AND 20CM x 20CM WITH IRISH SLATE INSERTS AS SHOWN

EXISTING STEPS TO BE REMODELLED USING GRANITE TREADS ON STEP

EXISTING GRANITE WALL TO REMAIN UNPAINTED

N

SCALE 1:50

TO FRONT GARDEN

HOUSE

SECOND ACCESS POINT FROM FRONT GARDEN TO TERRACE. GRANITE STEPS. RISER 16CM. TREAD 40CM

SCENTED PLANTING AND LOW-GROWING EVERGREEN SHRUBS

DOOR TO BE REINSTATED

EXISTING GATE TO BE REMOVED WITH GATE MADE GOOD AND ALL PLANTING TO 50CM AT ACCESS POINT TO POTAGER

CIRCULAR GRANITE STEPS LEADING TO REINSTATED HOUSE DOOR

CIRCULAR POOL WITH RENDERED WALLS TO 80CM. STANDARD TREE PLANTED IN FIRME GLOBE CONTINUER

TO GREENHOUSE AND UTILITY AREA

RENDERED WALLS INITIALLY 120CM HIGH RISING TO 30CM FOR CIRCULAR SEATING AND UP TO 80CM ON CENTRAL BORDER FALLING TO 50CM AT ACCESS POINT TO POTAGER

CENTRAL CIRCULAR BORDER (80CM HIGH) PLANTED WITH STANDARD TREE AND EARLY SUMMER-FLOWERING SHRUBS AND PERENNIALS

EXISTING FIG TREE TO BE RE-POSITIONED AND TRAINED INTO A FAN SHAPE

SEATING AREA IN IRISH SLATE ON RENDERED WALLS (50CM)

EXISTING ACACIA

EXISTING 3M WALL TO BE PAINTED IN POWDER BLUE

EXISTING GRANITE WALL TO REMAIN UNPAINTED

TO GARAGE AND POTAGER

Colour brings a plan to life and defines the areas of planting and hard landscaping. In this watercoloured plan, the foliage greens are varied and patches of appropriate flower colour have been included. The use of light and dark tone creates an almost three-dimensional impression that reflects the effect of the finished planting scheme.

VISUALIZING AND CONSTRUCTING THE DESIGN

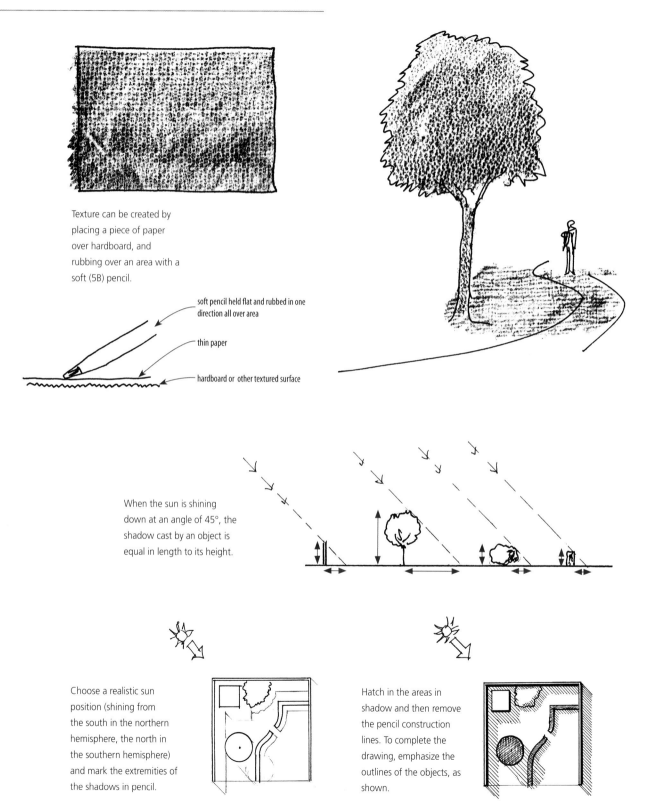

Texture can be created by placing a piece of paper over hardboard, and rubbing over an area with a soft (5B) pencil.

soft pencil held flat and rubbed in one direction all over area

thin paper

hardboard or other textured surface

When the sun is shining down at an angle of 45°, the shadow cast by an object is equal in length to its height.

Choose a realistic sun position (shining from the south in the northern hemisphere, the north in the southern hemisphere) and mark the extremities of the shadows in pencil.

Hatch in the areas in shadow and then remove the pencil construction lines. To complete the drawing, emphasize the outlines of the objects, as shown.

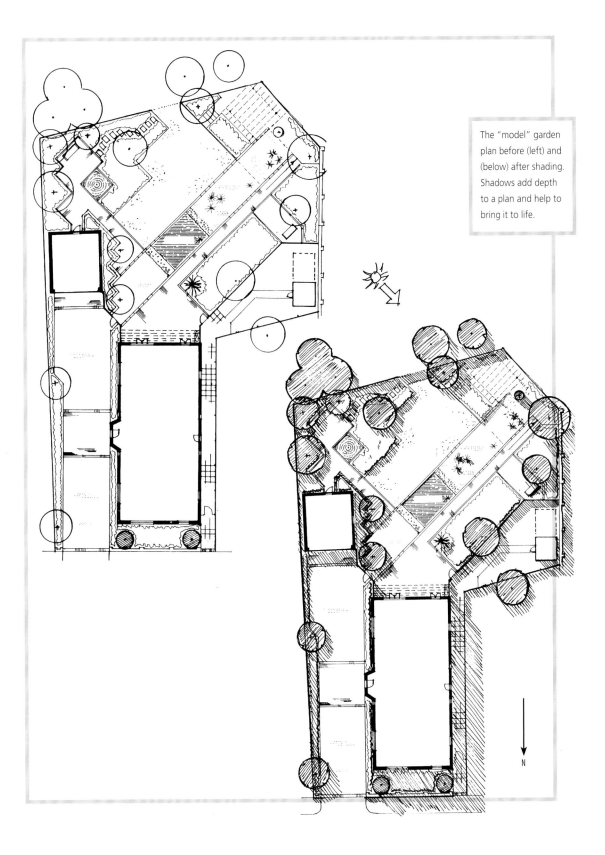

The "model" garden plan before (left) and (below) after shading. Shadows add depth to a plan and help to bring it to life.

N

Using Photographs

Cameras, whether film or digital, are useful working tools. It is worth considering that although computers and digital cameras offer the designer a lot of scope, in creating "before" and "after" effects they tend to short-cut the hands-on process that will give you closer contact with the actual business of design.

A photographic overlay is a freehand drawing showing proposed changes to a garden. It is created on tracing paper stuck down over an enlarged photograph of the existing site and is a simple and quick method of showing the site before and after the redesign. This type of quick sketch can produce a striking and easily understood impression of your intentions. These drawings are simple to set up, very effective and do not involve creating time-consuming perspective charts. This technique is an easy method of creating perspective drawings of your intended ideas, and, when used earlier in the design process, can be a useful method in helping you to decide which views to frame and which to screen.

Photographic overlays will enable you to "see" proposed views of any area of the garden (from the house to the garden, from the garden back to the house or from the house into the garden beyond, for instance).

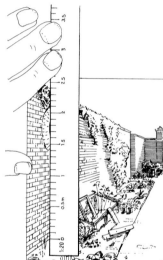

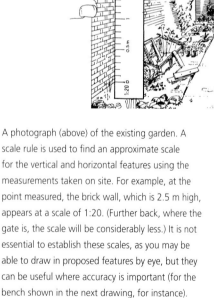

A photograph (above) of the existing garden. A scale rule is used to find an approximate scale for the vertical and horizontal features using the measurements taken on site. For example, at the point measured, the brick wall, which is 2.5 m high, appears at a scale of 1:20. (Further back, where the gate is, the scale will be considerably less.) It is not essential to establish these scales, as you may be able to draw in proposed features by eye, but they can be useful where accuracy is important (for the bench shown in the next drawing, for instance).

Right: The completed overlay showing the proposed new elements, together with the existing items that are being retained.

"Before and after": A sketch on tracing paper laid over the "before" photograph shows the site transformed. Note how the tree in the neighbour's garden has been retained as an integral part of the new design and this shows through the tracing paper.

Creating a Photographic Overlay

1. Study the garden layout plan and choose an area to illustrate. This could be a vertical element, such as a trellis, pergola, arbour, statue, urn, trees, border or even a garden shed. Lawns, paths and pools can also be shown, but as they are on the ground plane, they look less effective.

2. Look at the photographs that you took when doing the site survey (see Chapter 1). Choose the most suitable ones, either a single shot or a panoramic view. Digital photographs can be printed in many sizes, so select the size you want to use. If using an SLR or non-digital camera and the prints are small, have them enlarged as black-and-white or colour prints, or enlarge on a photocopier or scanner.

3. With masking tape, stick the photos down onto the drawing board using the graph-paper backing sheet as a guide to align them.

4. Using a scale rule, try to find an approximate scale for some of the horizontals or verticals in your photographs. These may be, for instance, a brick wall at 2 m (6.6 ft.) high (remember that by counting the number of brick courses, you can arrive at the overall height), a pergola at 3 m (9.8 ft.) high or a garden shed at 3 m (9.8 ft.) high by 6 m (19.7 ft.) wide. Note down the nearest approximate scale.

5. Over each photograph stick down A4 (8.5 × 11 in.) tracing paper.

6. Check back to the layout plan. Note how high and wide the proposed horizontal and vertical elements will be in the area of the photograph—perhaps steps, walls, pergolas and arches.

7. On the tracing-paper overlay, mark the position of the four corners of each photograph. This will help you to position the overlay later, once it has been reproduced.

8. Using a pencil and your chosen scale, pinpoint these dimensions on your tracing-paper overlay.

9. Draw in the proposed elements using a pen and varying the thickness of line to bring the sketch to life.

10. Trace, if you wish, any existing items that are being retained, such as patio doors or trees.

11. Title and date each sheet, and if possible, have it copied either onto tracing paper or onto a clear acetate sheet.

12. With glue, adhesive tape or staples, fix your "after" overlay over the "before" photograph. You will now be able to see the effect of your proposals.

Mood Boards

A mood board can be helpful in identifying the type of mood, style and look you are aiming to achieve in your new garden design. A form of visual stimulus, it is usually a large board covered with images that is designed to represent a mood, atmosphere or feeling. Often used in interior and architectural design, a mood board lends itself well to garden design and can be a very effective tool to explain design ideas.

Although usually used as a presentation tool by the designer, the person for whom the garden is being designed may also prepare a board. This often amounts to a collage of different ideas taken from magazines or journals to show the designer what type of garden they would like to have. A mood board is usually worked up after the garden layout and planting plans are complete and presented with them as an explanatory visual. A mood board can also be used before firming up on the design, as a means of establishing mutual goals between the designer and the garden owner in pictorial form.

A mood board can help to illustrate some proposed planting combinations and to give a sense of the proposed style. For instance, if the new garden is to be formal, the mood board can reflect this by being laid out in a similar manner, whereas an informal design may be better illustrated in a relaxed or contemporary style. It can demonstrate how plant colours and combinations will look together, or it can show how the planting will change with the seasons.

A mood board is constructed by using a selection of pictures cut from magazines and catalogues of objects, colours, plants, paving samples or fabrics that you plan to use in the garden. Generally a large sheet of heavyweight paper or card (cardboard) is used, and the cut-outs are mounted onto this. The size depends on the size of the project, but A2 (17 × 22 in.) is usually the most manageable.

The board should focus on portraying the main elements of the design arranged in a similar layout to your plans and should communicate your design ideas in a visually appealing and representative manner.

Making a Mood Board

You will need heavy-duty coloured card (cardboard) for mounting the main material, lightweight card (cardboard) or foam board for mounting cut-outs, double-sided adhesive tape or spray glue to stick down photographs or cut-out material, a reduced or small-scale plan of the garden, ink drawing pens for lettering and photographs or manufacturers' brochures.

1. Assemble the material that you are going to use, including a copy of the garden layout plan that has been reduced on a photocopier or scanner to a scale that matches the scale of the photographs that you will place around it on your board (usually less than 200 mm [8 in.]). Place the plan centrally on the board.
2. If you are doing the work for a friend or a client, remember to include your title block to ensure that you, as the designer, are credited for your work.
3. Associate areas of the board with areas of the garden. If the garden has only one main area, lay out the samples in the general order of the space. For example, position paving at the bottom of the board, furnishings and planting at the middle and arbours or anything that lies overhead at the top of the board. By grouping things together, you will create a clearer idea than sticking samples randomly over the board.
4. Arrange the photographs around the plan according to where each item is located on

the plan. Avoid photographs overhanging the edge of the board, as these will be damaged when transporting the board. Draw a border and organize the material neatly within in it.

5. The size of the samples should generally reflect how much space the material will take up in reality. For example, avoid filling the board with several photographs of a type of plant if it only occurs once on the plan.

6. By framing some photographs with a border, you increase their importance. Photographs can be stuck to lightweight foam board to add a sense of depth.

7. Use paint swatches to show colours for plantings, walls, furniture and so on.

8. Instead of searching out mood board material for each new occasion, keep a file of high-quality photographs of materials and plants for later use. Avoid torn edges by using a scalpel to cut them cleanly.

9. When you are satisfied with the board layout, use double-sided tape or spray glue to stick the images onto the board.

10. When using natural samples such as sticks, rocks or twigs, be careful not to venture into the world of dollhouse making. Too much novelty will detract from the message you are trying to convey.

The design of this mood board is well balanced. The reduced plan is placed to the left, two atmospheric photographs depict the garden style, a title block is placed to the bottom right of the board, and a range of plant images give colour and interest.

Drawing Sections and Elevations

A section is a scaled drawing of a vertical plane that is constructed from a line that cuts through a plan; it can include the area below ground level if this is needed. Sections are used for two reasons: for a designer to experiment on paper with different spatial compositions, and to supplement the information on a plan, showing details of vertical and overhead elements that cannot be illustrated on a plan drawing. They can be made from any scaled drawing. An elevation is any vertical view of a feature, group of plants or part of the garden, not necessarily along one line (see page 228).

At a chosen cut line (or section line) on the plan, the three-dimensional elements on this line are projected up to scale. Any vertical or overhead features that are close behind this line can also be shown. Some surface detail can be added to bring the drawing to life.

These drawings are quick and easy to complete because, unlike a perspective drawing, all the vertical and overhead elements are shown at their correct scale, no matter how far they are from the cut line. You will probably have drawn your plan at a scale of 1:50 or 1:100, too small a scale to illustrate anything meaningful, such as a change of level, or a pergola. To show enough detail, the scale should be enlarged or doubled, perhaps to 1:20. This will obviously take up more space across the drawing, so instead of showing the whole section across the garden (much of which may be irrelevant), you may prefer to only show a specific area, perhaps one of vertical interest. In this case, mark clearly on the plan where the section begins and ends and indicate your direction of view with arrows.

There is no point in drawing a section unless it is going to show some detail or change of level that cannot be clarified on the plan. Normally, two sections across the garden are enough for a small or average-sized garden, but use as few or as many as needed to explain your intentions. It is crucial that you choose section lines where any major alterations in level, or a reasonable amount of vertical interest, occur. This is usually one line along the length and one line along the width of the garden.

Drawing a Section Through a Garden Layout Plan

1. Study the garden layout plan and consider any changes in level or vertical and overhead features. By twisting the plan around to look at it from all angles, decide where a line can be drawn across the plan, or part of the plan, to show these features.

2. Stick down the garden layout plan, and over this, stick down a fresh sheet of tracing paper. Ensure that the plan is positioned centrally below the tracing paper, and consider the layout of the sheet. You will need to leave room for the title block, but it is unlikely that you will need an information panel on this drawing. Make sure you position the sections suitably on the sheet. It usually looks better to have a longer section nearer the bottom. If you have room, you may wish to include these sections on the garden layout plan instead of on a separate sheet.

3. Mark the beginning and end of the section line on the tracing paper. Is the scale large enough to show sufficient detail, or does it need to be enlarged? If so, you may only have enough space on your sheet to show part of the section line (obviously the area where most of what you need to show occurs).

4. Now draw the section line in pencil across the plan. To do this, use a T-square, parallel motion or, if the section line is at an angle, a set square.

continues on page 261

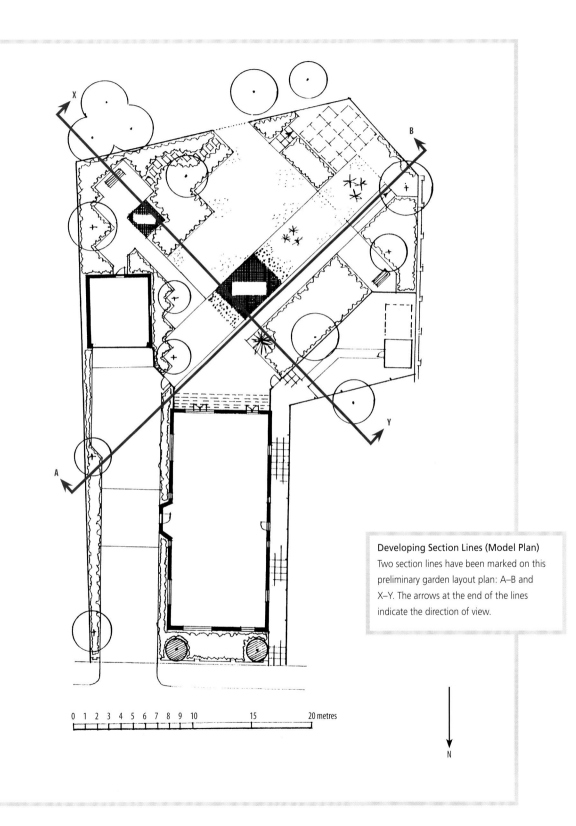

Developing Section Lines (Model Plan)
Two section lines have been marked on this preliminary garden layout plan: A–B and X–Y. The arrows at the end of the lines indicate the direction of view.

0 1 2 3 4 5 6 7 8 9 10 15 20 metres

N

VISUALIZING AND CONSTRUCTING THE DESIGN

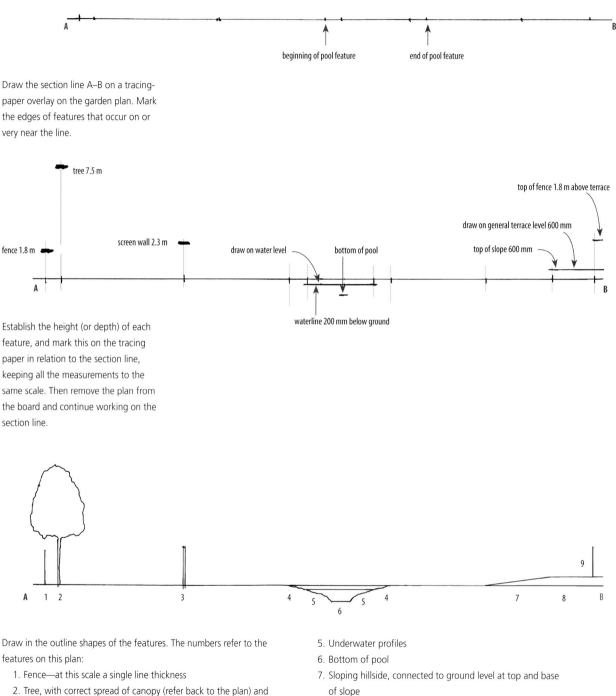

Draw the section line A–B on a tracing-paper overlay on the garden plan. Mark the edges of features that occur on or very near the line.

Establish the height (or depth) of each feature, and mark this on the tracing paper in relation to the section line, keeping all the measurements to the same scale. Then remove the plan from the board and continue working on the section line.

Draw in the outline shapes of the features. The numbers refer to the features on this plan:

1. Fence—at this scale a single line thickness
2. Tree, with correct spread of canopy (refer back to the plan) and height from ground
3. Wall indicated by two parallel lines. Note the section actually passes through a gateway
4. Edge details of pool—in this case a pebble "beach"

5. Underwater profiles
6. Bottom of pool
7. Sloping hillside, connected to ground level at top and base of slope
8. Terrace level
9. Fence

5. Beginning at one end of the section line, progress along this line, projecting vertical pencil lines upwards from the edges of any changes in level or any vertical features that are either on or just beyond the section line.

6. Use the measurements noted on the plan or in your notebook and a scale rule to establish the heights of these features, drawing in horizontal lines to indicate the top and bottom of the features.

7. Draw in and show some detail of the foreground structures, including the outline form of any planting. If they are not totally obscured by the structures in the foreground, draw in any vertical or overhead features beyond the cut line. If there are any significant trees beyond the boundary of your garden, it is useful to show these as well, as it gives the drawing some scale reference. Write down the measurements if this will help clarify the drawing.

8. Once you have drawn everything in pencil, remove the plan from the drawing board. On a new sheet of tracing paper, trace over the section drawing in pencil or pen. Use a fainter pencil or smaller pen size to indicate more distant features that do not fall exactly on the section line.

9. Adding a person, also drawn to scale, often improves this type of drawing. Remember to add your title block.

10. Remove this section drawing and have it printed. Adding colour to the print may help bring it to life (see page 249).

11. Mark on the garden layout plan where the sections begin and end, indicating this with arrows showing the direction of view. As you will already have had prints made from your original plan, perhaps this can be added to your print.

Use a pen with a fairly thick nib, and draw the ground profile or outline only. Draw in the fences with another thick line, but less thick than the ground. Erase pencil construction lines. You now have a cross-section.

Take the cross-section and lay it over the plan again, aligning the ground level on the cross section with the section line on your plan. Look from left to right along the section line. Look hard at the plan. Do you see any objects (or plants) behind the section line that are not obscured by others?

VISUALIZING AND CONSTRUCTING THE DESIGN

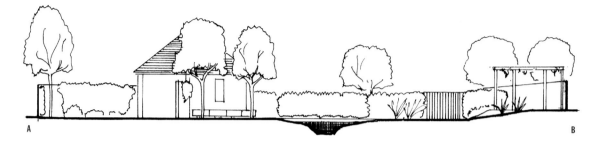

Following the same stages, draw in first the nearest items, and then those further away from the section line. The foreground items may partially obscure those in the background. You have now built up a picture of the garden beyond the actual line of section.

To make the section "read" more clearly, hatch in any features that fall on the actual section line, or emphasize their outline with a thick nib.

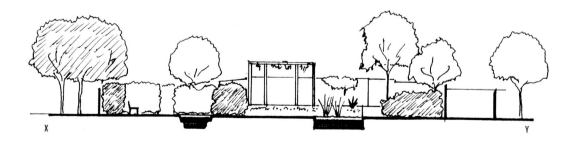

Here section X–Y has been developed in the same way.

Axonometric Projections

An axonometric projection is a type of perspective drawing that creates a three-dimensional impression in which all the planes are described and related to one another. It is relatively easy to set up because it is developed directly from a plan drawing.

An axonometric projection is usually set up by first tilting a garden layout plan, then projecting up the vertical elements, keeping the lines parallel. The plan is usually tilted at forty-five degrees, which produces an angled view of the garden from above, similar to what you would see from the second floor window of a neighbouring house.

If drawing at this angle does not show enough detail (perhaps because the garden design is done on the diagonal), try altering the angles (see below, right). Remember that the angles you choose must add up to 90°.

In axonometric projections, the length, breadth and height of any objects will all be drawn to the same scale, and so the view will look unrealistic and lacking in perspective, although it will be technically correct. As they are essentially technical drawings, they do not depend very heavily on artistic ability for their success. As long as you know the height of any object in the garden (which you will certainly need to know if it is to be built), you should be able to create these drawings without difficulty.

A completed axonometric will show clearly how the different components of a garden—buildings, walls, steps and fences—interrelate. Once mastered, this is a quick and easy method of visualizing your design or checking any construction details.

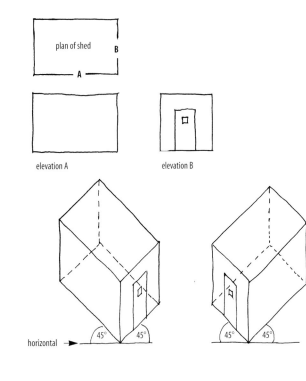

elevation A   elevation B

plan of shed B

A

horizontal →

Above: Most guides to drawing axonometric projections will advise using a 45° tilt, as shown by these two alternative views. The advantage of this angle is that you can see both elevations uniformly and without much distortion. However, you can use any angle you wish and should experiment to find the best view.

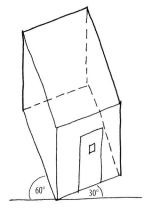

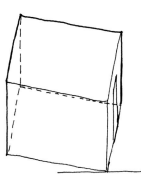

Below: Experimenting with different angles. Note that the plan (the "floor" of the shed) always remains rectanglar.

Drawing a Brick in Axonometric Projection

This exercise is designed to help you understand the concept of axonometric projection. The principles can be applied to objects of any size.

1. Set a brick beside you. Measure it and draw this accurately as a plan, at a scale of 1:1 (life size).
2. Using a parallel rule and set square, draw the plan of your brick at forty-five degrees on your graph-paper backing sheet. Stick this down with masking tape.
3. Using the parallel rule and set square, draw up the vertical lines. Do this by measuring, with your scale ruler at 1:1, the height of the brick, starting at the lowest level. Mark these points off on each vertical line.
4. Join up each of these points.
5. Rub out any unwanted lines hidden by the mass of the brick.

Drawing a brick in axonometric

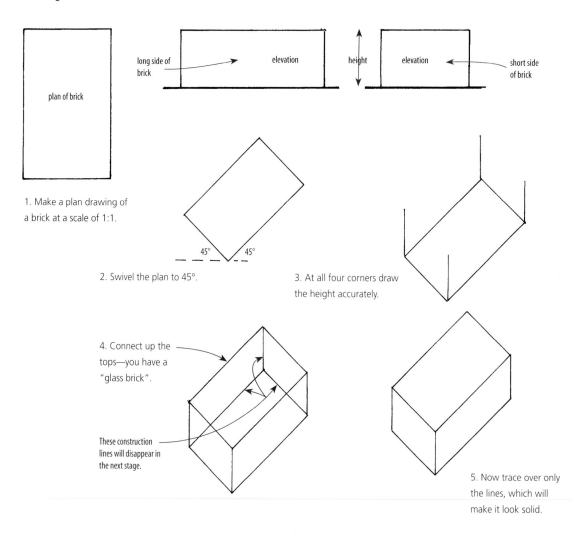

1. Make a plan drawing of a brick at a scale of 1:1.

2. Swivel the plan to 45°.

3. At all four corners draw the height accurately.

4. Connect up the tops—you have a "glass brick".

These construction lines will disappear in the next stage.

5. Now trace over only the lines, which will make it look solid.

Drawing a Tree in Axonometric Projection

When drawing trees in axonometric projection, use a circle template to construct the drawing of the leaf canopy. The resulting drawing will look something like an egg on a stick, but with a little artistic licence (and the addition of an outline to indicate foliage) you should be able to make it look more like a tree. Shrubs can be drawn in the same way, but since there is no trunk, the lower circle (representing the bottom of the canopy) is drawn at ground level.

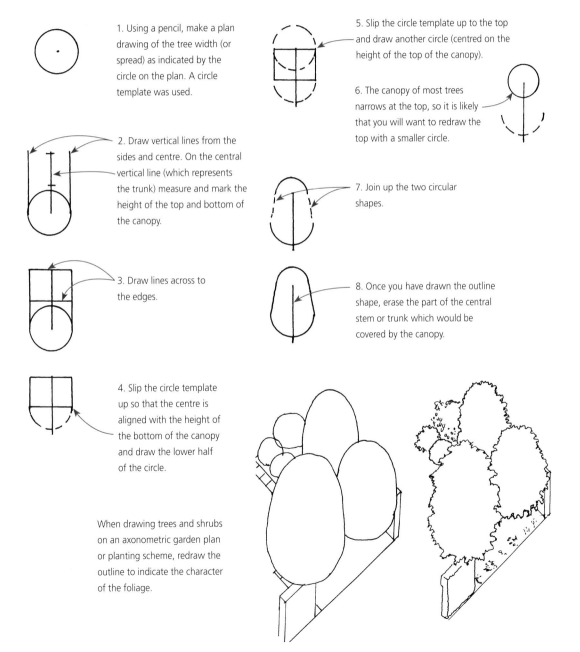

1. Using a pencil, make a plan drawing of the tree width (or spread) as indicated by the circle on the plan. A circle template was used.

2. Draw vertical lines from the sides and centre. On the central vertical line (which represents the trunk) measure and mark the height of the top and bottom of the canopy.

3. Draw lines across to the edges.

4. Slip the circle template up so that the centre is aligned with the height of the bottom of the canopy and draw the lower half of the circle.

5. Slip the circle template up to the top and draw another circle (centred on the height of the top of the canopy).

6. The canopy of most trees narrows at the top, so it is likely that you will want to redraw the top with a smaller circle.

7. Join up the two circular shapes.

8. Once you have drawn the outline shape, erase the part of the central stem or trunk which would be covered by the canopy.

When drawing trees and shrubs on an axonometric garden plan or planting scheme, redraw the outline to indicate the character of the foliage.

Plan

Elevation

Choosing the Viewpoint

Neither the plan nor the elevation drawing could convey the design of a sheltered alcove within a garden to best effect, so an axonometric projection was constructed. The first attempt was unsatisfactory because the statue is almost entirely concealed. In the second attempt, however, where the chosen viewpoint is from the opposite direction, the statue, and its relationship to the bench and plant, is clearly revealed.

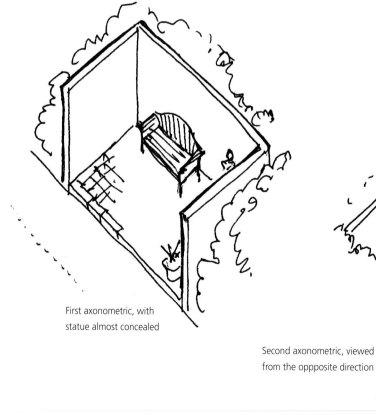

First axonometric, with
statue almost concealed

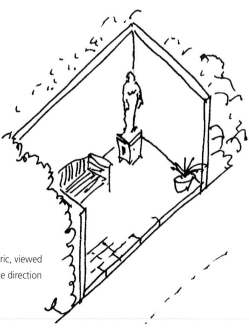

Second axonometric, viewed
from the oppposite direction

Raised seating corner

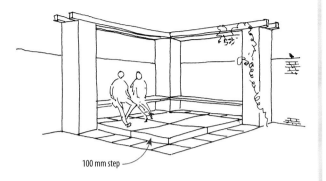

100 mm step

Although it may seem obvious, you need to know the design of every feature of the garden before you draw the axonometric. Thumbnail sketches and details will help. This page shows examples of sketches done before starting the axonometric.

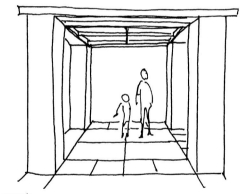

Part of the pergola

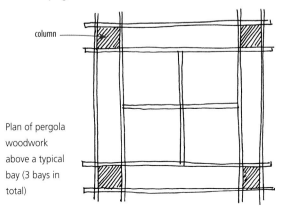

column

Plan of pergola woodwork above a typical bay (3 bays in total)

Drawing an Axonometric Projection from a Garden Layout Plan

1. Using your parallel rule or T-square, and an adjustable set square, fix down the garden layout plan at your chosen angle with, if possible, the lowest level of the garden or the terrace nearest the bottom of the page.
2. Stick a sheet of tracing paper over this. This sheet will contain the draft axonometric plan as it develops.
3. Use the scale rule to measure the vertical lines round the boundaries or exterior of the site, and project up from each corner the height of any structure—building, walls, fence—at these points.
4. Using a set square, join up these points, showing the structure nearest to you as a broken line. This will indicate its presence but allow you to "see through" it on the drawing.
5. Proceed in the same way with the interior of the plan, starting at the lowest level or terrace, which should, if possible, be nearest to you, working up gradually through each construction and change of level. Some more distant features may be hidden behind those in the foreground. At present only show hard landscaping—the plants can be added later. In this drawing, each vertical measurement should be taken from the level of your starting point. If your garden includes several changes of level, it may be easier and quicker, once the first level has been drawn, to slip the tracing-paper overlay up or down to the height of the new level. This will save having to remember to add on, or subtract from, the earlier dimensions each time.
6. All circles on your plan, such as round pools, pots or tables, will appear as the

same true circles in an axonometric. Slip your drawing up or down to the correct height and trace off.

7. When you have finished drawing all the hard landscaping, including pots, pergolas and garden furniture, you may have accumulated so many lines that your drawing is rather confusing. Sometimes it is easier to lay a further sheet of tracing paper over the drawing and trace off only the lines that you actually want.

8. Now draw in the plantings. These can be added to the same sheet or done on an overlay with the two later being combined for the final drawing. Again, begin by moving to the lowest part or terrace of the garden, and locate the planting position of an adjacent tree. Project a vertical line up from the centre point of the trunk to the height of the top of the tree, marking on the trunk where the tree canopy begins. Using that point as the centre, draw a circle to indicate the width or spread of the tree canopy. Normally the tree canopy will narrow at the top of the tree—draw another circle, using the highest point of the tree as the centre of the circle. Join up the two as shown on page 265. This will leave only a small amount (or none) of the tree trunk showing, and although it may look a little odd, it is correct.

9. Proceed in the same way with other trees and shrubs. Climbers and herbaceous plants are normally indicated by showing an outline of their height and spread. Keep your plant outlines simple, and avoid confusing the drawing with details of stems or leaves.

10. Try to make your axonometric drawing look more natural by softening the outlines of the plants, representing the texture of their foliage.

11. For your final drawing, stick down a fresh sheet of tracing paper over the draft axonometric. Trace over all the relevant lines, adding further lines if necessary to help make the drawing appear as three-dimensional and realistic as possible.

12. Remove your new axonometric drawing and have three copies of it printed so that you can experiment with colouring or rendering techniques.

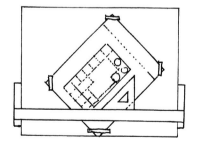 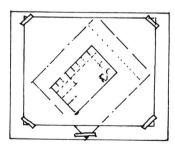 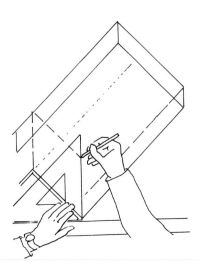

Set up an axonometric projection by attaching the garden plan to the board at 45° (left) and then taping down a tracing paper overlay (right).

Draw verticals after measuring them with a scale rule.

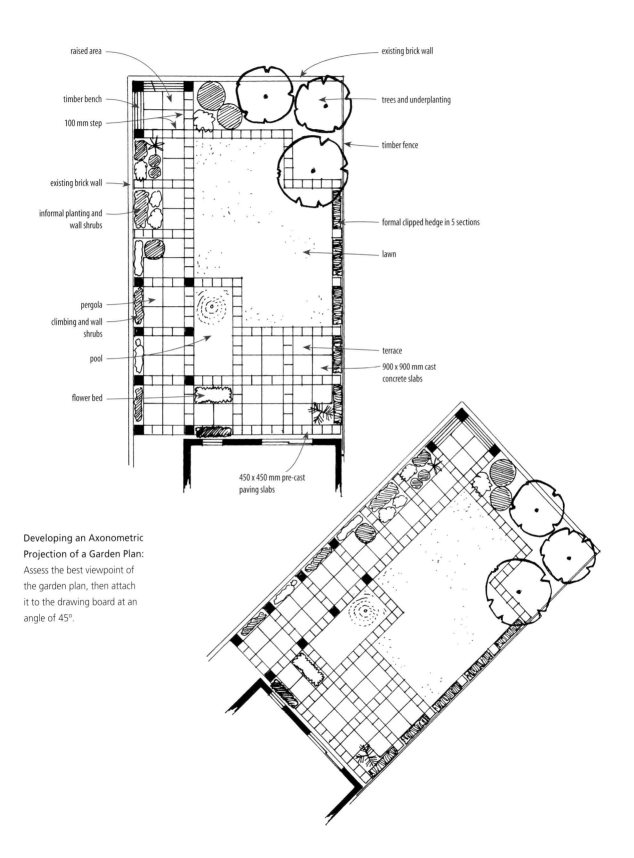

raised area

existing brick wall

timber bench

trees and underplanting

100 mm step

timber fence

existing brick wall

informal planting and wall shrubs

formal clipped hedge in 5 sections

lawn

pergola

climbing and wall shrubs

terrace

pool

900 x 900 mm cast concrete slabs

flower bed

450 x 450 mm pre-cast paving slabs

Developing an Axonometric Projection of a Garden Plan: Assess the best viewpoint of the garden plan, then attach it to the drawing board at an angle of 45°.

On a sheet of tracing paper laid over the plan, project the boundary walls at each corner and then connect them.

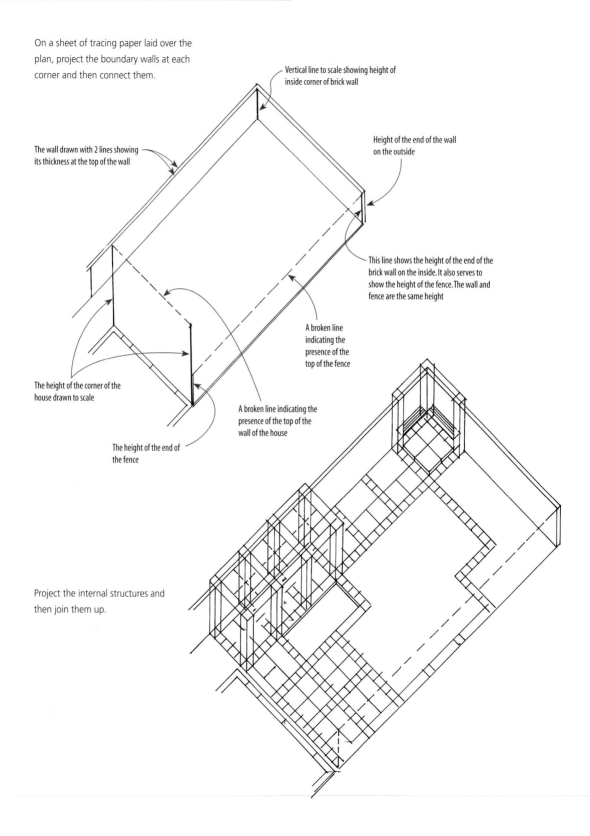

Vertical line to scale showing height of inside corner of brick wall

Height of the end of the wall on the outside

The wall drawn with 2 lines showing its thickness at the top of the wall

This line shows the height of the end of the brick wall on the inside. It also serves to show the height of the fence. The wall and fence are the same height

A broken line indicating the presence of the top of the fence

The height of the corner of the house drawn to scale

A broken line indicating the presence of the top of the wall of the house

The height of the end of the fence

Project the internal structures and then join them up.

Add the trees and shubs. A further
sheet of tracing paper is then laid over
the axonometric and it is redrawn
omitting all "invisible" lines.

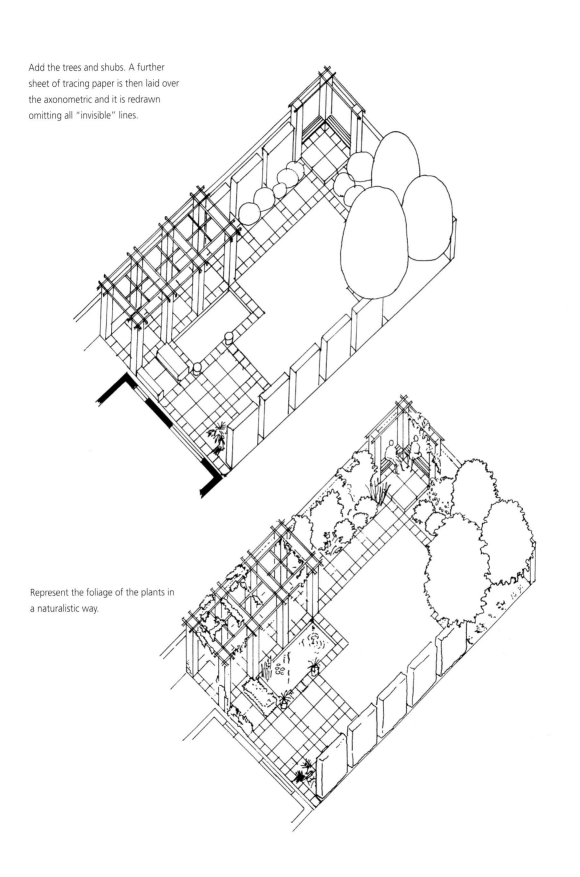

Represent the foliage of the plants in
a naturalistic way.

Adding texture and shadow gives the drawing a more solid appearance. This style of rendering is only one of many you can choose from. The light comes from a definite position, casting well-defined shadows. The figures add a sense of scale.

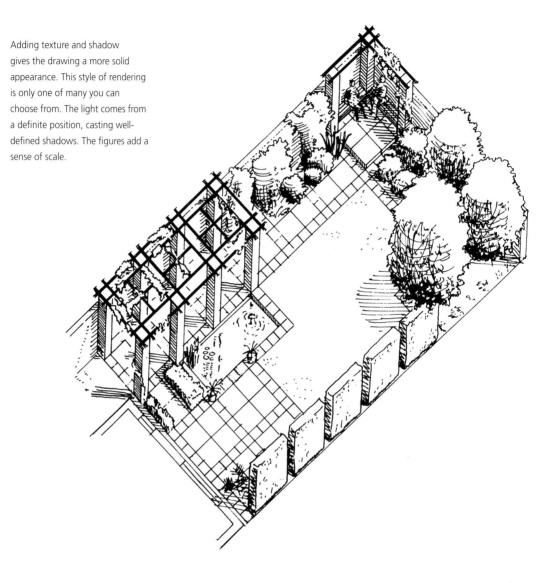

Construction, Planting and Maintenance

How you go about having the garden design built will depend largely on the garden layout plan. If it is an ambitious design that includes new terracing, steps, lawn, pergolas and garden buildings, for instance, it would be wise to hire a contractor. If it involves simply a realignment of existing borders and new plantings, you and your family or friends may be able to carry out most of the work.

Doing the Work Yourself

If you plan to do the construction work yourself it is worth consulting some of the informative do-it-yourself books that are available, which will point out details you might overlook, such as ensuring that the terrace has a cross fall to a drain or gulley to carry away excess water.

The position of new planting beds can be pegged out in accordance with your garden layout plan. Sometimes it is helpful to mark out the proposed line

Axonometric Drawing (Model Plan)

An axonometric drawing made from the planting plan and the final garden layout plan reveals how the design will work. The overhead view shows the relationship between the horizontal elements (such as the pool, lawn, and paths), and the vertical elements (such as the arbour, trees, and the seating).

with sand or a length of garden hose, lifting the turf to this guideline.

All areas to be planted must be well dug over and cleared of any perennial weeds, and unless the soil is in good condition, fertilizer and organic material should be incorporated to improve the soil texture and quality. Trees may need staking as protection from wind, and climbers and wall shrubs may need supporting with a framework of wires attached to walls and fences with vine eyes or wall nails.

Hiring and Using a Contractor

If much hard construction work is required, you may wish to bring in outside contractors to build your garden. These may be house builders or a garden construction company who will work to your specifications. Quotations for the work can vary enormously, so try to make sure that they are all quoting for the same work—for the same depth of gravel, the same type of stone, the same foundations and so on. The glossary includes terminology that may be useful in your discussions.

Many professionals write a detailed specification for large or complex sites, but for smaller works it is often best to seek quotations from a contractor who has a reputation for honesty and reliability. Make sure that you read any quotations carefully, comparing like with like, checking that nothing is overlooked.

A good contractor may be able to make alternative suggestions for some of the construction; this may even save you money. Be sure to ask to see examples of previous work before committing yourself, and, if in any doubt, ask the contractor for permission to contact one of his or her clients so that you can discuss reliability, keeping to the budget and other such details. Ask to see and approve samples of any hard-landscape materials before accepting the quotation—economizing on the quality of materials has ruined the carefully planned effect of many

gardens. Always try to use the best material you can afford.

Make sure that your contractor is familiar with ground preparation and planting and can supply good-quality plants. Always state, "No substitutes acceptable unless previously agreed", in case your contractor cannot supply your exact order. Most garden construction companies can supply plants at an advantageous price and prefer to quote for the whole job. An alternative is to ask your builder to prepare the borders but to obtain the plants and plant them yourself.

Supplying the Plants

For many designers and clients this is the most exciting part of creating a new garden. But plants vary in size, quality and cost. Obviously, larger plants will be more expensive. They may also take longer to become established, and there may be hidden costs such as bringing them in over the house by crane or requiring a fork-lift truck and manual labour to move them onto the allotted space. For large stock, preparing the planting holes in advance will not only save time but may also prevent deterioration through wind rock or frost. Be sure to have everything needed for planting, such as fertilizer, stakes and ties.

Whether buying through trade or retail, try to obtain all your plants from one source. A retailer may give you a discount for quantity, the plants may be superior, and you may be able to select them personally. If different suppliers are used, the plants may arrive at different times, and you will need to leave space for the later deliveries, which will make it more difficult to place the plants exactly where you want them.

Unless the garden is very large and trade prices would be more economic, it may be better to buy the plants locally. Several organizations grow on plants for their own regular horticultural society sales, or there may be a good farmers' market in your nearest town. Buying from a local source will reduce the carbon footprint of transport costs and encourage the livelihood of the local grower. Specialist nurseries, where the owner usually selects and raises his or her stock with loving care, tend to produce healthier and more interesting or unusual plants than the garden centre. Staff at specialist nurseries are also more likely to be able to pass on advice on what to choose and how best to grow the plant.

Maintenance and Future Development

After the garden has been built, it will need to be carefully maintained until established, usually over a period of about three years. Sufficient water and nutrients will need to be available for plant growth, and both hard landscaping and plants should be checked twice yearly for repairs or replacements due to weather and general wear and tear. Although in working up your planting plans you will have taken into account the local conditions, there are occasionally unforeseen reasons for certain plants not growing well, and these may need replacing or changing to another variety. As the garden matures and the plants grow, you may wish to make minor alterations to the original concept. Try to keep notes and a photographic record of the different seasonal effects. You may wish to adjust or add to some of your plant groupings, or perhaps experiment with different bulbs or annuals.

No garden is static, and the way your garden matures will largely depend on how well it is looked after, particularly in the early stages.

Your Role as Garden Designer

Designing for a Friend

Once your friends know that you design gardens, it is very likely that they will suggest that you experiment with their gardens. If you are inexperienced, this proposition may sound attractive, but it could lead to dissatisfaction, misunderstanding and a broken friendship. Try to avoid falling into this trap by providing only the plan and the planting plan and suggesting that your friend selects and employs his or her own contractor.

Both you (as the designer) and your friend (as the client) should be present at the meeting with the contractor to discuss the implementation, as only you will have a clear idea of desired finishes, such as, for instance, the pattern of brickwork. Thereafter you have a choice, either to oversee the work on your friend's behalf or to let your friend supervise the work. Although the latter course may not produce such a good finish, it may still be advisable—so much depends on the personalities involved.

Student Designers

There are various ways of beginning in the profession, but at the outset it can be a daunting and lonely experience. Students often begin by working together as a partnership, especially if they have different yet complementary skills. An alternative is to work in an established practice, spending time in the different departments to gain overall experience, or to work in a nursery where you will not only extend your plant knowledge but may also be asked to redesign a customer's garden to accommodate their new plants. A wide range of experience at an early stage is a valuable springboard for the future.

Newly Qualified Professionals

Even if you have trained at a college, accepting your first commission is a daunting prospect. Each job has its own idiosyncrasies, and clients vary in their attitude to a designer. It is essential that a client understands how a designer works and respects his or her professional skills. Most professionals produce a brochure detailing their services—for example, explaining the different stages, such as the garden layout plan, planting plan, visuals, supervision of the work and payment. Some also list and illustrate past work.

As gardens vary in size and complexity, it is usual to quote a daily rate or, for a once-only consultation, an hourly rate. Once you have seen the site and met the client, you should be able to sum up how long it will take you to complete the required stages. After the initial meeting, the client will expect a speedy written reply from you setting out your charges for the work involved, how and when you expect to complete the various stages and what the client can expect for his or her money. You may wish to give options such as supervising the whole job, or perhaps only overseeing at certain agreed stages. Most job relationships that founder do so because the exact responsibilities and expectations were not made clear at the outset. Be sure to put everything in writing, and insist on written agreement to your terms.

Semi-Professional Designers

Many good, often self-taught designers work part-time and have a more casual relationship with their clients. Often these are people well known in their own locality for providing a friendly, reliable local service at a reasonable price, business coming to them largely by word of mouth. Occasionally these designers work in tandem with a contractor or builder who wants someone to draw plans and liaise with the client while the work is carried out. In this case also it is vital that all parties involved know what is expected and when the work will be carried out, although, compared with the professional rules, the service may be more relaxed.

Professional Designers

You may wish to outsource the design and layout of your garden by using a professional or qualified designer. Many of these will have trained as landscape architects and will be accustomed to advising on large-scale work, but others may have carved out a well-deserved local niche or concentrate

on smaller scale work. Their style, rates, scope and way of working will vary enormously, and it is usually best to ask other people or visit gardens open to the public to find a designer whose style and work you like. Look at their web sites to find out their specializations, scale and type of work before contacting them. Some designers have a sole practice, others may employ a team of designers and specialists, while some may have their own landscape construction firm who carries out their work. Ask about where they have created gardens and who their past clients are, and try to see some of their work before deciding.

If you are to derive pleasure from your garden, it is vital that you and your garden designer have a sound working relationship from the outset, and that you have a clear understanding of their role and their responsibilities, of their charge rates, and the standard of work of any contractors they may use, such as tree surgeons or landscapers to build the garden. Garden design is now a highly skilled and competitive profession, and most professionals are keen to build up a rewarding working relationship with their clients.

Appendices

Keeping a Plant Notebook

Core Plant List

Glossary

Recommended Reading

Index

Keeping a Plant Notebook

Acquiring a good working knowledge of plants takes many years. There are so many variables, such as the preferred soil conditions, aspect and time of flowering. Even if your plant knowledge is good, perhaps you would like to try to extend it by increasing your repertoire. If plants are a new subject to you, building up your own reference notebook from personal observations will be more useful than looking through catalogues or books, although you will need to refer to these to find out more about each plant. Once you have begun your notebook, you may be surprised at how much you can learn.

Keeping a plant notebook will help you to develop a "palette" or repertoire of plants to use in your designs and planting plans. This will not only extend your plant knowledge but will also develop your skill in combining plants for form, texture, colour and seasonal effects. Try to select a range of reliable plants which you find particularly garden-worthy.

Using Plants in Garden Design

Although each plant may have certain outstanding features—form, texture, leaf or flower colour—these can be enhanced by careful grouping to contrast with other companion plants. A shrub, for instance, may well have flowers, berries or autumn leaf colour, and no single perennial herbaceous plant can serve as a complement or contrast to all three. An effective plant grouping might therefore include spring bulbs to accompany the shrub's early spring flowers, an early perennial to show off its foliage and a late-flowering perennial to contrast with its berries. Note which plants attract wildlife and insects as this will bring a further dimension into your gardens. A deep understanding of the special features of each plant and how it harmonizes or contrasts with its neighbours is an important part of getting to know your plants.

In preparing a plant notebook, go further than simply being familiar with a wide range of plants. Be selective and discerning in what you choose and how you use them. A garden designer's palette of plants will not necessarily include fashionable or unusual plants, but rather plants that will perform well over a prolonged season, that are easily grown and disease-resistant, and that combine well with other plants. To ensure that your chosen plants will be compatible and grow well together, look for their country of origin—plants that enjoy dry and sunny conditions may not thrive next to those that prefer damp shade. Your aim in preparing a plant notebook is to produce your own reliable planting palette.

For each plant, research information on characteristics, growth rate, propagation and other factors, as shown on the sample sheet (see page 281). Each of your plant sheets should include photographs or drawings of the plant and information on where and when it was seen.

It is useful to divide the information into two sections, the first including your own photographs or drawings and descriptions of individual plants in their specific categories, and the second including information about groups of plants that make effective combinations in specific situations.

Plant Categories

Choose and photograph different plants for each of the categories relevant to the garden you are designing. Set out the details of each plant on a plant sheet, and keep this with two photographs of the plant—one taken close up, one taken from a distance. It is useful to note the names of two additional plants that would combine with the plant to form an interesting grouping. Plants can be categorized as follows:

– Native trees and shrubs
– Smaller ornamental trees
– Evergreen shrubs
– Deciduous shrubs
– Conifers
– Plants for hedging and screening
– Climbers

- Wall shrubs
- Shrub roses
- Climbing and rambling roses
- Other roses (floribunda, hybrid tea, ground cover and so forth)
- Early-flowering perennials (up to early summer)
- Late-flowering perennials (midsummer onwards)
- Ground covers
- Bamboos
- Grasses
- Hardy ferns
- Aquatic and bog plants
- Bulbs, corms, tubers and rhizomes
- Annuals, biennials, half-hardies and bedding plants

Plant Information Sheet

Gather together information for each plant based on the list that follows. Use the example opposite as a guide to the level of information to include.

Full Latin name

The name must be accurate and up to date. Use a reliable reference, such the latest edition of the *RHS Plant Finder*. Pay particular attention to the correct use of upper and lower case and single quotes for cultivar names.

Synonym

Give well-known or commonly used alternative Latin name or names, if any.

Common name

Give the name or names the plant is commonly known by.

Origin

For a species, give the geographical origin. For a hybrid or cultivar, note the origin of the parent or parents and the nursery or garden in which the plant originated.

Plant family

This is given in the *RHS Plant Finder*, or use a reliable book which details the plant family.

References

Note the book or books where you found most information on the plant (may be noted in abbreviated form) so that you can refer back later if necessary.

Description

Under "General", identify the category and give a brief summary of the key features of the plant (for instance, "A vigorous, evergreen shrub with large scented flowers all summer"). Then note the important characteristics of foliage, flower, fruit and stem where these are significant. Technical botanical language is not necessary unless it helps your understanding of various features.

Period of interest

Shade in the chart as appropriate, using coloured pencils.

Form

A simple line drawing of the outline shape of the plant will help you to identify it in the future.

Height and spread

Assuming average growing conditions in your area, state the probable height and spread after a period of approximately five years after planting. This will vary, of course, depending on the sizes of plants available to you. Mature stock or larger plants can usually be supplied but are more expensive and may well take time to adapt to their new location. Smaller plants suffer less from wind rock, which slows down growth by preventing the roots from establishing firmly in the soil.

Plant Information Sheet

Latin name *Anemone ×hybrida* 'Honorine Jobert'
Synonym *A. japonica* 'Honorine Jobert' or *A. ×hybrida* 'Alba'

Common name Japanese anemone
Plant family Ranunculaceae
Origin Garden origin, sport of hybrid between parents from China and Nepal
References G.S. Thomas, *Perennial Garden Plants*

DESCRIPTION

General Late-flowering hardy perennial, slightly invasive giving a good show of flowers over a long period.
Important characteristics Flowers rounded, pure white with contrasting bunch of yellow stamens, on branching stems that rise well above the foliage.
Leaves rather coarse, three-lobed, pointed, dark green, in clumps. Herbaceous.

	J	F	M	A	M	J	J	A	S	O	N	D
leaf			✔	✔	✔	✔	✔	✔	✔			
flower							✔	✔	✔			
fruit												
stem												
period of interest	J	F	M	A	M	J	J	A	S	O	N	D

Form – height and spread
ultimate growth
10 years: 1.5 m × 3 m
5 years: 1.5 m × 1 m

CULTIVATION

Soil and moisture Prefers any retentive soil, not too dry; more invasive in light soils.
Aspect Full sun preferred; will tolerate light to moderate shade.
Maintenance and pruning Requires no staking (so useful where labour is limited); cut right down in winter.
Propagation By division of old clumps in spring; or root cuttings taken in dormant season or early spring.
Problems and drawbacks Normally trouble-free, but may take two years to establish.
Hardiness Fully hardy.

DESIGN USE AND ASSOCIATED PLANTING

Useful to give a fresh burst of colour in late summer and into autumn when many plants are looking a little tired. A good plant for a mixed border.

Complementary plants

Aster ×frikartii 'Mönch', a good blue-mauve daisy flower for colour contrast at same time of year.
Sedum 'Herbstfreude' (*S.* 'Autumn Joy'), a lower plant with pink flowers and solid fleshy leaves for contrast; grey-green foliage gives interest earlier in season, and dry
flower heads in winter.

Alternatives and substitutes

Many cultivars of *A. ×hybrida*, mainly in shades of pink, also the original pale pink *A. ×hybrida*.
Some good cultivars are: 'Königin Charlotte', large-flowered pink; 'Géante des Blanches', white; 'Margarete', deep pink semi-double. Also forms of *A. hupehensis japonica*, such
as 'Bressingham Glow', rosy-red semi-double; 'Prinz Heinrich', pink.

Notes

Hybrid of *A. hupehensis japonica* and *A. vitifolia*, the sport arose c.1858.
The original *A. ×hybrida* was raised at the R.H.S. garden, Chiswick, in 1848.

Cultivation

Give brief details of the various requirements listed. Under soil, include details of moisture and pH requirements.

Hardiness

This can be a complex area and will depend on the climate where you live. A plant can be fully hardy, frost-hardy, half-hardy or frost-tender. Find out how low the temperature in your area can reach before selecting plants.

Design use and associated planting

This is an important section. Give suggestions of situations where you might use the plant, and try to note two other plants that you believe would associate well with it. Give the reasons for your choice.

Alternative and substitutes

Name a few other plants that are similar to the subject but differ in some significant way, and describe the difference. These may be alternative colours of the same plant, other species of the same genus or plants of different genera that give the same effect in a different situation.

Notes

Add any miscellaneous information, such as notes on propagation, making sure that each sheet represents only one species. A clear system of cross-referencing is helpful. For example, *Taxus baccata* (English yew) could be included under native trees and shrubs, conifers, or plants for hedging and screening. The description of this species would appear in only one section, but a cross-reference could appear in the other sections.

Photographs or drawings

Accompany each master sheet with a separate sheet showing a distant and a close-up photograph of the plant. Beside each illustration give the name of the plant, the date or month when the photograph was taken and the location. A detailed drawing in place of the close-up may teach you more about the habit of the plant.

Plants for a Purpose

It is useful to extend your plant knowledge and to develop your awareness of plants that will look effective when combined. Start by looking at plants, considering good groupings. Confine each of your plant groupings to no more than three to six species, and aim for a wide range of situations in your locality. Choose plants that associate well and that will all grow easily in your specified conditions or tolerate similar conditions. The following are some typical situations:

- Dry shade
- Moist shade
- Dry, sunny situation
- Windy situation
- Shady walls
- Winter interest
- Ornamental stems or bark
- Autumn colour
- Thriving on specific soil conditions, such as lime-free, acidic or chalk
- Thriving by the coast
- Surviving pollution
- Attracting butterflies and bees
- Tolerating drought conditions

Create plant information sheets for these "Plants for a Purpose". Draw an outline elevation to show the shapes of the plants and how they interact. If possible, photograph the groupings, and take rough measurements of the plants and the distances between them to help you understand about spacing and rate of growth. Make a note of the location and the date, and the situation for which the group is intended. Write down the botanical name of each plant, details of features of interest (and the times of year that they occur), and cultivation information. Suggest other plants that might be linked with the plant group, perhaps to extend the season of interest or to continue the theme.

Core Plant List

If your plant knowledge is limited, this list can be used as a basis for making choices for your own plant palette. No plant list can be comprehensive, and most garden designers have their own favourite plants.

If the common name of a plant varies from region to region, only the Latin name is given. Where a variety of a particular plant is not stated, you will need to research the variety most suited to the needs of the garden design.

Structural Planting

Large, Native, Deciduous Trees

These can spread to 30 m (100 ft.).
Betula pendula (silver birch or European white birch)
Carpinus betulus (hornbeam)
Fagus sylvatica (beech)
Fraxinus excelsior (ash)
Quercus robur (oak)

Large, Decorative, Deciduous Trees

Betula varieties (silver birch)
Catalpa bignonioides (Indian bean)
Fagus sylvatica 'Purpurea' (copper beech)
Ginkgo biloba (maidenhair tree)
Liriodendron tulipifera (tulip tree)
Salix babylonica (weeping willow)
Ulmus glabra 'Pendula' (weeping elm)

Fast-Growing Trees

Acer lobelii (maple)
Ailanthus altissima (tree of heaven)
Alnus cordata (Italian alder)
Castanea sativa (sweet chestnut)
Eucalyptus in var. (gum)
Fraxinus excelsior (ash)
Gleditsia triacanthos (honey locust)
Juglans regia (walnut)

Platanus mexicana (plane)
Populus alba (white poplar)
Prunus avium (wild cherry)
Pterocarya fraxinifolia (wing nut)
Robinia pseudoacacia (false acacia or locust)
Salix alba varieties (willow)
Tilia americana (American lime or linden)

Vertical Conifers

Chamaecyparis lawsoniana 'Kilmacurragh'
Chamaecyparis lawsoniana 'Wissellii'
Juniperus scopulorum 'Skyrocket'
Juniperus communis 'Suecica' (Swedish juniper)
Taxus baccata 'Aurea' (golden yew)
Taxus baccata 'Fastigiata' (Irish yew)

Small Trees as Specimens or Focal Points

Betula varieties (birch)
Malus varieties (crab apple)
Prunus varieties (cherry)
Pyrus varieties (pear)
Sorbus varieties (ash or rowan)

Structural Shrubs or Small Trees

Arbutus unedo (strawberry tree)
Arundinaria varieties(bamboo)
Aucuba varieties (laurel)
Berberis thunbergii 'Atropurpurea' (barberry)
Bupleurum fruticosum (shrubby hare's ear)
Buxus sempervirens (box or boxwood)
Camellia varieties.
Choisya ternata (Mexican orange)
Cordyline australis (cabbage palm or cabbage tree)
Eriobotrya japonica (loquat)
Escallonia varieties
Fatsia japonica
Griselinia in var.
Hebe varieties (veronica)
Ilex varieties(holly)
Ilex aquifolium 'Pyramidalis' (holly)

Juniperus communis 'Hibernica' (Irish juniper)
Magnolia grandiflora 'Exmouth' (Exmouth magnolia)
Magnolia grandiflora 'Goliath' (magnolia)
Mahonia ×media 'Charity'
Olearia ×haastii (daisy bush)
Phormium tenax (New Zealand flax)
Photinia
Pittosporum
Rhododendron varieties (rhododendrons and azaleas)
Rhus varieties (sumach)
Sambucus varieties (elderberry)
Taxus baccata (yew)
Viburnum plicatum 'Mariesii'
Yucca

Key Planting

Shrubs as Seasonal Features

Acer varieties (maple)
Amelanchier (service berry)
Berberis (barberry)
Brachyglottis (ragwort)
Buddleja (butterfly bush)
Cornus (dogwood)
Corylopsis
Cotinus (smoke tree)
Daphne pontica (daphne)
Elaeagnus (silverberry)
Genista aetnensis (broom)
Hamamelis (witch hazel)
Hydrangea varieties
Itea ilicifolia (sweetspire)
Lavandula (lavender)
Ligustrum lucidum (privet)
Magnolia ×soulangeana (garden magnolia or saucer magnolia)
Magnolia stellata (star magnolia)
Mahonia
Myrtus (myrtle)
Olearia (daisy bush)
Paeonia delavayi (tree peony)
Philadelphus (mock orange)

Rosa (rose)
Rosmarinus varieties (rosemary)
Sarcococca (sweet box)
Skimmia varieties
Tamarix (tamarisk)
Viburnum varieties

Decorative Planting

Deciduous Shrubs (Including Wall Shrubs)

Caryopteris
Ceanothus
Chaenomeles
Cistus
Convolvulus cneorum
Cytisus
Deutzia
Fuchsia
Genista
Halimium
Lavandula
Lavatera
Spiraea
Syringa
Viburnum
Weigela

Decorative Climbers

Clematis
Cobaea
Hedera
Hydrangea anomala subsp. *petiolaris*
Lathyrus
Lonicera
Parthenocissus
Passiflora
Rhodochiton
Rosa
Solanum
Trachelospermum

Tropaeolum
Vitis
Wisteria

Rounded Plants

Berberis thunbergii 'Atropurpurea Nana'
Buxus
Genista hispanica
Hebe varieties
Lavandula angustifolia 'Hidcote'
Ruta graveolens
Santolina
Teucrium

Grasses

Arundo donax (giant reed)
Calamagrostis ×*acutiflora* 'Karl Foerster'
Carex elata 'Aurea' (Bowles' golden sedge)
Deschampsia cespitosa (tufted hair grass)
Festuca amethystina (sheep's fescue)
Festuca glauca (blue fescue)
Hakonechloa macra
Helictotrichon sempervirens (blue oat grass)
Milium effusum 'Aureum' (Bowles' golden grass)
Miscanthus sinensis (Chinese silver grass)
Molinia (purple moor grass)
Panicum virigatum (switch grass)
Pennisetum alopecuroides (fountain grass)
Stipa tenuifolia

Herbaceous Planting

Broad-Brush Herbaceous Perennials

Achillea
Aconitum
Agapanthus
Alchemilla mollis
Anemone japonica
Anthemis punctata
Artemisia

Aster
Astrantia
Bergenia
Campanula
Crocosmia
Dianthus
Diascia
Dicentra
Digitalis
Epilobium
Eryngium
Euphorbia
Geranium
Hemerocallis
Hosta
Iris
Kniphofia
Lobelia
Macleaya
Nepeta
Oenothera
Paeonia
Penstemon
Persicaria
Rodgersia
Romneya coulteri
Ruta graveolens
Salvia
Sedum
Sisyrinchium striatum
Thalictrum
Veratrum
Zauschneria californica

Plants with Fleeting Effects

(B) after the plant name denotes a bulbous plant.

Allium (B)
Alstroemeria
Amaryllis (B)
Anemone blanda (B)
Canna (half-hardy in Britain)
Chionodoxa (B)
Colchicum (B)

Cosmos
Crocus (B)
Cyclamen (B)
Dahlia (half-hardy in Britain)
Digitalis
Felicia
Fritillaria (B)
Galanthus (B)
Galtonia (B)
Gladiolus (B)
Hedychium (half-hardy in Britain)
Helichrysum
Lilium (B)
Lupinus
Malva moschata

Muscari (B)
Narcissus (B)
Nectaroscordum (B)
Nerine (B)
Nicotiana
Osteospermum
Papaver
Phlox
Pulsatilla
Ricinus (half-hardy in Britain)
Salvia
Scilla (B)
Tulipa (B)
Verbena
Viola

Glossary

Aggregate Small stone content of a given mixture.

Ashlar A facing of dressed stone blocks on a backing wall of brick, rough stone or concrete block.

Automatic valve A valve which can be remotely operated. The remote operation method may be electrical (the most common) or hydraulic. Automatic valves are commonly used as "control valves" for irrigation systems.

Ball valve A valve which controls the water by means of a rotating ball with a hole through the centre. When the hole is aligned with the water flow, the water moves freely through the valve with almost no friction loss. When the ball is rotated so that the hole is not aligned, the flow is completely shut off. Ball valves are used primarily as isolation valves. They tend to be very reliable and trouble-free, but ball valves as a group tend to require more effort to turn on and off than other valves. For largest pipes, butterfly valves are usually used rather than ball valves.

Ballast A mixture of sand and stone aggregate. Usually associated with the mixture used for making concrete.

Balustrade A complete railing system consisting of a top handrail supported by balusters (which sometimes rest on a bottom rail).

Batter The angle of a wall where it is made to lean inwards from the perpendicular.

Belt course A continuous horizontal course of flat stones marking a division in the wall plane.

Bentonite A natural clay product commonly used for a soil sealant in ponds. When hydrated, the bentonite granules swell into the voids surrounding soil particles, creating a tough watertight seal.

Blinding A layer of sand laid to cover sharp edges of stone, such as over a hardcore base, or when laying a liner for a pool.

Bond The way in which bricks or stone are laid to give structural strength.

Brick on edge A brick laid with the thin stretcher face uppermost, as when used as a trim to an edging or as a coping to a wall.

Brushed finish A textured finish obtained by brushing with a coarse rotary-type wire brush.

Brushed aggregate Concrete, the surface of which has been brushed before setting (when "green") to expose the selected stone aggregate to give a textured finish. Also referred to as exposed aggregate.

Bull nose The convex rounding of a stone member, such as a stair tread.

Bush-hammered finish A textured finish made by a pounding action.

Camber (of paths) A slightly arched surface.

Cement The medium used as the binding agent in mortar or concrete.

Chat-sawn finish A finish featuring irregular, uneven markings.

Concrete A mixture made up of cement, sharp sand and aggregate (usually gravel stone). The sand and stone are often referred to as ballast.

Controller A timer used to turn an automatic irrigation system on and off. Controllers range from very simple to extremely sophisticated computer systems that utilize modems, cell phones or radios and allow two-way communication between the controller and the units being controlled (valves, metres, weather stations, soil moisture and sensors, for example).

Coping The top course of a wall, usually made of brick, stone or concrete, designed to prevent water from seeping into the body of the wall.

Coursed Describes stone or brick laid in a particular pattern.

Critical curve The maximum extent to which a path can be curved without the need for cutting corners.

Cubic feet A measurement of liquid quantity, often used by water companies in the United States. A cubic foot is 1 foot long, 1 foot wide and 1 foot deep.

Curbing Slabs and blocks of stone bordering streets, walks and so forth.

Damp-proof course (DPC) A course laid near the base of a wall to prevent moisture rising within the wall. It can consist of a number of courses of high-density engineering bricks, two courses of overlapping tiles or a layer of bitumen-impregnated strip. Where there is a poured concrete foundation this can also be referred to as the "top of foundation".

Design pressure The pressure at which a specific piece of irrigation equipment is designed to operate.

Drip irrigation Any type of irrigation that applies water to the soil very slowly. Drip irrigation tends to be the most efficient irrigation technology in terms of both water and energy use.

Drip system An irrigation system that uses drip irrigation.

Dry-mix A mixture of sand and cement without any water added, sometimes used when laying brick or slab paving.

Emitter A small device, also known as a dripper, that controls the flow going to the soil during drip irrigation. Emitters come in many different flow rates and styles.

Fall The slight slope created to carry water off hard surfaces to prevent flooding and puddling. The fall, also referred to as the slope or grade, is directed towards open soil areas or specially sited drains and gullies.

Finish A surface treatment. Stones may be finished in a variety of ways. In general, smooth finishes emphasize colour and veining, while rough finishes subdue veining and markings.

Flagstone Thin slabs of stone used for flagging or paving walks, driveways, patios and so forth, generally consisting of fine-grained sandstone, bluestone, quartzite or slate, although other stones may be used.

Flamed finish A rough finish developed with intense heat.

Footing The load-bearing (underground) substructure of a wall—for example, with a wall, the excavated trench, foundation and lower courses.

Gallons per minute (GPM) A measurement of water flow primarily used in the United States.

Gauging A grinding process that results in the uniform thickness of all pieces of material to be used together.

Gnomon A rod or pin that indicates the time of day by the position of its shadow.

Gravity flow A water system that relies on gravity to provide the pressure required to deliver the water. Consists of a water source located at a higher elevation than the water delivery points.

Ground-water table The level at any given time of the water travelling through the soil. It varies according to the soil conditions and the time of year.

Gulley A shallow channel that carries away surface water. Sometimes used as another name for a drain, a gulley may also be known as a swale.

Hardcore A mixture of broken brick or stone used to create a firm base on which to lay concrete foundations, paving and so on. It should not include any soil or traces of vegetation. Can also be referred to as base course, bedding or sub grade.

Head to head Said of sprinklers spaced so that the water from one sprinkler throws all the way to the next sprinkler. Most sprinklers are designed to give the best performance when this kind of spacing is used.

Hoggin A mixture of gravel and clay used as the binding agent in gravel paths and driveways.

Honed finish A dull finish without reflections.

Hydro-zone An area of an irrigation system in which all the factors that influence the watering schedule are similar. Typical factors to be considered would be the type of plants, the precipitation rate of sprinklers or emitters, solar radiation, wind, soil type and slope.

In situ Constructed on site in the position shown. For example, a concrete wall is created in situ by pouring liquid concrete into a "form" using timber shuttering.

Liner A waterproof layer used to create water features ranging from small pools to lakes. This can be a variety of materials, including clay and sheeting made of butyl or PVC.

Litres per minute A metric measurement of water flow used worldwide.

Mainline The pipes going from the water source to the control valves.

Mortar A mixture of soft sand and cement used for walling, paving and so forth. Sometimes referred to as cement.

Natural cleft Stones formed in layers in the ground. When stones are cleaved or separated along a natural seam, the remaining surface is referred to as a natural cleft surface.

Nozzle The part of a sprinkler that the water comes out of. Usually a nozzle is carefully engineered to assure a good spray pattern. In most cases the nozzle is removable so that is can be easily cleaned or replaced. With plastic nozzles, replacement is generally preferred over cleaning, as small scratches in the plastic can cause big problems with water distribution uniformity.

Operating pressure The pressure at which a device or irrigation system is designed to operate. There can be "optimum operating pressure", "minimum operating pressure", "maximum operating pressure" and "operating pressure range".

Paver A "shin" brick specially manufactured for brick paving. It can also be used as a facing on walls.

Pea shingle A material dredged from sea and rivers, consisting of more rounded stones than gravel.

Planed timber Timber that has been cut to a nominal size with a saw and has a rough finish. Also referred to as sawn timber or rough-sawn lumber, this timber can be planed or sanded for a smooth finish. Timber sizes are quoted in sawn sizes unless otherwise stated. For example, after planing, it is "F4S" (Finished Four Sides): 50×100 mm (2×4 in.) is the rough-sawn dimension, but the actual piece of wood measures 37×87 mm (1.5×3.4 in.).

Polished finish A shiny finish with sharp reflections. This is the smoothest finish available, resulting in a high lustre (gloss).

Pop-up sprinkler head A sprinkler head that retracts below ground level when it is not operating.

Precipitation rate A measurement of water application, given in the depth of water applied to the soil—in other words, the depth that the water would be if it did not run off or soak into the soil. In the United States, precipitation rates are measured in inches per hour. In metric countries, they are measured in mm per hour.

Pressure gauge A device used to measure water pressure. The best pressure gauges are "liquid filled"; however, most inexpensive gauges work well enough for irrigation use.

Pump A device that increases water pressure or moves water.

PVC Polyvinyl chloride, a type of plastic used to make pond liners and water pipe. PVC is available in several colours. Purple indicates unclean or wastewater.

Quoins Stones at the external corner or edge of a wall emphasized by size, projection, rustication or by a different finish.

Random course Paving laid so that the roughly shaped stones are in a random pattern instead of in coursed lines. Various sizes of square paving can be laid in a random pattern, such as when using slate or York stone paving.

Resin bonded aggregate Gravel that is mixed with resin before it is laid. When set, it provides a firm base and allows water to drain through.

Riprap Irregular, broken and randomly sized pieces of rock used for facing abutments and fills.

Stones are thrown together without order to form a foundation, breakwater or sustaining wall.

Rise The height of stone (generally in veneer) or the vertical dimension between two successive steps.

Rock-face finish Also referred to as a pitch-face finish, this convex finish is similar to a split-face finish except that the face of the stone is given line and plane, producing a bold appearance that is considered to more closely resemble natural stone.

Sharp sand A sand that is washed to remove the silt content, used mostly for concrete and rendering. It is coarser, larger-grained, and lighter in colour than soft sand.

Slab A lengthwise cut of a large quarry block of stone, approximately 1.5 × 2.4 m (5 × 8 ft.).

Smooth finish A softened effect created by a saw, grinder or planer.

Snapped edge A style, also known as quarry cut or broken edge, that usually involves a natural breaking of stone either by hand or machine. The break should be at right angles to the top and bottom surface.

Soft sand A very fine sand with a relatively high silt content, often referred to as building sand and used to make mortar for brickwork.

Spall A stone fragment that has split or broken off the face of a stone, either by the force of a blow or through weathering. Sizes may vary from chip size to large stones. Spalls are primarily used for taking up large voids in rough rubble or mosaic patterns.

Split-face finish Also referred to as a sawed-bed finish, this finish is concave or convex, usually sawed on the stone bed and split by hand or machine so that the face of the stone exhibits the natural quarry texture.

Sprinkler A device that distributes water over a given area for irrigation.

Stretcher and header The different faces of a brick. The stretcher is the long face, either when seen as the narrow side in walling or when laid on edge, or the wider face when laid flat in paving. The header is the small, end face of the brick.

Thermal finish A coarse finish created by applying a mechanically controlled flame to a surface.

Tread A flat stone or surface used as the top walking surface on a step.

Valve A device used to control the flow of water. Isolation valves are used to shut water off for repairs. Control valves turn water on and off to the individual circuits of sprinklers or drip emitters. Check valves allow water to flow in only one direction. Master valves are located at the water source and turn water on and off for the entire irrigation system when not in use.

Veneer Any decorative facing material which is not meant to be load-bearing.

Water table The level at which water lies naturally in the soil.

Recommended Reading

You may wish to extend your understanding and skills in garden design through further reading on the subject. The books on these lists include both American and British titles. If a title is out of print, it is often possible to find a copy in a secondhand bookstore or on the internet.

History

Barlow Rogers, Elizabeth. 2001. *Landscape Design: A Cultural and Architectural History.* New York: Harry N. Abrams.

Hobhouse, Penelope. 2002. *The Story of Gardening.* London: Dorling Kindersley.

Otis, Denise. 2002. *Ground for Pleasure: Four Centuries of the American Garden.* New York: Harry N. Abrams.

Quest-Ritson, Charles. 1996. *The English Garden Abroad.* London: Penguin.

Design and Inspiration

Brookes, John. 2002. *Garden Masterclass.* New York: Dorling Kindersley.

Crowe, Sylvia. 1981 *Garden Design.* London: Gibson Packard.

Dickey, Page. 2003. *Breaking Ground: Portraits of Ten Garden Designers.* New York: Artisan.

Dixon, Trisha. 1998. *The Vision of Edna Walling.* Hawthorn, Victoria: Bloomings. Australia and New Zealand only.

Hayward, Gordon. 2003. *Your House, Your Garden: A Foolproof Approach to Garden Design.* New York: W. W. Norton & Co..

Hayward, Gordon and Mary Hayward. 2003. *Tending Your Garden.* New York: W.W. Norton & Co.

Lewis, Pam. 2005. *Sticky Wicket: Gardening in Tune with Nature.* London: Frances Lincoln.

Strong, Roy. 1989. *A Small Garden Designer's Handbook.* Boston: Little, Brown.

Strong, Roy. 1995. *Successful Small Gardens: New Designs for Time-Conscious Gardeners.* New York: Rizzoli.

Trulove, James Grayson, ed. 1998. *The New American Garden: Innovations in Residential Landscape Architecture: Sixty Case Studies.* New York: Watson-Guptill.

Verey, Rosemary. 1989. *Classic Garden Design: How to Adapt and Re-create Garden Features of the Past.* New York: Random House.

Drawing

Alexander, Rosemary, and Karena Batstone. 1996. *A Handbook for Garden Designers.* London: Ward Lock.

Reid, Grant W. 2002. *Landscape Graphics: Plan, Section, and Perspective Drawing and Landscape Spaces.* New York: Watson-Guptill.

Hard Landscaping

In addition to any of the collection of *Sunset* and *Ortho* books:

Alexander, Rosemary and Richard Sneesby. 2005. *The Garden Makers Manual.* London: Conran Octopus.

Archer-Wills, Anthony. 2002. *The Water Gardener: A Complete Guide to Designing, Constructing and Planting Water Features.* New York: Todtri.

Blanc, Alan. 1996. *Landscape Construction and Detailing*. New York: McGraw-Hill.

Van Sweden, James. 2003. *Architecture in the Garden*. New York: Random House.

Plants

Beales, Peter. 1997. *Classic Roses*. London: Harvill.

Blanc, Patrick. 2008. *The Vertical Garden: From Nature to the City*. W. W. Norton & Co.

Brickell, Christopher, and Trevor Cole, eds. 2002. *American Horticultural Society Encyclopedia of Plants and Flowers: The Definitive Practical Guide*. New York: Dorling Kindersley.

Chatto, Beth. *Beth Chatto's Gravel Garden*. London: Frances Lincoln.

Davis, Brian. 1987. *The Gardener's Illustrated Encyclopedia of Trees and Shrubs: A Guide to More Than 2000 Varieties*. Emmaus, Pennsylvania: Rodale.

Dorling Kindersley. 2000. *American Horticultural Society Great Plant Guide*. New York: Dorling Kindersley.

Hillier, John, ed. 2002. *Hillier Manual of Trees and Shrubs*. Newton Abbot, England: David & Charles.

Lancaster, Roy. 1997. *What Perennial Where*. London: Dorling Kindersley.

Phillips, Roger, and Martyn E. Rix. 1988. *Roses*. London: Pan.

Phillips, Roger, and Martyn E. Rix. 1989. *Bulbs*. Ed. Brian Mathew. London: Pan.

Phillips, Roger, and Martyn E. Rix. 2002. *Perennials: The Definitive Reference with over 2500 Photographs*. Toronto: Firefly.

Royal Horticultural Society. 2004. *RHS Plant Finder 2004—2005*. London: Dorling Kindersley. For British use only; reprinted annually.

Thomas, Graham Stuart. 1992. *Ornamental Shrubs, Climbers and Bamboos: Excluding Roses and Rhododendrons*. Portland, Oregon: Sagapress.

Thomas, Graham Stuart. 1993. *Perennial Garden Plants, or, The Modern Florilegium*. London: Orion.

Planting

Alexander, Rosemary. 2006. *The Essential Garden Maintenance Workbook*. Portland, Oregon: Timber Press.

DiSabato-Aust, Tracy. 2006. *The Well-Tended Perennial Garden: Planting and Pruning Techniques (Expanded Edition)*. Portland, Oregon: Timber Press.

Dunnett, Nigel and Noël Kingsbury. 2008. *Planting Green Roofs And Living Walls, Revised and Updated Edition*. Portland, Oregon, Timber Press.

Hunningher, Erica. 2002. *Gardens of Inspiration*. New York: Dorling Kindersley.

Johnson, Arthur T. and H. A. Smith. 2008. *Plant Names Simplified: Their Pronunciation, Derivation and Meaning*. Ipswich, Suffolk: Old Pond Publishing Ltd.

Lord, Tony. 1999. *Designing with Roses*. London: Frances Lincoln.

Nold, Robert. 2007. *High and Dry. Gardening with Cold-Hardy Dryland Plants*. Portland, Oregon. Timber Press.

Quest-Ritson, Charles. 2003. *Royal Horticultural Society Encyclopedia of Roses*. London: Dorling Kindersley.

Oudolf, Piet and Henk Gerritsen. 2003. *Planting The Natural Garden*. Portland, Oregon: Timber Press.

Oudolf, Piet and Noël Kingsbury. *Planting Design: Gardens in Time and Space*. Portland, Oregon: Timber Press.

Toogood, Alan. 1991. *The Hillier Guide to Connoisseur's Plants*. Portland, Oregon: Timber Press.

Warren, William. 2000. *The Tropical Garden*. London: Thames & Hudson.

Warren, William and Luca Invernizzi Tettoni. 2001. *Balinese Gardens*. Boston: Tuttle.

Irrigation

Smith, Stephen W. 1996. *Landscape Irrigation: Design and Management*. New York: John Wiley & Sons.

Lighting

Lennox Moyer, Janet. 1992. *The Landscape Lighting Book*. New York: John Wiley & Sons.

Raine, John. 2001. *Garden Lighting*. San Diego, California: Laurel Glen.

Index

Page numbers in *italic* type refer to photographs.

A

access, site 191
altitude 55
annuals 231
arbours 133, 134, 138, 171, 175–6
arches 133, 138
    mirrored *152*
    presentation plan 76
architectural salvage 179
arid environments 221, *239*
art, garden 138–9
aspect 52, 217
asphalt 123, 124
atmosphere, controlling 171–2
autumn effects 217
avenue-channelled space 98
awnings 171, 172
axonometric projections 249, 263–73

B

backdrops 140–1
background planting *238*
balls, ornamental 180
balustrades 180
barbecues *150*, 185
bark chippings 121, 122, 123, *150*
beds
    construction 272, 274–5
    curved 28, 147
    digging 274
    raised *239*
biodiversity 222
birdbaths and feeders 112, 180
block paving 126
bog gardens 150, *202*, 222
borders
    background planting 167–8, 170, 214
    planning 120
    service paths 120
boreholes 107, 194

boundaries 50–1, 156–7
boundary ownership 59
brick 121
    paving 124–6, 127, *151*
    walls *148*, 159, 162
bridges 108, 149, 180
broad-brush effects 231
    core plant list 286
buildings 133, 136–8, 155, 176–7
    green (living) roofs 137–8, *205*, *206*
    measuring 23–4, 26–7
    presentation plan 73
    site survey 23–4, 42
    softening outlines 49
    see also house
bulbs 231, 232, *246*
    core plant list 286–7
buttressing 160, 161

C

call-before-you-dig 60
cellular paving 126
cement 120–1
chalky soil 58
checklists 17–18
children
    play areas and equipment 15, 122, 130, 135, 136, 186–7, *239*
    safety 25, 114
    tree houses 186–7, *239*
chimney pots 179
circular themes 78–9, 91, 93, 95, 96, *150*, 200
circulation, directing 113, 156
cisterns 180
clair-voyées 181
clay soil 32
clearance, site 191
climate 54–5, 217–18
    change 54–5
    hardiness-zone system 54
    shadows and shade 53, 99
    water features 105, 106, 113
climbers 224, 229–30

core plant list 285–6
    supports 274
climbing frames 187
coastal locations 217, 221
cobbles 124, 125, 126, 127
colour *145*, 209, 214–15, *241–6*
    on drawn plans 249–50, 251
    foliage 214, *242*, *244*, *245*, *246*
    garden furniture 185
    hard landscaping 214
    and light 214–15
    owner's requirements 16
    spatial tricks 214
    water features 103, 104–5
compasses 37
compost 16, *206*
concept diagram 64–6, 69, 115
concrete 120, 121, 123–4
    cellular paving 126
    containers 206
    pavers 125, 126
    precast 127, 128
    walls 159, 162–3
conifers 77, 225–6, 284
conservation areas 58
construction and maintenance 272, 274–5
construction details 197
contractors, hiring and using 274
coping 159
copyright 70
cottage gardens 220
covenant communities 59
crazy paving 127
critical curve 119
curves 130
    measuring 28
curvilinear patterns 79, 95, 96
    paths 119
cut and fill 29, 135

D

damp-proof courses (DPCs) 117–18
deciduous plants 214, 217, 224, 225, 226
decking 117, 128–9, *145*, *205*

decorative planting 229–30
    core plant list 284, 285–6
depth, adding 80, 81–2
designer's role 275–6
desire lines 119
diagonal themes 78, 90, 91, 94, 97, 118
    repeat planting 224, 231
disclaimers 70
dock 59
doors 23, 24, 30, 118
    dummy 156–7, 182
    scale and proportion 101
dovecotes 181
drainage 56–7, 191–3
drains 30
drawing boards 35, 36
drawings
    axonometric 249, 263–73
    basic skills 35–8
    colouring 249–50, 251
    elevations 228, 249, 258–62
    full size 38
    orientation 40
    perspective 254
    photographic overlays 249, 254–5
    plant notebooks 279
    planting plan 233–7
    plants 76–7
    presentation plan 69–77
    scale, to 35, 37–43
    sections 249, 258–62
    texture, rendering 250, 252
    thumbnail sketches 267
    tone 250
    walls, fences and hedges 74, 77
dry stone walls 120–1
dry stream beds 122, *203*
dummy windows and doors 156–7, 182
dustbins 16
dynamic designs 80, 98

E

edging 122, 133
electricity supply 195

INDEX

elevations 228, 249, 258–62
entrances 141, 157–8
evergreen plants 217, 224, 225, 226
existing plants, using 18, 218, 225, *238*
experimental theme plans 95
extrovert gardens 47

F

fencing 140–1, *149*, 164–7
  chain-link 165
  closeboard 164
  concealing 50
  larchlap 164
  log-filled gabions 165
  measuring 24–5
  mesh 165
  metal 165
  ownership 59
  presentation plan 74
  representation on plans 25
  timber 165
  as windbreak 56, 156
filler plants 218–19
final garden layout plan 155–99
  back-up drawings 197
  colour 199
  drawing up 196–200
finials 180
fire pits 150, 185
flag stones 127, 128
fleeting effects 231
  core plant list 286–7
flow, creating 80, 99
flower pots *151*, 181
focal points 138–9, 155, 172, 183, 210, 227
  structural planting 284
foliage
  colour 214, *238–9, 242, 244, 245, 246*
  shape *245*
foreshortening 108
formal gardens *147*, 219, *238, 244*
  water features 107, 109

fountains 105, 114
framework, underlying 82
framing 47, 48, 100, *148, 152*, 181
French drains 192
friends, designing for 275
frost 55, 56
fruit, growing 211, 221
furniture 183–5, *205*
  storage 16, 183

G

garages 136
garden use 11, 15–18
  future changes 15
  paths 118–19
gateways 100, 141, 157–8, 180
glass chippings 122
granite setts 124, 126
graphic language 69
graphic symbols 73–5
grass 130–3
  mown paths 130
  rough grass and wildflower meadows 131, 133–4, 222
grasses *245*, 286
gravel 121, 122–3, 127, *148*
green (living) roofs 137–8, *205, 206*
greenhouses 16, 136–7
grey water 111, 193, 195
grids, designing with 80, 83–95
  diagonal 90
  directing ground plane 95
  grid size 84–90
  moving and turning grid 91, 94, 95, 97
  paths 118
  paving 118
  paving patterns 118
ground cover 219, 230
ground plane 115–33
  choice of materials 120–33
  directing 95
  see also surfacing materials
ground surfaces 75
  see also surfacing materials

grouping plants 212

H

ha-has 50, 167
half-hardy annuals 231
hard landscaping 69, 82, 115
  colour 214
  enhancing 209–10
  estimating quantity 195
hardiness-zone system 54
hedges 115, 140–1, *148*, 168–9, 209, *238*
  backgrounds to decorative planting 170
  clair-voyées 181
  cutting 170–1
  decorative 170–1
  green walls 168–70
  presentation plan 74, 77
  removal 18
  rose hedging 230
  service paths 119, 120
  structural planting 167–71
  tapestry 170
  as windbreaks 55, 56, 156
herb gardens 147, 211, 221
herbaceous planting 18, 218, 230–2
  core plant list 286–7
historic districts 58
hot tubs 106
house
  damp-proof course 117–18
  doors and windows 23, 24, 30, 48, 82, 87, 118
linking garden with 16, 82, 83, 115, 117, *145–7*, 156, 168, 172, 200
  measuring 23–4, 27
  presentation plan 73
  reflected light 113
  site survey 23, 42
  window sill heights 24, 48

I

informal gardens 220
water features 107, 109–11

information panels 72
introvert gardens 47
irrigation 193–5

J

jacuzzis 136
Japanese gardens 220, *241*

K

key planting 227–8
  core plant list 285

L

lap pools 106
lawns 130–2
layers, planting in 213
legal considerations 58–9
length, increasing apparent 80, 97, 161
lettering 71–2
level, changes in 134, 163, *201*
  measuring 29
  safety 117–18, 163
  terraces 115–18
  see also steps
liability for accidents 25
  disclaimer 70
light 99–100, *152*, 252
  and colour 214–15
  controlling 155–6, 171
  intensity 99
  mirrors *152*
  neighbours' right to 59
  quality 99
  reflected 49, 113, *152*
  rendering on plans 250
  seasonal considerations 52–5
  silhouettes 100
  and texture 213
  water features 103–5
lighting 16, 145, 187–90
  water features 106
loam 32, 57

M

maintenance considerations 16, 275

manhole covers 30
mass and void 81, 97–9, 115, 139, *148*
materials, choice of
  climate affecting 54
  estimating quantity 195
  ground plane 120–33
  local materials 121
  surfacing *see* surfacing materials
meadows 131, 133–4, 222
measuring 19–22
  baseline 20
  changes in level 29
  curves 28
  doors and windows 23, 24
  estimating measurements 26–7
  fences etc 24–5
  heights and widths of features 24–6
  house and buildings 23–4, 26–7
  offset 21, 23
  running dimensions 23
  sloping sites 29
  steps 24–6
  trees 27–8
  triangulation 22, 23–4
  walls 25, 26
measuring tapes 19
microclimates 54
mirrors 152, 181
modern-style gardens 220
mood boards 256–7
moonlighting 188
movement, water features 105, 111–12

N
native plants 222
natural gardens 220
naturalistic gardens 222, *239*
notebook, keeping 209, 278–82

O
optical illusions 80, 156–7, 182–3
ornaments 138–9, 178–83

overhead elements 133–41, 171–8, 204
  role 171–2
  sections and elevations 249, 258–62
owner's requirements
  checklist 17–18
  mood boards 256–7

P
panoramic views, photographic records 46
paper sizes 35, 36–7, 40
parallel motion rule 35
parking and turning spaces 16
parterres 147
paths 82, 118–20
  changing direction *201*
  critical curve 119
  curved 28
  edging 133
  lighting 188
  linking house and garden *146*
  mown 130
  service paths 119, 120
  surface materials 121–33
patterns and shapes 78–83
paved areas 82, 115–18, 121
  brick and paver patterns 125
  paving materials 123–33
  permeable materials 115, 117, 118, 128, *239*
  presentation plan 75
  scale and proportion 116, 117
pavers (paviours) 124–6
  imitation paving 127–8
pea shingle 123
peaty soil 32, 58
pebbles 122
perennials 231
  core plant list 286
pergolas 15, 101, 133, 138, 171, 172–4, 200
  presentation plan 76
permeable materials 115, 117, 118, 128, *239*
perspective drawings 254

axonometric projections 249, 263–73
pH value 32, 57–8
photographs
  panoramic views 46
  photographic overlays 249, 254–7
  plant notebooks 279
  recording site 45–6
pinch points 98
pivots 138–9, 227
plan sheets 70
planning regulations 58–9
plant information sheets 280–1
plant list
  core 284–7
  planting plan, accompanying 223, 236
plant notebook, keeping 209, 278–82
planting 120, 272, 274–5
planting plan 12, 209–46
  background planting 167–8, 214, *238*
  broad-brush effects 231, 286
  climatic conditions 217–18
  colour 209, 214–15
  decorative planting 229–30
  drawing up 223–37
  elevations 228, 249, 258–62
  existing plants, using 18, 218, 225, *238*
  filler plants 218–19
  fleeting effects 231, 286–7
  focal points 210
  garden surroundings, relating to 210
  herbaceous planting 218, 230–2
  key planting 227
  layers, planting in 213
  non-visual plant qualities 210–11
  plant list 223, 236
  principles of planting design 211–15
  repeat planting 227, 231

role 209–11
  scale and proportion 211–12
  seasonal changes 210, 216–17, 224
  shade 215
  shape and form 212–13
  soil conditions 217, 218
  spacing plants 218
  stages involved in 223–4
  structural planting 167–71, 209, 224–7
  texture 100, 211, 213, *245*
planting styles 219–23
plants
  buying 274–5
  categories 279–80
  choosing 11, 209
  established 18
  grouping 212
  local, harmonizing with 49–50
  moving 18, 218
  owner's requirements 16
  shape 11, 212–13
  soil indicators 57–8
  spacing 218–19
  specific conditions, for 282
  specific purpose, for 282
  water 112
  see also planting plan
play areas and equipment 15, 135, 136, 186–7, *239*
pleached trees 169
pollution 217, 226
ponds *see* pools and ponds; water features
pools and ponds 75, 103–14, *150*, 191
  angle of sides 114
  blanket weed 109
  climate 113
  depth 104, 112
  edging 114, 133
  location 112–13
  naturalistic 109–10
  overflow 114
  planting schemes *244*
  plants 112

raised 109
Roman style 109
safety 108, 114
size 112
sun and shade 113
underwater lighting 188
see also water features
pre-excavation responsibilities 60
preliminary garden layout plan
141–4
privacy 47, 185

R
ragwort 59
ramps 102, 135, 163
rectilinear themes 78, 91, 92, 95
recycled materials 120, *150,*
206, 239
reflections
mirrors *152,* 181
water features 103–4, 106, 113
repeat effects 210, 213, 219,
224, 227, 231
reproduction ornaments 179
research and preparation 11
resin bonded aggregate 123
rhododendrons 57, 58
romantic style 220
rooftop gardens 54
root pruning 218
roses 230, *238, 242, 243, 245,*
246

S
safety 46, 102, *149*
changes in ground level 117–
18, 163
disclaimer 70
hedge-cutting 119
paths 119
ramps 163
steps 25, 102
water features 108, 114
sandpits 186
sandy soil 32, 58
scale, drawing to 35, 37–43
choosing a scale 39–40

scale and proportion 101–2,
211–12
controlling scale 171–2
paved areas 116, 117
scented plants 210, 223, *241*
screening 47, 49, 155, 166–7,
169–71
sculpted terraces 136
sculpture 133, 138–9, 155, 179
lighting 187
seasonal considerations 52–5,
210, 216–17, 224
shrubs as seasonal features 285
seating 133, 134, 138, 183–5,
205
presentation plan 76
sections 249, 258–62
security lighting 188–9
septic tanks 193
set squares 35, 36
setting and surroundings 15
character 47
choice of materials 120–1
outward views 47–8
relating garden to 49–50, 156,
210, 227
zone of visual influence 46, 50
setts 124, 126
shade 52–4, 99–100
creating 53–4
planting plan 215, 225
pools and ponds 113
providing 155–6, 171, 172,
175
umbrellas 185
shadows 53, 99–100, 171
rendering on plans 250, 252–3
shape and form 11, 212–13
sheds 16, 136–8, *205, 206*
shelterbelts 55–6
shingle 122
shrubs 133
accenting with 238
core plant list 284–5
decorative planting 229–30,
285
presentation plan 76–7

as seasonal features 285
site survey 30
spacing 218–19
structural planting 167–71,
209, 224–7, 284–5
wall 224, 274, 285
silhouette lighting 188
silhouettes 100
site appraisal 11, 64, 69, 115
altitude 55
climate 54–5
drainage 56–7
drawing up 62–3
legal considerations 58–9
light and shade 52–4
recording existing conditions
52–9
site inventory 11, 44–61, 64, 69
checklist 44–5
drawing up 60–1
photographic record 45–6
recording existing conditions
52–9
site survey 11, 64, 69
aspect 52–3
changes in level 29
curves 28
drawing 35–43
full size drawing 38
house and buildings 23, 42
light and shade 52–3
making 18–34
orientation 40
paper sizes 35, 36–7, 40
pools 108
scale, drawing to 35, 37–43
shrubs 30
sketch plan 30–1
slopes 29
soil, testing and recording
32–4
trees 27–8, 30, 43
sloping sites 135–6
construction and maintenance
136
drainage 56–7
levelling 29, 135

measuring 29
snow cover 54
soakaways 57, 192
soft landscaping 69, 115
soil 217, 218
organic matter 58
pH value 32, 57–8
preparation 191, 274
site assessment 57–8
site survey 32–3
structure 32, 58, 191
substrata 58
temperature 58
testing and recording 32–4
soil indicators 57–8
solar-powered water features 106
sound
plants 210
water features 103
space 97–9
avenue-channelled 98
and colour 214
dynamic 98
enclosing 155, 209
foreshortening 108
increasing apparent 47, 51, 80,
151, 181
lengthening 80, 97, 161
outdoor 97
static 98
subdividing 51, 90, 115, *148,*
166–8
swirling 98
widening 80, 161
spas, outdoor 136
spotlighting 187–9
spring effects 217
sprinkler systems 194
square as basis of design 78–9,
96
static designs 80, 98
statuary *see* sculpture
stepping stones 104
steps 82, 101–2, 133, 135, *150,*
163, *201, 204*
balustrades 180
building materials 163

changing direction *201*
handrails 25
lighting 187, 188
measuring 25–6
presentation plan 26, 76
safety 25, 102
tread overhang 25
stone paving slabs 127, 128, *150*
stone walls 162
storage 16
streams *240*
dry stream beds 122, *203*
structural planting 167–71, 209, 224–7, *238*
colour 214–15
core plant list 284–5
evergreen and deciduous plants 225
existing plants, using 225, 238
plant size 226
repeat planting 227
shrubs 227
substrata 58
summer effects 217
summerhouses 136, 186
sundials 182, *204*
sunlight *see* light
surfacing materials 120–33
fluid 121, 123–4
loose 121, 122–3
rigid 121, 124–9
sustainable gardens 220–1, 222
swimming pools 106
swirling space 98

T
T-squares 35, 36
tactile plants 211
telephone wires 49
terraces 115–18
balustrades 180
changes in level 117–18
decking 128–9
planting 117
sculpted 136

size 116, 117
texture 100, 211, 213, *245*
rendering on plans 250, 252
thistles 57, 59
thorny plants 46
thumbnail sketches 267
tile drainage 192–3
timber decking *145, 205*
timber edging 122
title blocks 70–2
tone, drawing on plans 250, 253
topiary 138–9, *145, 147, 148,* 170, 182, *238, 244*
traffic pollution 217
tree houses, swings and ropes 186–7, *239*
trees 133, 138–9, 177–8
accenting with *238*
axonometric projection 265
bark and stems 214, 226
buying and ordering 227
choosing 226
core plant list 284–5
dangerous 59
deciduous 214, 217, 224, 225, 226
decorative 226–7, 284
evergreen 217, 224, 225, 226
existing, using 18, 218, 225, 238
fast-growing 284
fastigiate 168, 169, 178, 226
as focal point 155, 284
harmonizing with local 49–50
measuring 27–8
moving 18, 218
outline shape 28, 226
overhanging neighbouring land 59
overhanging a water feature 113
paved areas 124, 126
planting 274

pleached 169
presentation plan 76–7
pyramid 77
removal 18, 59
root pruning 218
shade, provision of 53–4
site survey 28, 30, 43
size 226
spacing 219
structural planting 167–71, 209, 224–7, 284–5
tree preservation orders (TPOs) 59
tree screens 169–70
weeping 226
trelliswork (treillage) 166–7, 182
trompe l'oeil 156–7, 182–3
turf banks 120–1

U
umbrellas 185, *204*
uplighters 187
urns and vases 133, 138, *151,* 172, 183, *242*
use *see* garden use

V
vegetable gardens 211, 221, *239*
vertical elements 133–41, 155–61
axonometric projections 249, 263–73
materials for 162–3
presentation plan 76
role 155–61
sections and elevations 249, 258–62
trees 284
views 47–8, 141
blending in with 49
clair-voyées 181
directing and screening 155
framing 47, 48, 100, 148, *152,* 181
Japanese gardens 220

light and shade 100
linking garden with surroundings 156
photographic records 46

W
walls 82, 133, 140–1, 158–9
building materials 162–3
buttressing *149*
clair-voyées 181
climbers and wall shrubs 224, 274, 285–6
dry stone 120–1
dummy windows and doors 156–7, 182
freestanding 159–60
green 168–70
height 159
house 156–7
measuring 25, 26–7
ownership 59
presentation plan 25, 74
retaining 133, 134, *148,* 159–60
water butts 193, *203*
water features 69, 103–14, *202–3, 240*
blanket weed 109
boreholes 107
cascades 112
climate 105, 106, 113
colour 103, 104–5
decking with 129
directing circulation 113
formal 107, 109
historical 103
informal 107, 109–11
light, reflected 103–5
lighting 106
location 112–13
movement 105, 111–12
overhanging trees 113
presentation plan 75
reflections 103–4, 106, 113
safety 108, 114
size 112
solar-powered 106

sound 103
sustainable and biodiverse
    gardens 222
underwater lighting 188
using grey water 111
water restrictions 106
see also pools and ponds
water points, siting 193

water supply 191, *203*
    boreholes 107, 194
    grey water 111, 193, 195
    irrigation 193–5
    rainwater 193–4
watering systems 193–5
waterlogging 56–7, 58
weeds 122, 191, 274

legal requirements 59
widening apparent space 61,
    80
wild areas 131, 132–3, 222
wildflower meadows 131,
    133–4, 222
wildlife 16, *203*, 222
wind 55

fountains 105
wind tunnels 55–6
windbreaks 55–6, 155–6
winter effects 217, 223, 226

Z
zone of visual influence (ZVI)
    46, 50